Cultivating Wellbeing and Community through Writing in Academia

This book revolutionises our understanding of academic and creative writing processes. This groundbreaking collection, the first of two volumes, explores how Shut Up & Write! (SUAW) sessions transform solitary writing into a powerful tool for community building, personal growth, and enhanced wellbeing.

Featuring 17 diverse chapters from global contributors, the book unveils SUAW's evolution from a simple productivity technique to a comprehensive approach for nurturing writer wellbeing. Organised into four key sections, it examines SUAW's role in fostering community, supporting academic development, transcending institutional boundaries, and driving innovative wellbeing practices. From graduate students to established academics, university writing centres to national writers' retreats, this book offers a kaleidoscope of perspectives on implementing and adapting SUAW. It challenges the notion of writing as an isolating pursuit, instead presenting it as a collaborative, supportive endeavour that boosts creativity, builds resilience, and cultivates a sense of belonging.

This essential read provides both practical strategies and theoretical insights, making it invaluable for writing program administrators, academic developers, researchers, and anyone interested in innovative approaches to supporting writers' wellbeing.

Narelle Lemon is Professor and Vice Chancellor Professorial Research Fellow at Edith Cowan University, Australia, where she leads the Wellbeing and Education Research Community, and is an interdisciplinary scholar across arts, education, and positive psychology. She is also Creative Director of Explore & Create Co.

Aaron Bolzle is Co-Founder of Writing Partners and President of its flagship initiative, Shut Up & Write! He also serves as an Innovation Fellow at the Cambridge University ThinkLab, where he collaborates on community-focused initiatives that support connection and wellbeing. Bolzle's work centres on creating inclusive, thriving global writing communities that foster belonging, resilience, and sustainable practice. Under his leadership, Shut Up & Write! has expanded to hundreds of cities and universities in over 60 countries.

Wellbeing and Self-care in Higher Education
Editor: Narelle Lemon

Passion and Purpose in the Humanities
Exploring the Worlds of Early Career Researchers
Edited by Marcus Bussey, Camila Mozzini-Alister, Bingxin Wang and Samantha Willcocks

Supporting and Promoting Wellbeing in the Higher Education Sector
Practices in Action
Edited by Angela Dobele and Lisa Farrell

Understanding Wellbeing in Higher Education of the Global South
Contextually Sensitive and Culturally Responsive Perspectives
Edited by Youmen Chaaban, Abdellatif Sellami and Igor Michaleczek

The Making Academic
Perspectives on Expressive Practice and Wellbeing in Higher Education
Edited by Narelle Lemon, Sharon McDonough and Mark Selkrig

Creating Wellbeing
The Role of Making Practices in Academic Contexts
Edited by Narelle Lemon, Sharon McDonough, and Mark Selkrig

Cultivating Wellbeing and Community through Writing in Academia
Shifting the Culture with Shut Up and Write
Edited by Narelle Lemon and Aaron Bolzle with Malaika Santa Cruz and Rennie Saunders

Fostering Wellbeing through Collective Writing Practices
Shut Up and Write in Higher Education Settings
Edited by Narelle Lemon and Aaron Bolzle with Malaika Santa Cruz and Rennie Saunders

For more information about this series, please visit: www.routledge.com/Wellbeing-and-Self-care-in-Higher-Education/book-series/WSCHE

Cultivating Wellbeing and Community through Writing in Academia
Shifting the Culture with Shut Up & Write!

Edited by Narelle Lemon and
Aaron Bolzle with Malaika Santa Cruz
and Rennie Saunders

LONDON AND NEW YORK

Cover image: Getty Images

First published 2026
by Routledge
4 Park Square, Milton Park, Abingdon, Oxon OX14 4RN

and by Routledge
605 Third Avenue, New York, NY 10158

Routledge is an imprint of the Taylor & Francis Group, an informa business

© 2026 selection and editorial matter, Narelle Lemon, Aaron Bolzle, Malaika Santa Cruz, and Rennie Saunders; individual chapters, the contributors

The right of Narelle Lemon, Aaron Bolzle, Malaika Santa Cruz, and Rennie Saunders to be identified as the authors of the editorial material, and of the authors for their individual chapters, has been asserted in accordance with sections 77 and 78 of the Copyright, Designs and Patents Act 1988.

All rights reserved. No part of this book may be reprinted or reproduced or utilised in any form or by any electronic, mechanical, or other means, now known or hereafter invented, including photocopying and recording, or in any information storage or retrieval system, without permission in writing from the publishers.

Trademark notice: Product or corporate names may be trademarks or registered trademarks, and are used only for identification and explanation without intent to infringe.

British Library Cataloguing-in-Publication Data
A catalogue record for this book is available from the British Library

ISBN: 978-1-041-05991-2 (hbk)
ISBN: 978-1-041-05990-5 (pbk)
ISBN: 978-1-003-63333-4 (ebk)

DOI: 10.4324/9781003633334

Typeset in Galliard
by SPi Technologies India Pvt Ltd (Straive)

Contents

List of Figures   x
List of Images   xi
List of Tables   xii
Contributor Bios   xiii
Foreword   xxix
Series Preface   xxxvii
Acknowledgements   xl

SECTION 1
Foundations and Frameworks   1

1 Where Wellbeing Science Meets Writing Practice: The Intersection of Shut Up & Write! and Self-Care   3
  NARELLE LEMON

2 "It's About Accountability More Than Community": Embedding Co-Working within Graduate Research Training   20
  REBECCA HOWE, CLAIRE AKHBARI, BIANCA WILLIAMS, AND ELEANOR BENSON

3 Writing in Company: Looking at the Screen, Looking at Each Other   32
  CALLY GUERIN

SECTION 2
SUAW as a Tool for Academic Development and Wellbeing 45

4 Expanding a Creative Writing Practice to Foster Connection, Wellbeing, and Engagement across Multiple Disciplines 47
KRISTYN HARMAN, LUCY CHRISTOPHER, CAYLEE TIERNEY, PHILIPPA MOORE, STEPHANIE RICHEY, AND MANDY PINK

5 The Power of Writing in Community: Fostering Wellbeing and Self-efficacy among Postgraduate Researchers 59
SARAH KNEEN, PADMA INALA, LILY PEARSON, NICOLA TOMLINSON, AND CHARLOTTE EVANS

6 Shared Goals, Collective Growth: Developing Shut Up & Write! Communities of Practice 71
LYN LAVERY AND REBECCA GEORGE

7 Pomodoro and ePortfolio: An Unlikely but Perfect Pair 84
CLAIRE BOWMER AND DANA BUI

8 Community Support: Practical Strategies for Professional Self-Care and Wellbeing 97
DEWI WAHYU MUSTIKASARI, MASLATHIF DWI PURNOMO, AND ANUGRAH IMANI

SECTION 3
SUAW across Institutional Boundaries 107

9 Shut Up & Write! at Varuna, The National Writers' House 109
NAOMI PARRY DUNCAN AND AMY SAMBROOKE

10 Shutting Up and Staying Well: Reflections on Community, Belonging, and Mattering from SUAW Exeter 120
KELLY LOUISE PREECE AND JO SUTHERST

11 SUAW and Creating Inclusive Student Learning Communities 133
SIAN ROBINSON

SECTION 4
Innovative Approaches to SUAW for Wellbeing — 145

12 Writing Together Online: A History of Online SUAW
    in the Southern Hemisphere — 147
    KATHERINE FIRTH

13 Writing 'Alone Together' in a Nourishing and Supportive
    Online Environment — 159
    ANDI SALAMON, NATALIE THOMPSON, AND BELINDA DOWNEY

14 The Time of Our Lives: SUAW as a Space for Academic
    Writing Wellbeing — 172
    ABIGAIL WINTER, JENNA GILLETT-SWAN, NAOMI BARNES,
    CATHERINE CHALLEN, KERI FREEMAN, DANIELLE GORDON, TESSA
    RIXON, TOM LONG, ZOE MELLICK, JANE TURNER, ALETHEA BLACKLER,
    JULIE ARNOLD, CASSANDRA CROSS, NICOLE VICKERY, STINE JOHANSEN,
    DAVID PYLE, EMILY WOODMAN-PIETERSE, AND DANNIELLE TARLINTON

15 Sprinting Towards Academic Writing Wellbeing: Reflections
    from a Care-full and Compassionate Friday Writing
    Community — 185
    ABIGAIL WINTER, JENNA GILLETT-SWAN, DEANNA GRANT-SMITH,
    FRANCIS BOBONGIE-HARRIS, MICHELLE JEFFRIES, AND SOPHIA
    MAVROPOULOU

16 Fear of a Blank Page: Discovering My Writing Superpowers
    in a Two-Day Pomodoro Writing Workshop — 198
    NADEZHDA CHUBKO

17 The HDR Writer's Wellbeing Lounge: A Community-Driven
    Approach to Enhancing Writing Productivity and Wellbeing
    for Higher Degree Research Students — 209
    NATASHA KITANO, OWEN FORBES, AND KIRSTEN BAIRD-BATE

18 Connection, Momentum, and Growth: Exploring the Benefits
    and Challenges of 'Shut Up & Research' for Researcher
    Wellbeing — 221
    ANNALISE ROACHE, JANE GEORGE, AND LISA M. BAKER

Figures

10.1   Mapping SUAW wellbeing   128

Images

1.1	SUAW understood through a wellbeing science lens	4
2.1	Collective artworks created during the 2022 retreat	25
3.1	The sense of companionship and connection is captured in a screenshot of the Zoom participants – a grid of squares with faces all directed towards us as the writers look at their documents appearing on their screens	33
4.1	Achievements from our SUAW	48
5.1	An attendee's reflective drawing of what the writing retreat means to them (Heslop, 2024)	64
6.1	Proposed model for SUAW vCoP development	73
7.1	SUAW for belonging by Claire Bowmer	84
8.1	Community support-based SUAW framework	99
9.1	Pink flannel flowers (*Actinotus forsythii*) at Narrow Neck, Katoomba in January 2021. These diminutive flowers, pale feathered stars with pink button centres, only bloom the summer after a big fire. They are a sign of regeneration after devastation	110
10.1	Mattering (photo collage by Dr Elsa Urmston)	126
11.1	Body doubling for an ADHD Brain	134
12.1	My hand, my laptop, my cat	147
13.1	Foreground (writing "alone together" online) and background (teaching, research, life)	160
14.1	A framework for academic writing wellbeing	176
15.1	Mosaic of care	193
16.1	Imaginary chain of self-doubt	198
17.1	Taking breaks by walking on the beach helped me become more conscious of how I maintained productivity and focus and supported my wellbeing	217
18.1	Venn diagram of intersecting themes that connect SU&R practice with participants' wellbeing	224

Tables

1.1 The five dimensions of self-care and their manifestation in SUAW 8
15.1 Typical sequence of activities occurring in SUAW sessions 186

Contributor Bios

Claire Akhbari is from a white settler background, a trans and queer person with lived experience of disability, and lives on the stolen lands of the Dja Dja Wurrung People of the Kulin Nation. They are currently undertaking a Master of Social Work at La Trobe University. Between 2019–2022 they were employed by the Indigenous Settler Relations Collaboration and the Australian Centre at the University of Melbourne where they were involved in developing and then coordinating the Interdisciplinary Graduate Research Program in Indigenous Settler Relations. The desire to individually reject and collectively dismantle the personal and structural privilege gained from the foundational and ongoing genocide and dispossession of Aboriginal and Torres Strait Islander peoples informs their work.

Julie Arnold is a lecturer in education, specialising in English curriculum, pedagogy, and assessment. She explores students' classroom experiences and teachers' responses to professional learning, to make recommendations for improving teacher practice and student agency. Her current projects include the ARC Linkage Accessible Assessment; Accessible Assessment for Learning in English and Mathematics; and Dialogues for Inclusive Assessment and Learning. Other research interests are in English curriculum and pedagogy, especially building teacher linguistic subject knowledge for writing instruction. Before and beyond university, Julie was a long-time English Head of Faculty and she co-authors Cambridge's Essential English for Queensland Schools. In her role as Vice President of the English Teachers Association of Queensland, Julie takes an active interest in instructional leadership and curriculum development.

Lisa M. Baker has been a teacher, learner, and researcher in early childhood education for over 35 years and is currently working with the Research in Effective Education in Early Childhood (REEaCh) Centre at the University of Melbourne. She holds a Bachelor of Education, specialising in Early Childhood, Masters of Applied Positive Psychology (MAPP), Graduate Certificate in Education Research, and is currently completing a PhD. Lisa's PhD with the Centre for Wellbeing Science University of Melbourne is researching the application of Wellbeing Literacy to early childhood education in Australia. Her presentations and publications highlight the synergies between the fields of early childhood and wellbeing science, combining theory and practice for educators.

Kirsten Baird-Bate is an educational researcher with a strong interest in wellbeing, inclusive education, and visual research methodologies. Her PhD research explored how families of autistic children conceptualise wellbeing and used innovative, visual narrative methods, to help bring forward their voice. Previous research has explored the effectiveness of photographic journaling as a reflective tool for mothers of autistic children. Kirsten has previously lectured in autism and inclusive education and is a carer representative with Carers NSW. She is also mother to three children. Kirsten completed her PhD through Queensland University of Technology (QUT) and met Tasha and Owen through the HDR Writer's Wellbeing Lounge. She credits their friendship and the dedicated writing space provided by the Lounge as instrumental to successful completion as an external student.

Naomi Barnes is a senior lecturer interested in how crisis influences education politics. With a specific focus on moral panics, she has demonstrated how online communication has influenced education politics in Australia, the US and the UK. She has analysed and developed network models to show the effect of moral panics on the Australian curriculum and how it is taught. Naomi is also regularly asked to comment on how Australian teachers should respond to perceived threats to Australian nationalism, identity, and democracy. Naomi lectures future teachers in modern history, civics and citizenship and writing studies. She has worked for Education Queensland as a senior writer and has worked as a secondary humanities and social science teacher in the government, Catholic, and independent schooling sectors.

Eleanor Benson is Research Coordinator at the Australian Centre. She is a settler living and working on the unceded lands of the Wurundjeri and Boonwurrung peoples of the Kulin nations. Eleanor completed a Bachelor of Arts degree with Honours at the University of Melbourne exploring the relationship between incarceration and settler colonial sovereignty. She has tutored in gender studies and sustainability studies and worked as a research assistant on the ARC Discovery Project, Revitalising Indigenous-State Relations in Australia.

Alethea Blackler is a professor within the School of Design at QUT. As the world leader in intuitive interaction research, she pioneered and published the first empirical work in the field and edited a journal issue and a book on intuitive interaction. As an early career researcher, she led a nationally funded project on Facilitating Intuitive Interaction for Older People. Her research projects include older people and technology (including PhD supervisions and commercial research) and design for dementia (including an international EU Horizon project, Mindful Design for Dementia). She has also worked on interaction for gaming and for children. She has always worked with researchers from a range of disciplines and has often acted as a bridge between HASS and STEMM researchers and as a leader in mixed methods approaches.

Francis Bobongie-Harris is a senior lecturer in the School of Education at Queensland University of Technology. Her research focus is on Australian South Sea Islander and Indigenous Australian Education and community-led approaches. She has recently been awarded an Indigenous Discovery (2025–2029): Community-Led Approaches to Teaching Australian South Sea Islander History grant.

Aaron Bolzle is Co-Founder of Writing Partners and President of its flagship initiative, Shut Up & Write! He also serves as an Innovation Fellow at the Cambridge University ThinkLab, where he collaborates on community-focused initiatives that support connection and well-being. Bolzle's work centres on creating inclusive, thriving global writing communities that foster belonging, resilience, and sustainable practice. Under his leadership, Shut Up & Write! has expanded to hundreds of cities and universities in over 60 countries.

Claire Bowmer is a learning designer with a background in graphics and teaching. The third space is an exciting new and dynamic place for her as it is about bringing people together, celebrating ideas, and communicating creatively. She found parallel writing and SUAW sessions to be a source of encouragement and mentoring across her career chapters. In writing curriculum or marking as a together activity in schools to having accountability in developing instructional design and project portfolios, writing is a way of making sense of the world and learning. Claire has a creative practice writing comics and zines. Strangely, she also finds joy in writing technical instructions as there is a link with improving the learning experience for academics and students. Claire holds a Master's in Education which included interviewing regional teachers about lifelong learning and their access to peer support.

Dana Bui is an educational designer in the Faculty of Medicine, Nursing and Health Sciences at Monash University. She specialises in creating hands-on, engaging, and feedback-driven workshops that critically evaluate educational practice. As a Senior Fellow of the Higher Education Academy, she creates support resources that unpack contextually appropriate educational practice that integrates institutional policies and frameworks. She is also passionately focused on embedding inclusive educational practice in higher education and analysing implicit bias.

Catherine Challen is an educator committed to increasing access and equity in education by centring students and engaging teachers as powerful agents of change. She leverages ten years of experience in the biotechnology sector and seven years as a classroom teacher to coach teachers and leaders on how to analyse and use data regularly to inform instructional practices and school-wide decision-making. She supports new mathematics teachers to interrogate the status quo based on data, give students a voice, and teach for social justice.

Lucy Christopher is Senior Lecturer in Creative Writing at the University of Tasmania. An award-winning writer for young people, Lucy's research interests centre on creative writing, with specific focus on writing for young people, empathy, psychology, place, and ecocriticism. Lucy has taught in many countries and for many organisations, including residential tutoring for Arvon Writing Centres, Ty Newydd Writing Centre, and for Loutro Writers. She established Mexican Writing Retreats, luxury creative writing courses run in the central highlands of Mexico. She frequently visits schools to talk about her work for young people and participated in the recent, successful bid for Hobart to be recognised as a UNESCO City of Literature.

Nadezhda Chubko is a mixed methods researcher and learning designer with industry experience. She has a profound interest in education research involving teaching and learning English for specific purposes and scientific literacy acquisition. Her research projects are in curriculum materials design, gender and education, multilingual education, STEAM, ICT, and digital storytelling. As an action researcher, Nadezhda's aim is to translate theory into practice through constant improvement based on previous experience.

Cassandra Cross is currently Associate Dean (Learning & Teaching), Faculty of Creative Industries, Education and Social Justice and Professor in the School of Justice, QUT. In 2021, she completed a Senior Research Fellowship, with the Cybersecurity Cooperative Research Centre (CRC) on the topic of romance fraud. Previously, Professor Cross worked as a research/policy officer with the Queensland Police Service, where she commenced research on the topic of online fraud and was awarded a Churchill Fellowship in 2011. Since taking up her position at QUT in 2012, she has published in this area across several journals and continued her research into online fraud focusing across the prevention, victim support, and policing aspects of this crime. She has received over AUD $1.5 million in grants and industry funding to further this work, and co-authored (with Professor Mark Button) the book *Cyber frauds, scams, and their victims* (Routledge 2017).

Belinda Downey is a lecturer in early childhood education in the Faculty of Arts & Education at Charles Sturt University. She has taught across a broad range of age groups and programs in regional NSW and in Darwin, NT. Her initial focus was primary teaching; she then began working in a long day care service teaching birth to 3 years, later becoming a director in the long day care sector. This led to a role in university that included early childhood pedagogy, professionalism, and professional experience coordination. Belinda returned to the early childhood sector and most recently worked as educational leader in a community-based preschool before returning to academia to complete her PhD. Her research focuses on retention of educators in the early childhood workforce.

Naomi Parry Duncan is a writer, adjunct researcher at the Universities of Tasmania and Western Sydney, and accredited professional historian who lives and works on Dharug and Gundungurra Country in the Blue Mountains. She was the Hazel Rowley Fellow in 2022–23 and her book on the Aboriginal warrior Musquito will be published by Allen & Unwin in 2026. She participated in a Lamplight Residency at Varuna, The National Writers' House, during COVID-19 lockdowns in 2020, which introduced her to the concept of Shut Up & Write.

Charlotte Evans has worked in teaching and learning development roles at the University of Manchester for the past ten years. Her core passions are developing learning content and activities which are inclusive and accessible and creating and holding spaces where all feel safe to learn and reach their potential. Her areas of particular interest are trauma-informed pedagogy and universal design for learning. She is a member of the ALN (Academic Libraries North) Copyright and Academic Skills Communities of Practice and regularly reviews papers for the *Journal of Learning Development in Higher Education* (JLDHE).

Katherine Firth has been developing research writers for over 15 years. A co-founder of the award-winning Thesis Bootcamp program, she maintains a writing blog, *Research Degree Insiders*. She is Senior Lecturer in Research Education and Development at La Trobe Graduate Research School. She is co-author of the books *How to Fix your Academic Writing Trouble* (Open University Press 2018), *Your PhD Survival Guide* (Routledge 2020), and *Level Up your Essays* (New South 2021). Her new book is *Writing Well and Being Well for Your PhD and Beyond* (Routledge 2023).

Owen Forbes is a translational data scientist whose work spans statistical analysis, ecology, and mental health research. His current work involves applying data science to ecological questions, examining biological specimen data to understand ecosystem changes and climate impacts. He has participated in community wellbeing and student mental health initiatives, and volunteers with community organisations including the Good Data Institute and Palliative Care ACT. SUAW groups have been a core part of Owen's writing practice throughout his PhD and continue to be a valued component of his research practice today, helping him maintain productivity across a range of projects.

Keri Freeman is Senior Lecturer and HDR Language and Learning Educator at QUT who provides writing support to HDR students across QUT. Her teaching philosophy is to offer engaging, inclusive, and student-centred learning environments for HDRs to gain a deep understanding of the research and academic literacy skills relevant to their field of study. Her research interests focus on academic literacy development, building HDRs' sense of belonging and positive researcher identities, and the development of feedback literacy within a community of practice.

Jane George works at the intersection of rural health equity and workforce sustainability in Aotearoa (New Zealand). With roots in social work practice and a doctorate focused on allied health recruitment and retention in rural settings, Jane brings both practical leadership experience and rigorous research to her current work. Through independent research initiatives and collaborations with universities across New Zealand and Australia, she addresses complex workforce challenges facing rural communities. Jane challenges urban-centric assumptions about healthcare delivery and champions the unique strengths and opportunities of rural practice. She believes that when we get the rural workforce right, we create pathways to better health outcomes for all communities, regardless of geography.

Rebecca George is a health leadership consultant specialising in digital health, clinical digital governance and the allied health, scientific, and technical professions. A registered occupational therapist, she is experienced in leading and implementing digital health innovations, contributing to national programmes of work and policy development. Engaging across workforce professions to support and enable change, she works to empower others to lead and innovate. Working in collaboration with Lyn Lavery, she has participated in leading the Research Accelerator community. She will shortly complete her doctorate in health systems leadership and will publish her recommendations for enabling allied health clinicians to take up health systems leadership roles.

Jenna Gillett-Swan's research at QUT focuses on wellbeing, rights, voice, inclusion, and participation. She also specialises in qualitative child-centred participatory research methodologies. Jenna is the co-leader for the Health and Wellbeing Research Program within the Centre for Inclusive Education (C4IE). She is an active member of the Research in Children's Rights and Education Network of the European Educational Research Association and is Co-Convenor for this network. Jenna is a Senior Fellow of the Higher Education Academy and an Associate Fellow (Indigenous Knowledges) of the Higher Education Academy. She is current Chair of the Faculty of Creative Industries, Education, and Social Justice Equity Committee.

Danielle Gordon is a lecturer and PhD candidate in the School of Teacher Education and Leadership at QUT. With 12 years of teaching experience, she has also contributed three years to the Queensland Curriculum and Assessment Authority, where she played a pivotal role in developing syllabuses and external assessments across various curriculum subjects. Danielle's PhD thesis by publication investigates the impact of Curriculum and Assessment Reform on pre-service and early career teachers in Queensland.

Utilising a longitudinal, mixed-method research design, her work provides valuable insights into how these reforms influence teaching practices and educational outcomes. Passionate about education and teacher development, Danielle is dedicated to enhancing the teaching profession and supporting educators in navigating curriculum changes effectively.

Deanna Grant-Smith is Professor of Management in the School of Business and Creative Industries at the University of the Sunshine Coast where she conducts research on work across a range of dimensions, including the potential for exploitation associated with unpaid internships, work-integrated learning, emerging forms of contemporary labour, and multilevel marketing. She has a particular interest in the conditions and expectations associated with work that diminish or support worker wellbeing.

Cally Guerin is a researcher developer in the Research Education and Development Unit at La Trobe University. She has been teaching, researching, and publishing on doctoral education since 2008, working with both supervisors and HDRs to develop effective research practices. Much of her time is spent translating the mysteries of academic research cultures for newcomers. Her research interests include research writing, supervision practices, and doctoral education. She is Joint Executive Editor of *HERD* journal and a founding co-editor of the *DoctoralWriting* blog. Recent publications include a book on *Creating, Managing, and Editing Multi-Authored Publications* with co-authors Claire Aitchison and Susan Carter; a chapter on "Supervising a thesis by publication" co-authored with Ngoc Nuyen; and a chapter on "Finding confidence in writing: Doctoral writing groups" written with Claire Aitchison.

Kristyn Harman is a professor in history at the University of Tasmania. Prior to becoming Chair of Academic Senate in mid-2024, she was the Associate Head of Research in the School of Humanities and, in this capacity, was a member of the College of Arts, Law and Education (CALE) Research Committee. A social historian, Kristyn is an award-winning expert on cross-cultural encounters across Britain's 19th-century colonies with a particular focus on law, punishment, and incarceration. Kristyn's expertise and experience as a university learning designer, developer, and teacher has been recognised by numerous awards, most recently a Vice-Chancellor's Teaching Excellence Award (2019), a CALE Teaching Excellence Award (2019), and a CALE Citation for Outstanding Contributions to Student Learning (team teaching award, 2021). She publishes in the field of SoTL both as sole author and as a co-contributor to research teams.

Rebecca Howe With an extensive history working in the LGBTIQASB+ youth homelessness and health policy sectors, Rebecca Howe is a lecturer in Social Work and Human Services at RMIT University. Her research focuses on approaches to depathologisation in trans health policy and, in doing so, considers the governing of gender within contemporary settler colonialism. Rebecca is a settler Australian and a queer, cis person who experiences a chronic illness and reads science fiction.

Anugrah Imani is currently a lecturer at Islamic University of Sunan Gunung Djati Bandung, Indonesia (UIN SGD). She graduated from the School of Education of Western Sydney University, Australia. Ima has been teaching in the Faculty of Education at Islamic University Bandung Indonesia for more than 10 years. Her research interests are in English language teaching (ELT) and English for young learners (EYL). Since 2009 she has been involved in Tutorial Center Bandung to help young learners learn English.

Padma Inala is a teaching and learning librarian at the University of Manchester. She is a chartered librarian with over 20 years' experience working in higher education in the UK. Her main areas of work are content creation, development, and delivery of teaching sessions to students and researchers to support their information literacy and academic skills. Her particular areas of interest are in supporting and engaging online and distance learners, developing inclusive practice and EDI in teaching and learning. She is an active member of CILIP – the UK's library and information association and also a committee member on the CILIP Information Literacy Group as their HE Sector rep and EDI representative, supporting members to gain better knowledge and practice of information literacy.

Michelle Jeffries is a postdoctoral research fellow in the School of Teacher Education and Leadership at Queensland University of Technology, Brisbane, Australia. Her predominant area of research is in the area of gender and sexuality diversity in education. Her current research explores the experiences of gender and sexuality diverse (GSD) teachers in regional, rural, and remote Australia. Michelle's doctoral study explored the enablements and constraints experienced by GSD parents within the context of their child/ren's primary school/s. She received a QUT Executive Dean's Commendation for Outstanding Doctoral Thesis for this work. Her research interests also include exploring public discourses about queer-related issues across traditional and social media. Michelle is currently a co-convenor of the Gender, Sexualities and Cultural Studies SIG (Australian Association of Research in Education). She is an associate editor of *Teachers and Teaching: Theory and Practice*.

Stine Johansen is an assistant professor in the Department of Computer Science, Aalborg University. Her research focuses on designing interactions with complex technical, cyber-physical systems such as robots and sound zone systems. This includes designing human-robot collaboration, sonification of robot movements, and supporting interaction with spatial sound through dynamic visualisations. Her research relies on design-based and physical prototyping methods. Stine has a PhD in computer science, focusing on human-computer interaction. Throughout her research career, Stine has maintained close collaborations with industry, including Bang & Olufsen, Soundfocus, Cook Medical, and Stryker.

Natasha Kitano is a language and learning educator with the Graduate Research Education + Development (GRE+D) team at QUT. She founded the HDR Writer's Wellbeing Lounge in 2020 to support research students' mental health and writing practice, coinciding with the onset of COVID-19 and lockdown, which intensified the sense of isolation often experienced by research candidates. Natasha has developed an understanding of the importance of creating spaces where PGR students can engage in focused writing sprints, reflect on their academic writing practices, and safely discuss wellbeing topics relevant to their research journey. She is passionate about supporting PGR students throughout candidature.

Sarah Kneen has been passionate about research-informed learning development since her first entry into teaching during her PhD at the University of Manchester (UoM). Now working at UoM Library, she loves seeing the results of building close partnerships with students and researchers to co-create and deliver their training offer, and is always looking for ways to build a more inclusive, supportive, and empowering learning environment. A particular area of interest is researcher wellbeing and how to boost confidence and efficacy in academic writing and co-leading the development of the Library's community-writing offer of Shut Up & Write and writing retreats.

Lyn Lavery is the Director of Academic Consulting, a New Zealand–based research and training company, which she established following a successful career in the tertiary sector. Her PhD was in educational psychology, specifically examining the area of self-regulated learning. Her research interests are more widely in the areas of learning and motivation, particularly in relation to adult learning contexts and social learning. She has been teaching research methods and data analysis software across New Zealand and Australian universities for over 25 years, and more recently, established the Research Accelerator community as a way to make research methods training more accessible to doctoral and early career researchers.

Narelle Lemon is an internationally recognised researcher, coach, and educator specialising in positive psychology and building non-medicalised self-care into the everyday. Narelle is series editor and founder of this Routledge book series on wellbeing and self-acre in higher education. As Lead of the Wellbeing and Education Research Community at Edith Cowan University, she brings together insights from education, arts, and positive psychology to transform how we approach personal and professional wellbeing. Through her work at Explore & Create Co, podcasting, and innovative projects like "Citizen Wellbeing Scientist," Narelle champions practical, evidence-based approaches to flourishing amid life's challenges. Her expertise has been recognised through various awards, including an Australian Awards for University Teaching (AAUT) National Teaching Citation, and she currently leads significant initiatives including the SHESpeaks project, amplifying diverse voices in women's wellbeing. In 2024, she published her first solo book, sharing her research and insights on self-care. Narelle practices what she teaches, maintaining her own wellbeing through mountain bike riding, photography, camping adventures, and daily rituals of self-compassion and intention-setting. You'll often find her exploring nature trails with a trusty flask of green tea in hand, embodying her belief that self-care is a daily practice rather than a destination.

Tom Long is a dedicated researcher in the fields of human-robot interaction (HRI), human-centered design (HCD), and research through design (RtD). Currently pursuing a thesis titled "Design for Collaboration: Redesigning the Cobot Welding Experience for More Human-Centered Human-Robot Collaboration," Tom focuses on enhancing the synergy between humans and collaborative robots (cobots). Their work aims to create more intuitive and effective interactions in industrial settings, particularly in welding applications. By integrating the principles of HCD and RtD, Tom seeks to develop innovative solutions that prioritize the needs and experiences of human operators, ultimately fostering more creative and engaging applications of industrial cobots.

Sophia Mavropoulou is an Associate Professor at the School of Education in the QUT Faculty of Creative Industries, Education and Social Justice. Sofia is passionate about creating autism-friendly environments to accommodate the strengths and preferences of persons with autism to promote their inclusion, independence and well-being.

Zoe Mellick is a lecturer in fashion in the School of Design at Queensland University of Technology. Zoe's research has delved into the complexities of sustainability within the global textile and apparel value chain. This has included thorough investigations into sustainability within Australian cotton value chains, the development of circular school uniforms, and studying the effects of circular fashion business models including rental, resale, and repair. Zoe also has over a decade of experience in retail with Australian fashion brands and continues to work with industry as a sustainability and impact advisor.

Allison Miller is Director and Lead Consultant of Digital Capability, Founder of the PARE sessions. Digital Capability is an organisation which specialises in cutting edge online learning and online business strategies and solutions. Allison holds a Master of Learning and Development (Organisational Development), Graduate Certificate in Innovation and Entrepreneurship, Bachelor of Education (Secondary Business), Graduate Certificate in Learning and Teaching (Higher Education) Diploma of VET, Certificate IV in Training and Assessment, Diploma of Business, Certificate IV in Business Administration, and Certificate III in Government. She has been involved in education and training for nearly 30 years as an educator, online learning leader, and innovator and as disruptive change manager. She leads ePortfolios Australia – a professional network that aims to support the use of ePortfolio practice in Australia and beyond through professional development activities and the sharing of research, resources, ideas, and practice. In this role, she works with individuals from leading educational institutions, both within Australia and in Europe, New Zealand, and North America. Allison has written about ePortfolios for academic and professional audiences, most recently contributing to the educational podcast, *Create, Share, Engage*.

Philippa Moore is an award-winning Hobart-based writer and a PhD candidate in creative writing and history at the University of Tasmania. As a novelist, poet, and journalist, her work appears regularly in consumer magazines, international media, literary journals, and online, including *The Guardian* and *Womankind*. As a historian, Philippa is passionate about telling the stories of lesser-known women from the past in creative and provocative ways. Her research spans colonial Australia to post-war Britain, with specific research interests in feminist history, creative history, deep mapping methodologies, and convict history. Her academic work is published in *TEXT* and *The Australian Journal of Biography and History* (forthcoming). Philippa's PhD project received a 2023 KSP Residential Fellowship and she was the joint winner of the 2022–23 Van Diemen History Prize. Philippa has also worked on a number of public projects aiming to promote Tasmanian history and raise awareness of its heritage sites.

Rory Mulcahy is an associate professor in the UniSC School of Business and Creative Industries. His research interests currently focus on digital communities, including misinformation, online trolling, social media believability, and deepfakes. He is also interested in the role of emotions in explaining consumer behaviour. Rory's work has been published in journals such as the *Journal of Service Research*, *Journal of Advertising*, and *European Journal of Marketing*. He also serves as an associate editor for the *Journal of Services Marketing* and is a co-cluster lead for the Work, Live and Play research group.

Dewi Wahyu Mustikasari is an academic at UIN Salatiga, a government university in Central Java, Indonesia. Dewi graduated from University of Technology Sydney, Australia. She has been teaching for more than 13 years in the higher education sector. Her research interests include technology-enhanced language learning, blended and online learning, learning design, and teacher practice. She is available for joint lecture and research collaboration.

Lily Pearson: At the time of writing this chapter, Lily Pearson was a member of the University of Manchester Library's student team and also a final year PhD researcher in history. Supporting SUAW sessions allowed her to reflect on her dual perspectives as both staff and PGR to really appreciate the benefit that SUAW could bring to herself and fellow researchers in terms of productivity and writing confidence, but importantly also community building and creating a sense of shared experience.

Mandy Pink is Research Program Manager in the College of Arts, Law and Education at the University of Tasmania. With over 12 years of experience in research management, she is passionate about supporting research, particularly in its many interdisciplinary forms. She is an active member of the Australasian Research Management Society and has presented at ARMS conferences on research and creative practice, streamlined research administration, and best practice in supporting collaborative and interdisciplinary research.

Kelly Louise Preece is the Head of Educator Development at the University of Exeter, where she oversees the Educator Development team and supports the Education Leadership Team in achieving the goals of the Education Strategy. With 15 years of experience in higher education, Kelly Louise has held roles as an academic, researcher, and researcher developer. Kelly Louise also directs the EduExe Framework, accredited by AdvanceHE, which includes the ASPIRE Professional Recognition Pathway and Learning and Teaching in Higher Education and Academic Professional programmes. From 2015 to 2022, she led the Researcher Development Programme for PGRs at Exeter, taking a holistic and inclusive approach. In 2022, she was awarded a National Teaching Fellowship for her outstanding support for postgraduate researchers. Kelly Louise's interests are in doctoral education, online and blended learning, and wellbeing, and she has published and presented widely on these topics.

Maslathif Dwi Purnomo is an associate professor in the Faculty of Tarbiyah and Teachers Training of UIN Sumatera Utara Medan. He graduated from Charles Sturt University, Australia. His research interests are linguistics, discourse analysis, critical discourse analysis, political discourse analysis, and communication arts.

David Pyle is a lecturer in QUT's School of Creative Arts and Principal Curator, Digital Initiatives at Queensland Museum. Following a successful career in music, theatre, radio, and television, David has worked extensively in museums and interpretive centres as a producer of content and senior manager. His background in creation and installation (especially video and digital media) makes him a highly qualified source of practical professional advice. His recent university-based research projects include QUT's ScanCave and application of 3D-scanning techniques such as photogrammetry for preservation, display, and exhibition of objects, artefacts, and specimens in the museum sector. In addition to digitising QM's vast collections, his work also involves dissemination using both immersive displays (VR/AR) and more traditional interactive techniques.

Stephanie Richey is a lecturer in the Bachelor of Education (Primary) at the University of Tasmania (UTAS). She enjoys the rich cross-discipline collegiality and close-knit community of her regional campus. Stephanie completed both her Bachelor of Education (First Class Honours) and PhD at UTAS. She is passionate about access to languages education for everyone, especially students, and her research focuses on Anglophone English speakers' motivation for and attitudes towards learning additional languages. Stephanie's other key research area is in the field of Scholarship of Teaching and Learning (SoTL), primarily focusing on enhancing higher education student participation, engagement, and retention.

Tessa Rixon is a practitioner-researcher in digital scenography and Australian performance design. As Senior Lecturer in Scenography at Queensland University of Technology, her research into digital scenographies, ecoscenographic practice and pedagogy, and Australian design has been published in leading publications including the *International Journal of Performance Arts and Digital Media*, and *Theatre and Performance Design*. She is the inaugural Chair of ScenoLab Australia, Chair of the Research Commission for the International Organisation of Theatre Designers, Architects and Technicians, and the National Secretary for the Australasian Association for Theatre, Drama and Performance Studies. In 2021, she guest-edited the first special edition in over a decade to highlight Australian scenography (*Scene Journal* (Intellect)), and in 2023 Tessa curated the Australian Hub for the International Theatre Engineering and Architecture Conference.

Annalise Roache is a Positive Psychology practitioner, credentialed coach, and wellbeing researcher dedicated to fostering personal and workplace growth. She specialises in solution-focused, evidence-based approaches grounded in Positive Psychology and is committed to advancing ethical standards in the field. Annalise develops psycho-educational courses and online resources that promote active engagement with wellbeing practices. She holds a Master of Science in Applied Positive Psychology and Coaching Psychology from the University of East London and completed her Doctorate at Auckland University of Technology, where she explored lay people's conceptions of wellbeing, comparing them to academic approaches to enhance the relevance of policy and intervention.

Sian Robinson is a Senior Lecturer in Human Resource Management at the University of Exeter Business School. Sian has been teaching in higher education since 2020 and teaches across a range of areas in HRM and business and management. She is also a programme director and is passionate about improving the student experience for inclusivity, linked with her experiences of having ADHD, and for widening participation. She holds undergraduate and postgraduate degrees in business, management and HRM. She has co-authored a textbook titled 'Strategic Learning and Development Practice' with Graham Perkins. Sian also works with the CIPD as a moderator for their qualifications at levels 3 and 5 and is a non-executive director for SBA CIC, who support enterprise and business success.

Andi Salamon is a senior lecturer in early childhood pedagogy in the Faculty of Education at the University of Canberra. Taking a respectful, reciprocal, and participatory approach and using the theory of practice architectures, her research focuses on infant cognitive, social, and emotional development and how these come together in holistic communicative and playful practices. She is a keen practice theorist who sees transformation in everyday actions and interactions (practices). Andi incorporates her research into her teaching to help advocate for and transform infant pedagogy and uphold infants' rights to quality early childhood education. She keeps children and families at the front of her mind in her work and encourages pre-service teachers, colleagues, and early years leaders to do the same.

Amy Sambrooke is a writer, producer, and facilitator who was formerly the Creative Director of Varuna, the National Writers' House and Artistic Director of the Blue Mountains Writers' Festival (2017–2023). Amy has held senior roles in program leadership, education, and communications in the arts and in public policy. Amy started her career as a producer at ABC Sydney. She is a graduate of Macquarie University and the Australian Film, Television and Radio School (AFTRS). Amy has served on advisory committees for visual arts, heritage, and not-for-profit organisations and on community boards. She is based in Katoomba and is part of a weekly Shut Up & Write group.

Malaika Santa Cruz served as a key early team member at Shut Up & Write!, growing the community back when Shut Up & Write! was only a few thousand members across eight chapter cities. A decade later, her operational expertise and dedication to fostering meaningful partnerships has been pivotal in maintaining the inclusive culture as Shut Up & Write! has expanded to hundreds of cities and universities worldwide.

Rennie Saunders is the founder and CEO of Shut Up & Write!, a global organization that hosts free writing events for authors worldwide. What began as a personal quest to find creative community in San Francisco has grown into a movement supporting nearly 100,000 writers across 53 countries. A lifelong science fiction enthusiast who wrote his first story at age 12, Rennie is passionate about providing writers with the resources, community, and accountability they need to succeed.

Jo Sutherst is a part-time PhD student at the University of Exeter, originally from Coventry and now residing in the Forest of Dean, Gloucestershire. Her PhD research focuses on the influence of selfies on identity construction on social media and the narrative techniques artists employ on these platforms. Jo's multidisciplinary background spans engineering, teaching, and professional photography, enriching her exploration of identity narratives in her ongoing doctoral studies. Her current research builds on themes from her MA project, "Fractured Identities." Beyond her research, Jo is an active member of the academic community at Exeter University, where she coordinates and frequently facilitates the PGR Study Space group (formerly Shut Up & Write!). In this role, she fosters a collaborative writing environment that supports the advancement of postgraduate researchers, demonstrating her commitment to both her scholarly and peer communities.

Dannielle Tarlinton is a PhD candidate specialising in the study of tangible, embedded, and embodied interactions (TEI) designed to enhance active play among young children. Their research is grounded in a Research

Through Design methodology, emphasising iterative design and the continuous interaction between users and their environments. With a background in industrial design and research within the field of human-computer interaction, Dannielle brings a unique perspective to the development of innovative and adaptive play systems that support the physical and cognitive development of young children.

Natalie Thompson is a Lecturer in Education in the Faculty of Arts & Education at Charles Sturt University. Natalie's teaching and research is positioned within critical theories of education, particularly in relation to literacies, disability, inclusion, and teacher education. She is interested in promoting dialogue around education as a public good, the purpose of education, and the relationship between pedagogy and politics.

Caylee Tierney has been involved in various forms of collaborative writing and manifestations of SUAW while working across academic and professional roles at the University of Tasmania and as a creative writer. Her current research focuses on writing and publishing children's fantasy fiction, and she writes YA fantasy and romance fiction.

Nicola Tomlinson is a learning developer in the University of Manchester Library with over 10 years' teaching experience in tertiary education settings. She is passionate about supporting students to explore their approaches to learning, with the aim of inspiring a growth mindset and a lifelong love of learning. Having benefited from attending Shut Up & Write! sessions as a postgraduate student, Nikki finds the opportunity to be part of a community of writers that these events provide immensely valuable. Her current research interests include embodied learning and fostering academic writing communities, particularly among postgraduate researchers.

Jane Turner's research and practice explores game design, and the game engines and systems that underlay production, as cultural objects. Jane was involved in the Australasian CRC for Interaction Design (ACID) Indigenous game world project Digital Songlines. She has been exploring cultural geographies of the imagination via use of high-end game engines in projects. Her work explores the autocracy of software and potential participatory options to exploit the spatial metaphors of game worlds to re-connect digital storytelling to place. Her recent projects continue exploration of cultural geographies of the imagination and ontological design – the power of design to tell stories.

Nicole Vickery is a lecturer of visual communication and an early career researcher at the School of Design, Faculty of Creative Industries, Education and Social Justice, QUT, where her research focuses on design for children's health. An enthusiastic advocate for holistic academic practices, Dr. Vickery is a devoted supporter of the Shut Up & Write! sessions within the Faculty. These structured writing sessions, which she has actively promoted and participated in, foster a communal and supportive environment that enhances productivity and mental wellbeing among academics. Having met most of her collaborators through these faculty-run sessions, Dr. Vickery credits much of her research inspiration and success to the interdisciplinary connections and focused writing time they provide. Her commitment to integrating well-being practices into academic life not only benefits her own research pursuits but also nurtures a healthier, more collaborative atmosphere in the academic community.

Bianca Williams is a Ngemba woman and the Research Centre Manager at the Australian Centre, living and working on the unceded lands of the Wurundjeri and Boonwurrung peoples of the Kulin nations. She holds a Bachelor of Arts (Indigenous Studies) and a Master's in Justice and Criminology from RMIT. Her minor thesis explores the criminalisation of coercive control and its disproportionate impact on First Peoples women. Her academic work engages with themes of policy making, Indigenous sovereignty, and coloniality, with contributions to teaching and research RMIT and the University of Melbourne.

Abigail Winter is a results-driven academic writing wellbeing coach, mentor, and independent researcher, skilled in the analysis of words and data for user needs. She has expertise in evaluation methods in higher education, both from her own research and in various forms of student and corporate evaluation, at all levels from subject to whole-of-degree program accreditation, and institutional review. She is a confident researcher trainer, and leader, with over 20 years' experience in quality assurance, and change and project management. While her PhD focused on what helps workers in higher education cope with large-scale organisational change, and she was part of the small team that created and developed the concept of academagogy (the scholarly leadership of learning), her more recent research has focused upon professional identity, developing writing wellbeing, and reflective practice.

Emily Woodman-Pieterse is a senior lecturer in optometry and vision science in the Faculty of Health at Queensland University of Technology. Emily has a clinical, teaching, and research focus centred on myopia aetiology and control. Her PhD investigated the influence of accommodation and near-work on ocular structures that are correlated with myopia development, such as axial length, choroidal, and scleral thickness. This was followed by a 3-year industry-sponsored Postdoctoral Research Fellowship that focused on myopia control contact lens design and environmental influencers of myopia development. Emily combined her experience as a therapeutically qualified clinical optometrist, interest in contact lens practice, and strong background in myopia research to develop and implement the first Australian university-based Myopia Control Clinic in 2015 within the QUT Optometry Clinic.

Foreword

Words That Hold Us: Writing as a Practice of Wellbeing and Belonging in Academia

Narelle Lemon
Edith Cowan University

Introduction

In the contemporary landscape of higher education, where academic pressures intensify and isolation permeates scholarly communities, the need for transformative approaches to writing practice has never been more urgent. Traditional paradigms of academic writing – characterized by solitary struggle, competitive individualism, and productivity-focused metrics – have inadvertently contributed to widespread burnout, imposter syndrome, and mental health challenges among writers across all career stages (Lemon, 2024; Winter et al., 2024). Against this backdrop, Shut Up & Write! (SUAW) sessions have emerged not merely as a productivity technique, but as a revolutionary reimagining of what writing can be when grounded in community, care, and collective flourishing.

This collection represents the first comprehensive examination of SUAW as a wellbeing practice, drawing together voices from across the globe to illuminate how structured, communal writing sessions create ecosystems of support that nurture both scholarly output and human thriving. The chapters within this volume demonstrate that SUAW transcends its seemingly simple premise – writers gathering to work silently together – to become something far more profound: a practice of radical care that challenges the neoliberal academy's emphasis on individual competition and instead fosters collaborative resilience.

The significance of this work extends beyond academic writing circles to encompass broader questions about how we conceptualize productivity, community, and wellbeing in professional contexts. As Tronto's (2013) ethics of care framework suggests, genuine care involves not only attending to immediate needs but also creating conditions for sustained flourishing. The contributors to this volume reveal how SUAW sessions embody this deeper understanding of care by establishing rhythms of accountability, creating spaces for vulnerability, and building networks of mutual support that extend far beyond individual writing sessions.

What makes this collection particularly timely is its response to the seismic shifts in academic work patterns accelerated by the COVID-19 pandemic. As universities grappled with remote work, social isolation, and unprecedented stress, SUAW communities demonstrated remarkable adaptability, transitioning to virtual formats while maintaining their core commitment to collective care (Firth, 2023; Sambrooke & Duncan, 2024). These adaptations revealed not only the resilience of SUAW practices but also their fundamental flexibility – their capacity to meet writers where they are, whether geographically dispersed, managing caring responsibilities, or navigating neurodivergent needs.

Chapter Introductions

It is an honour to present an entry point into each chapter featured in this book that illuminates how wellbeing and community is cultivated through writing in the higher education setting.

The opening chapter foregrounds the vision of this book and its partner within the series. Narelle Lemon examines SUAW sessions through the lens of wellbeing science, demonstrating how this seemingly simple writing practice naturally incorporates all five dimensions of Lemon's self-care framework: mindful awareness, self-compassion, empowerment, time, and habits. The analysis reveals SUAW as more than a productivity technique – it represents a relational ecosystem of care that transforms writing from a potentially stressful individual activity into a regenerative communal practice where participants simultaneously support their own wellbeing and contribute to others' flourishing. Through case studies and theoretical frameworks, the chapter positions SUAW as an exemplar of non-medicalised self-care that addresses both individual needs and structural academic challenges, creating spaces where productivity and psychological wellbeing become mutually reinforcing rather than competing priorities.

Chapter 2 explores how SUAW sessions are embedded within the Australian Centre's Interdisciplinary Graduate Research Program in Indigenous Settler Relations as an intentionally stepped process that supports students in disrupting colonial relations through accountability and relationality. Howe, Akhbari, Williams, and Benson examine three key program activities – welcome sessions, mid-year writing retreats, and annual student feedback – demonstrating how SUAW becomes more than a wellbeing initiative by grounding the practice in anti-colonial analysis and creating opportunities for students to practice new forms of accountability that challenge traditional academic power structures.

The chapter by Guerin called "Writing in Company" examines online adaptation of SUAW at an Australian university, analysing how specific structural elements – including 50minute writing sprints, goal-setting practices, physical activity breaks, and online delivery— – contributed to participants' physical, emotional, psychological, and intellectual wellbeing over 2.5 years. Notably, the study reveals facilitator wellbeing as a significant but previously overlooked benefit of SUAW groups, demonstrating how these sessions created a reciprocal care-full community that reinforced both participants' and the facilitator's scholarly identity and sense of belonging within the research community.

Harman, Christopher Tierney, Moore, Richey, and Pink explore the "November Write In," a month-long online SUAW initiative at the University of Tasmania that adapted creative writing methodologies to foster connection and wellbeing across multiple disciplines and geographically dispersed campuses. Through personal reflections from participants across different roles and career stages, the study demonstrates how daily 50-minute writing sessions with structured goal-setting, peer hosting, and collaborative sharing created a supportive interdisciplinary community that enhanced both productivity and belonging, particularly during challenging periods of institutional change and post-pandemic isolation.

Kneen, Inala, Pearson, Tomlinson, Evans, and Pink examine how the University of Manchester Library implemented SUAW sessions and writing retreats to address widespread wellbeing concerns among postgraduate researchers (PGRs), using an emancipatory pedagogy approach that positioned library staff as "third space professionals" who could provide academic support without assessment responsibilities. Through analysis of feedback from over 1,000 participants across 1,634 total attendances, the authors demonstrate how writing in community fostered wellbeing through cross-disciplinary connection, improved writing self-efficacy through structured goal-setting and reflection, and empowered researchers to develop independent writing practices and advocate for their own wellbeing.

Lavery and George examine in Chapter 6 how embedding SUAW within a community of practice (CoP) framework can extend benefits beyond individual writing sessions, using their Research Accelerator virtual community as a case study to demonstrate sustainable community building. Drawing on Wenger's CoP model, they provide a practical roadmap for developing thriving SUAW communities through six key steps: identifying a shared domain, establishing community connections, developing shared practices, implementing participative leadership, creating inclusive environments, and measuring success while adapting to member needs.

Bowan in their chapter explores the Plan, Act, Reflect and ePortfolio (PARE) sessions – a unique SUAW format that combines Pomodoro-style writing sessions with ePortfolio development to support wellbeing and professional development among third space professionals in higher education. Through participant vignettes, the research demonstrates how PARE creates a sense of belonging, accountability, and community connection for professionals working across academic and administrative boundaries, helping them develop reflective writing practices while combating isolation and supporting career development in an increasingly challenging higher education landscape.

The MoRA Academic Writing Club, an online community created by academics from three Indonesian universities to support master's students facing mandatory publication requirements for thesis examination eligibility, is described by Mustikasari, Purnomo, and Imani. Drawing on SUAW framework cores of connections, belongings, and accomplishments, they implemented four strategic programs (lead and co-author formation, regular sessions, guest lectures, and sharing sessions) to foster professional self-care and wellbeing, though they encountered significant challenges including student burnout, time management issues, and inconsistent participation that required adaptive strategies and lowered expectations to achieve modest successes.

Varuna, The National Writers' House in Australia's Blue Mountains, was forced to close its doors during COVID-19 lockdowns in 2020, prompting creative director Amy Sambrooke and her team to pivot to virtual "Lamplight Residencies" that incorporated SUAW sessions to maintain their writing community. The initiative, described by Sambrooke and alumnus Naomi Parry Duncan, began with small cohorts but expanded to free weekday SUAW sessions serving over 200 writers across Australia when Victoria entered extended lockdown in August 2020. These sessions became a vital lifeline for geographically isolated writers like poet Meg Mooney from Alice Springs, demonstrating how SUAW could reduce barriers of geography, disability, and caring responsibilities while supporting writer wellbeing and productivity during unprecedented times of crisis.

The SUAW Exeter community for Postgraduate Researchers at the University of Exeter is examined by Preece and Sutherst (2024), who trace its evolution from small Write Clubs to a thriving worldwide peer-led community that grew 4484% in engagement between 2017–2020. Through narrative vignettes from community members, they demonstrate how SUAW Exeter combats isolation and creates wellbeing through community building, belonging, and "mattering" – where PGRs not only feel valued but add value by taking leadership roles in facilitating and coordinating sessions, ultimately developing what they term the SUAW Exeter Manifesto with principles for creating inclusive, flexible, and supportive writing environments.

Robinson explores how focus/writing retreats function as both a revolutionary productivity tool for neurodivergent academics through body doubling and an effective method for creating inclusive student learning communities in large undergraduate programmes. The chapter demonstrates how these retreats support student wellbeing by fostering autonomy, competence, and relatedness whilst providing structured environments that particularly benefit neurodivergent learners and help address challenges of scale, community building, and individualised support in higher education.

Firth traces the history of online SUAW programmes across the southern hemisphere from the early 2010s, demonstrating how these initiatives emerged as pragmatic responses to geographic distance, caring responsibilities, and time constraints rather than simply copying northern hemisphere models. The chapter reveals how online SUAW evolved from early text-based social media formats through to video conferencing platforms during COVID-19, creating inclusive writing communities that persist today and serve diverse populations including regional researchers, carers, and neurodivergent writers who benefit from flexible, accessible writing support.

The chapter by Salamon, Thompson, and Downey uses Aboriginal and Torres Strait Islander concepts of "Storying" as both framework and methodology to explore how three academics at different career stages experienced Academic Writing Fortnight (AcWriFo), an intensive online writing initiative that built upon existing Shut Up & Write! sessions. Their individual and collective stories reveal how AcWriFo transcended mere productivity interventions to create a community of practice grounded in care, inclusion, and mutual support, demonstrating how collaborative online writing environments can foster wellbeing and resist neoliberal academic pressures whilst enabling meaningful scholarly work.

Winter and colleagues present reflections from 18 cross-disciplinary academic writers at a large Australian metropolitan university, analysing how their regular SUAW sessions support academic writing wellbeing through a framework combining Joan Tronto's Ethics of Care (1993, 2013) and Narelle Lemon's Dimensions of Self-Care (2021, 2024). The authors demonstrate that SUAW functions as more than a productivity tool, creating a caring community of practice that provides emotional support, role modelling, creative management, and instrumental assistance whilst fostering what they term "communitas" – a safe, subversive space where academics can share writing challenges and celebrate achievements together.

In a complimentary chapter from the preceding, Winter joins with another group of colleagues to reflect on their Friday writing sprint community during COVID-19, analysing through Joan Tronto's Ethics of Care framework how these full-day structured writing sessions supported their wellbeing, productivity, and connection as women academics during a time of global crisis. The authors demonstrate how their Friday sprints functioned as both self-care practice and resistance against neoliberal academic pressures, creating what they term a "mosaic of care" where individual contributions combined to form a supportive interdisciplinary writing community that sustained participants through uncertain times.

Chubko reflects on her experience with writer's block during the early stages of her PhD, describing how participation in a two-day Shut Up & Write! Pomodoro technique workshop helped her overcome self-doubt and complete her entire PhD proposal literature review section within that timeframe. The chapter explores the psychological barriers behind writer's block, particularly in academic settings where high expectations and lack of guidance create anxiety, and demonstrates how structured writing communities using the Pomodoro technique can transform the blank page from an intimidating void into a manageable writing opportunity that supports both productivity and wellbeing.

Kitano, Forbes, and Baird-Bate describe the HDR Writer's Wellbeing Lounge at Queensland University of Technology, a community-driven initiative that adapts Shut Up & Write! principles specifically for postgraduate research students through a "write, reflect, relate, repeat" model combining Pomodoro writing sessions with structured wellbeing discussions. The chapter demonstrates through educator and student perspectives how this programme addresses the unique challenges of postgraduate research – including isolation, anxiety, and writing productivity – by creating a supportive hybrid community that fosters both academic progress and mental health resilience, particularly for remote students during and after the COVID-19 pandemic.

Roache, George, and Baker explore Shut Up and Research (SU&R) sessions within the Research Accelerator community, an evolution of the traditional Shut Up and Write model that encompasses broader research activities beyond writing, analysing qualitative data from participants to examine impacts on researcher wellbeing and productivity. Their findings reveal three key themes – connection, momentum, and growth – demonstrating how these structured virtual co-working sessions combat academic isolation, enhance productivity through focused work intervals, and foster researcher identity development, whilst also addressing challenges such as boundary management and imposter syndrome that participants encounter in balancing individual research needs with communal virtual working.

Conclusion

As this collection powerfully demonstrates, SUAW sessions represent far more than a writing technique – they constitute a form of collective resistance to academic cultures that privilege individual achievement over community wellbeing. Through the diverse experiences and insights shared across these chapters, we witness the emergence of a new paradigm for scholarly practice, one that recognizes writing as inherently relational and understands productivity as inseparable from care.

The evidence presented throughout this volume reveals SUAW's unique capacity to address multiple dimensions of academic wellbeing simultaneously. Writers report not only increased productivity and improved writing habits but also enhanced sense of belonging, reduced isolation, greater self-compassion, and stronger professional networks (Winter et al., 2024; Lavery & George, 2024). These outcomes suggest that SUAW sessions succeed precisely because they refuse to compartmentalize human needs – instead creating integrated experiences where personal wellbeing and professional development become mutually reinforcing.

Perhaps most significantly, this collection illuminates how SUAW practices embody principles of inclusive community building that extend far beyond writing contexts. The emphasis on accessibility, the celebration of diverse writing practices, the commitment to non-hierarchical structures, and the integration of care ethics offer valuable insights for anyone seeking to create more supportive professional environments. In an era marked by increasing awareness of systemic inequities in higher education, SUAW communities provide concrete examples of how seemingly simple practices can generate profound cultural shifts.

The global perspectives represented in this volume – spanning institutions across Australia, North America, Europe, and Asia – reveal both the universal human needs that SUAW addresses and the importance of culturally responsive adaptations. Whether embedded within Indigenous frameworks of relationality, adapted for postgraduate researchers navigating precarious employment, or integrated into institutional wellbeing initiatives, SUAW practices demonstrate remarkable flexibility while maintaining their core commitment to collective care.

Looking forward, the insights gathered in this collection point towards transformative possibilities for academic culture more broadly. As institutions grapple with ongoing challenges related to mental health, retention, and belonging, the SUAW model offers a scalable, sustainable approach to community building that requires minimal resources while generating significant impacts. The practices documented here provide blueprints for creating caring academic communities that honour both individual needs and collective flourishing.

Ultimately, this collection calls us to reconceptualize writing not as a solitary act of individual genius but as a fundamentally social practice that thrives within supportive communities. By documenting the transformative potential of writing together, these chapters contribute to a growing movement towards more humane, sustainable, and joyful approaches to scholarly work. In doing so, they remind us that the words we write are indeed words that hold us – binding us together in webs of care, accountability, and shared purpose that extend far beyond any single text or session.

References

Firth, K. (2023). *Writing together online: A history of online SUAW in the southern hemisphere.* In N. Lemon, A. Bolzle, M. Santa Cruz, & R. Saunders (Eds.), *Shut up and write: Fostering wellbeing through collective writing practices.* (In this collection). Routledge.

Lavery, L., & George, R. (2024). Shared goals, collective growth: Developing SUAW communities of practice. In N. Lemon, A. Bolzle, M. Santa Cruz, & R. Saunders (Eds.), *Shut up and write: Fostering wellbeing through collective writing practices.* (In this collection). Routledge.

Lemon, N. (2024). *The 'how' of self-care for teachers: Building your wellbeing toolbox.* Routledge.

Lemon, N. (2021). Illuminating five possible dimensions of self-care during the COVID-19 pandemic. *International Health Trends and Perspectives, 1*(2), 161–175.

Preece, K. L., & Sutherst, J. (2024). Shutting up, speaking up and staying well: Reflections from supporting PGR writing at the University of Exeter. In N. Lemon, A. Bolzle, M. Santa Cruz, & R. Saunders (Eds.), *Shut up and write: Fostering wellbeing through collective writing practices.* (In this collection). Routledge.

Sambrooke, A., & Duncan, N. P. (2024). Shut up & write at Varuna, The National Writers' House. In N. Lemon, A. Bolzle, M. Santa Cruz, & R. Saunders (Eds.), *Shut up and write: Fostering wellbeing through collective writing practices.* (In this collection). Routledge.

Tronto, J. (1993). *Moral boundaries: A political argument for an ethic of care.* Routledge.

Tronto, J. (2013). Joan Tronto: Interview. *Ethics of care: Sharing views on good care*. https://ethicsofcare.org/joan-tronto

Winter, A., Gillett-Swan, J., Barnes, N., Challen, C., Grant-Smith, D., Bobongie-Harris, F., Budby, S., Henderson, L., Lee, J., Liang, J., Lye, D., Malone, P., Mannix, M., Moseley, G., Ng, C., Olsen, A., Renton, M., & Saunders, K. (2024). The time of our lives: SUAW as a space for academic writing wellbeing. In N. Lemon, A. Bolzle, M. Santa Cruz, & R. Saunders (Eds.), *Shut up and write: Fostering wellbeing through collective writing practices*. (In this collection). Routledge.

Series Preface

As academics, scholars, staff, and colleagues working in the context of universities in the contemporary climate we are often challenged with where we place our own wellbeing. It is not uncommon to hear about burnout, stress, anxiety, pressures with workload, having too many balls in the air, toxic cultures, increasing demands, isolation, and feeling distressed (Berg and Seeber, 2016; Lemon & McDonough, 2018; Mountz et al., 2015). The reality is that universities are stressful places (Beer, et al., 2015; Cranton & Taylor, 2012; Kasworm & Bowles, 2012; Mountz et al., 2015; Ryan, 2013; Sullivan & Weissner, 2010; Wang & Cranton, 2012). McNaughton and Billot (2016) argue that the "deeply personal effects of changing roles, expectations and demands" (p. 646) have been downplayed and that academics and staff engage in constant reconstruction of their identities and work practices. It is important to acknowledge this, as much as it is to acknowledge the need to place wellbeing and self-care at the forefront of these lived experiences and situations.

Wellbeing can be approached at multiple levels including micro and macro. In placing wellbeing at the heart of the higher education workplace, self-care becomes an imperative both individually and systemically (Berg & Seeber, 2016; Lemon & McDonough, 2018). Self-care is most commonly oriented towards individual action to monitor and ensure personal wellbeing, however it is also a collective act. There is a plethora of different terms that are in action to describe how one approaches their wellbeing holistically (Godfrey et al., 2011). With different terminology comes different ways self-care is understood. For this collection self-care is understood as "the actions that individuals take for themselves, on behalf of and with others in order to develop, protect, maintain and improve their health, wellbeing or wellness" (Self Care Forum, 2019, para. 1). It covers a spectrum of health-related (emotional, physical, and/or spiritual) actions including prevention, promotion, and treatment, while aiming to encourage individuals to take personal responsibility for their health and to advocate for themselves and others in accessing resources and care (Knapik & Laverty, 2018). Self-love, -compassion, -awareness, and -regulation are significant elements of self-care. But what does this look like for those working in higher education? In this book series authors respond to the questions: *What do you do for self-care? How do you position wellbeing as part of your role in academia?*

In thinking about these questions authors are invited to critically discuss and respond to inspiration sparked by one or more of the questions of:

- How do we bring self-regulation to how we approach our work?
- How do we create a compassionate workplace in academia?
- What does it mean for our work when we are aware and enact self-compassion?
- What awareness has occurred that has disrupted the way we approach work?
- Where do mindful intentions sit?
- How do we shift the rhetoric of "this is how it has always been" in relation to overworking, and indiscretions between workload and approaches to workload?
- How do we counteract the traditional narrative of overwork?
- How do we create and sustain a healthier approach?
- How can we empower the "I" and "we" as we navigate self-care as a part of who we are as academics?
- How can we promote a curiosity about how we approach self-care?
- What changes do we need to make?
- How can we approach self-care with energy and promote shifts in how we work individually, collectively and systemically?

The purpose of this book series is to:

- Place academic wellbeing and self-care at the heart of discussions around working in higher education.
- Provide a diverse range of strategies for how to put in place wellbeing and self-care approaches as an academic.
- Provide a narrative connection point for readers from a variety of backgrounds in academia.
- Highlight lived experiences and honour the voices of those working in higher education.
- Provide a visual narrative that supports connection to authors' lived experience(s).
- Contribute to the conversation on ways that wellbeing and self-care can be positioned in the work that those working in higher education do.
- Highlight new ways of working in higher education that disrupt current tensions that neglect wellbeing.

References

Beer, L. E., Rodriguez, K., Taylor, C., Martinez-Jones, N., Griffin, J., Smith, T. R., Lamar, M., & Anaya, R. (2015). Awareness, integration and interconnectedness. *Journal of Transformative Education, 13(2)*, 161–185.

Berg, M., & Seeber, B. K. (2016). *The slow professor: Challenging the culture of speed in the academy.* Toronto: University of Toronto Press.

Cranton, P., & Taylor, E. W. (2012). Transformative learning theory: Seeking a more unified theory. In E. W. Taylor & P. Cranton (Eds.), *The handbook of transformative learning* (pp. 3–20). San Francisco, CA: Jossey-Bass.

Godfrey, C. M., Harrison, M. B., Lysaght, R., Lamb, M., Graham, I. D., & Oakley, P. (2011). The experience of self-care: A systematic review. *JBI Library of Systematic Reviews*, 8(34), 1351–1460. Retrieved from http://www.ncbi.nlm.nih.gov/pubmed/27819888

Lemon, N. & McDonough, S. (Eds.). (2018). *Mindfulness in the academy: Practices and perspectives from scholars.* Singapore: Springer.

Kasworm, C., & Bowles, T. (2012). Fostering transformative learning in higher education settings. In E. Taylor & P. Cranton (Eds.), *The handbook of transformative learning* (pp. 388–407). Thousand Oaks, CA: Sage.

Knapik, K., & Laverty, A. (2018). Self-care individual, relational, and political sensibilities. In M. A. Henning, C. U. Krägeloh, R. Dryer, F. Moir, D. R. Billington & A. G. Hill. (Eds.). *Wellbeing in higher education: Cultivating a healthy lifestyle among faculty and students.* Oxon, UK: Routledge.

McNaughton, S. M., & Billot, J. (2016). Negotiating academic teacher identity shifts during higher education contextual change. *Teaching in Higher Education*, 21(6), 644–658.

Mountz, A., Bonds, A., Mansfield, B., Loyd, J., Hyndman, J., & Watton-Roberts, M. (2015). For slow scholarship: A feminist politics of resistance through collective action in the neoliberal university. *ACME: An International E-Journal of Critical Geographies*, 14(4), 1235–1259.

Ryan, M. (2013). The pedagogical balancing act: Teaching reflection in higher education. *Teaching in Higher Education*, 18, 144–155.

Self Care Forum. (2019). Self Care Forum: Home. Retrieved July 27, 2019, from http://www.selfcareforum.org/

Sullivan, L. G., & Weissner, C. A. (2010). Learning to be reflective leaders: A case study from the NCCHC Hispanic leadership fellows program. In D. L. Wallin. (Ed.), Special issue: *Leadership in an era of change. New directions for community colleges*, No. 149 (pp. 41–50). San Francisco: Jossey-Bass.

Wang, V. C., & Cranton, P. (2012). Promoting and implementing self-directed learning (SDL): An effective adult education model. *International Journal of Adult Vocational Education and Technology*, 3, 16–25.

Acknowledgements

Declaration of AI Use:
 The authors of Chapters 4, 6, 16, and 18 used various AI tools under human oversight. Specifically, Chapter 4 used Claude to assist in identifying pertinent secondary literature (which was then read and written up by the authors); Chapter 6 used ChatGPT/Notion AI for minor editorial work (spelling, grammar, paragraph structure, and word count reduction); Chapter 16 used ChatGPT for brainstorming ideas and resources for the literature review; and Chapter 18 used ChatGPT for thematic analysis of anonymised survey responses and revision suggestions, and Grammarly for grammar, punctuation, and style consistency. No primary writing was done using AI.

Section 1
Foundations and Frameworks

1 Where Wellbeing Science Meets Writing Practice

The Intersection of Shut Up & Write! and Self-Care

Narelle Lemon

Introduction: Beyond Productivity Tools

In contemporary higher education environments characterised by intensifying productivity demands, diminishing institutional support, and unprecedented mental health challenges, academic writers increasingly find themselves navigating seemingly contradictory imperatives: produce more while preserving wellbeing (Sword, 2017; Murray, 2015; Papen & Thériault, 2018). This paradoxical landscape has catalysed interest in alternative writing communities that might address both productivity and wellbeing concerns simultaneously. Among these alternatives, Shut Up & Write! (SUAW) has emerged as a particularly significant phenomenon, transcending its origins as a simple productivity technique to become a global movement with profound implications for academic wellbeing (Mewburn et al., 2014). While SUAW's deceptively simple structure – timed writing sprints in shared physical or virtual spaces without critique or discussion during writing periods—might suggest a purely pragmatic approach to productivity, closer examination reveals a practice that embodies sophisticated wellbeing principles (Image 1.1).

This chapter examines SUAW through the lens of a non-medicalised conceptualisation of self-care defined as "anything you do proactively that helps you develop, protect, maintain and improve health, wellbeing or wellness" (Lemon, 2024a, p. 51). Specifically, we explore how SUAW naturally incorporates all five dimensions of Lemon's (2024a) self-care framework: mindful awareness, self-compassion, empowerment, time, and habits. This analysis reveals SUAW as more than a clever productivity hack – it represents a profound wellbeing intervention addressing both individual needs and structural challenges within academia. Furthermore, I position SUAW as an exemplar of relational self-care, challenging individualistic conceptions that position wellbeing as purely personal responsibility. By transforming the traditionally solitary act of writing into a communal practice, SUAW embodies what Schulz et al. (2022) describe as community care – taking care of people together for everything from basic physical needs to psychological and spiritual ones. And that indeed SUAW could be seen as a tool in the self-care toolbox that boosts

Image 1.1 SUAW understood through a wellbeing science lens.

one's wellbeing while engaging in relational acts – caring for self in order to care for others in one's life personally and professional, engaging in an act of self-care that involves others, and where one is motivate and inspired by others). The chapter extends beyond dimensional analysis to explore four innovative conceptual frameworks for understanding SUAW: as an ecosystem of care, as collective permission-giving practice, as institutional change catalyst, and as a vehicle for identity transformation. Together, these frameworks illuminate how SUAW operates at multiple levels – from individual psychology to institutional culture – creating spaces where writing becomes not just productive but profoundly nourishing.

Theoretical Framework: The Five Dimensions of Self-Care in SUAW

Research has examined self-care across multiple populations, revealing both shared patterns and significant contextual differences (Slemon et al., 2021). Recent reconceptualisations of self-care have moved beyond deficit-oriented, medicalised models emphasising disease prevention toward more holistic frameworks focused on proactive wellbeing (Narasimhan et al., 2019; Lemon, 2024b; Magyar-Moe, 2014), and this is where I position the work I do in this space. I argue that there is a notable gap in promoting self-care as a proactive action to thrive rather than merely preventing disease or managing deficits (Narasimhan et al., 2019). The growing interest in making time for self each day to process stressors and worries, and to focus on key life goals that align with meaning and purpose, represents a significant area requiring further research (Magyar-Moe, 2014). Approaches that support the act of self-care in everyday life to empower choice that broadens and builds resources for participants (Fredrickson, 2001) rather than focusing on preventing disease warrant further investigation. I thus propose reconceptualising care through what Giddens (1986) and Bondi (2005) describe as a networked understanding of self. This framework moves beyond individualistic approaches to wellbeing, positioning care as inherently relational (Lemon, 2021). I propose that my five-dimensional framework represents this shift. Firstly, I propose that we define self-care as "a proactive action to support, maintain, and protect wellbeing, wellness and health that draws from diverse areas of wellbeing science while acknowledging the process is of self-discovery, not perfectionism or comparing yourself to others" (Lemon, 2024, p. 51). With this approach I propose a toolbox theory, that is in order to draw on diverse areas of wellbeing science we need a variety of tools (strategies, practices, activities) to support our self-care across varying contexts, with then five dimensions – mindfulness, self-compassion, time, habits, and empowerment operating as interconnected pathways to sustainable wellbeing practices (or the how).

This framework provides a valuable lens for understanding SUAW's wellbeing impacts beyond mere productivity. First, let's look at the five dimensions, and then see them in action through case studies located in higher education.

SUAW and the Five Dimensions: Persona-Based Case Studies

Mindful Awareness

Mindfulness – present-moment, non-judgmental awareness – forms a cornerstone of contemporary wellbeing science (Kabat-Zinn, 2003; Brown & Ryan, 2003). SUAW sessions naturally cultivate this quality through their structure and norms. The dedicated focus time creates what neuroscientists call a "trigger for state change" – transitioning from scattered thinking to concentrated attention (Brewer, 2021). The deliberate absence of evaluation or critique during sessions allows writers to develop what Mason (2002) termed the "discipline of noticing" – metacognitive awareness of writing patterns, barriers, and enablers without judgment.

Research by Garland et al. (2015) on mindfulness-to-meaning theory helps explain why this aspect of SUAW proves so beneficial. Their work demonstrates how mindful awareness creates space for positive reappraisal and meaning-focused responses to challenges – precisely what academic writers need when facing inevitable writing difficulties. By maintaining silent, focused attention during writing periods, SUAW participants practice "being present with your needs to help you be the best version of yourself today" (Lemon, 2024, p. 51).

Self-Compassion

Self-compassion encompasses self-kindness, recognition of common humanity, and mindful awareness of difficult emotions without over-identification (Neff, 2003). SUAW sessions foster these qualities by normalising writing challenges and creating spaces where perfection is neither expected nor valued. The collective agreement that writing need not be perfect to be valuable directly counters the harsh internal critic many academics battle.

Particularly significant "permission-giving" as collective practice – where statements like "I give myself permission to write imperfectly" become shared values rather than isolated aspirations (Lemon, 2024). When participants witness others struggle and persist, it reinforces that difficulty is normal rather than personal failing – embodying the "common humanity" component of self-compassion (Neff, 2011).

Research by MacBeth and Gumley (2012) demonstrates that self-compassion significantly improves both psychological wellbeing and academic performance. For academic writers specifically, self-compassion mediates the relationship between performance pressures and wellbeing outcomes (Fong & Loi, 2016) – explaining why the self-compassionate environment of SUAW sessions contributes to both productivity and psychological health.

Empowerment

Self-determination theory identifies autonomy, competence, and relatedness as fundamental psychological needs (Ryan & Deci, 2000). SUAW sessions support all three needs – particularly autonomy through participant choice regarding attendance, writing projects, and participation style. This voluntary structure transforms writing from obligation to choice, fostering what Sheldon and Elliot (1999) term "self-concordant" goals – those aligned with intrinsic values rather than external pressures.

Furthermore, SUAW creates what writers often lack: feedback-free zones where ideas can develop before facing evaluation. This psychological safety – defined by Edmondson (1999) as feeling able to take interpersonal risks without fear of negative consequences – proves essential for authentic academic voice development. By protecting writing time from immediate critique, SUAW empowers participants to experiment and take creative risks necessary for original thought.

Importantly, this empowerment operates within community rather than in isolation. As Lemon (2024) emphasises, self-care is not purely individualistic but relational – "we care for self in order to care for others" (p. 52). SUAW embodies this principle by creating conditions where individual agency flourishes within supportive community structures.

Time

Academic time typically exists as a chronically insufficient resource – something writers never have enough of and must defensively protect. SUAW fundamentally reimagines this relationship through structured yet flexible writing periods. The pomodoro-like format (typically 25–60 minutes) demonstrates that meaningful progress doesn't require vast uninterrupted blocks – an especially significant lesson for academics with fragmented schedules.

Research on brief wellbeing interventions supports this approach. Studies by Hülsheger et al. (2015) and Parks and Biswas-Diener (2013) demonstrate that even short, intentional practices can significantly impact psychological outcomes. Similarly, research on micro-breaks shows how brief recovery periods throughout workdays substantially improve wellbeing and performance (Zacher et al., 2014).

By treating writing time as a communal asset rather than a scarce individual resource, SUAW transforms what Grant (2017) calls "stolen time" – moments wrested from overwhelming demands – into legitimate, celebrated practice. This temporal reframing addresses one of the most significant barriers to self-care implementation: the perception that one lacks time for wellbeing practices (International Self-Care Foundation, 2019).

Habits

Sustainable behaviour change requires more than motivation – it demands habit formation through consistent cues, routines, and rewards (Clear, 2018; Wood & Neal, 2007). SUAW sessions provide ideal conditions for writing habit development: the cue of arriving at designated space (physical or virtual), the routine of focused writing during timed sessions, and the reward of both social connection and writing progress.

Regular participation develops what Clear (2018) terms "identity-based habits" – practices rooted in self-conception rather than external goals. As participants transition from "people who have to write" to "people who write", motivation shifts from extrinsic pressure to intrinsic identity alignment. This transformation addresses what Lemon (2024) identifies as crucial for sustainable self-care: practices becoming integrated aspects of identity rather than additional tasks on overwhelming to-do lists.

Research by Neal et al. (2012) on habit formation in supportive social environments further explains SUAW's effectiveness. Their work demonstrates that habits formed in community contexts show greater persistence than those attempted in isolation, explaining why the social accountability of SUAW creates more durable writing patterns than solitary resolutions.

Table 1.1 summarises how each dimension of Lemon's (2024) self-care framework manifests within SUAW practices and connects to relevant wellbeing science concepts.

Table 1.1 The five dimensions of self-care and their manifestation in SUAW

Self-care dimension	Manifestation in SUAW	Connection to wellbeing science
Mindful awareness	Silent, focused writing periods; attention to writing process without judgment	Mindfulness-to-meaning theory (Garland et al., 2015); metacognitive awareness (Shapiro et al., 2006)
Self-compassion	Normalisation of writing challenges; permission to write imperfectly; shared humanity of writing struggles	Self-compassion theory (Neff, 2003, 2011); buffer against academic stress (Fong & Loi, 2016)
Empowerment	Choice in attendance, writing projects, and participation style; psychological safety to develop ideas before critique	Self-determination theory (Ryan & Deci, 2000); self-concordant goals (Sheldon & Elliot, 1999)
Time	Structured yet flexible writing periods; redefinition of productivity as process rather than output volume	Brief intervention efficacy (Parks & Biswas-Diener, 2013); micro-break research (Zacher et al., 2014)
Habits	Regular sessions with consistent cues, routines, and rewards; identity reinforcement as writer	Habit loop theory (Duhigg, 2012; Clear, 2018); identity-based habits (Clear, 2018)

To illustrate how SUAW naturally embodies the five dimensions of self-care for different academic contexts, the following case studies explore how participation addresses specific wellbeing challenges through distinct academic career stages.

Case Study 1: International PhD Student Navigating Isolation

Li Wei, an international PhD student in education from China, struggled with isolation in her first year at an Australian university. Her supervisor suggested joining the weekly SUAW sessions hosted by the graduate school.

Mindful Awareness Dimension: The focused writing periods helped Li Wei develop awareness of her scattered attention patterns. "Before each session, my mind raced with homesickness and anxiety," she explained. "During SUAW, I learned to notice when my thoughts wandered and gently return to writing. This skill transferred to managing homesickness in other contexts."

Self-Compassion Dimension: The normalised struggles she witnessed in the SUAW community helped Li Wei reframe her challenges. "Seeing established academics also struggle with writing gave me permission to be imperfect," she noted. "I stopped berating myself for writing blocks and started treating myself with kindness I would offer a friend."

Empowerment Dimension: The autonomous nature of SUAW sessions allowed Li Wei to reclaim agency amidst overwhelming PhD demands. "In structured programs, I always felt I was writing to please others," she reflected. "At SUAW, I choose what to work on each week—sometimes dissertation chapters, sometimes reflective journal entries. This choice feels revolutionary."

Time Dimension: The time-bounded writing sprints transformed Li Wei's relationship with academic writing. "I used to postpone writing until I had entire days free—which never happened," she said. "Now I know meaningful progress happens in 25-minute chunks. This changed everything."

Habits Dimension: Regular attendance established a writing rhythm previously lacking. "SUAW became my anchor point each week," Li Wei reported. "Even during difficult periods, I maintained this one commitment, which created stability amid PhD chaos."

Case Study 2: Early Career Researcher Transitioning from PhD

Dr. James Thomas had recently completed his PhD in chemistry and faced the pressure of publishing from his dissertation while teaching a heavy course load. Initially skeptical about "another writing group," he joined his department's SUAW sessions out of desperation.

Mindful Awareness Dimension: The silence during writing sessions revealed James's tendency to interrupt his own writing with self-criticism. "I never realized how harsh my internal dialogue was until these quiet sessions," he reported. "Observing these thoughts without judgment became powerfully transformative."

Self-Compassion Dimension: The social breaks between writing periods created space for normalizing publication challenges. "Hearing senior colleagues discuss their rejection experiences made me realize difficulty isn't evidence of incompetence," James reflected. "I stopped catastrophizing about reviewer comments and developed healthier perspective."

Empowerment Dimension: The absence of external evaluation during sessions allowed James to reconnect with intrinsic motivation. "In the publish-or-perish environment, I'd lost connection with why I loved chemistry," he said. "SUAW gave me space to write from curiosity rather than fear, which ironically improved my publication quality."

Time Dimension: The protected time of SUAW sessions challenged James's belief that writing required perfect conditions. "I discovered I could make meaningful progress in 60-minute sessions between classes," he noted. "This completely shifted my perception of what's possible within a busy schedule."

Habits Dimension: The consistent cues and rewards of SUAW helped James develop sustainable writing patterns. "The routine of arriving early, preparing my writing space, and celebrating progress afterward built powerful associations," he explained. "Now I automatically enter focused writing mode when following similar routines at home."

Case Study 3: Mid-Career Professor Rediscovering Purpose

Professor Sarah Martinez, tenured in sociology, found herself increasingly disengaged from writing twenty years into her career. "I was going through the motions, but felt disconnected from my research identity," she explained. A university-wide SUAW initiative became the unexpected catalyst for renewal.

Mindful Awareness Dimension: Regular SUAW participation helped Sarah notice patterns in her writing avoidance. "I realized I'd been using administrative work to escape deeper questions about my research direction," she reported. "The quiet writing periods created space to reconnect with my scholarly curiosity."

Self-Compassion Dimension: The non-judgmental atmosphere helped Sarah address her inner critic. "Academia rewards hyper-critical thinking, which I'd turned against myself," she explained. "In SUAW, I practiced kindness toward myself when exploring new research directions, treating uncertainty as natural rather than threatening."

Empowerment Dimension: The absence of external expectation in SUAW sessions allowed Sarah to experiment. "I gave myself permission to write exploratory pieces without clear publication targets," she noted. "This freedom led to my most innovative research direction in years—one I wouldn't have discovered under productivity pressure."

Time Dimension: The temporal structure challenged Sarah's all-or-nothing thinking. "I'd convinced myself meaningful writing required semester breaks," she reflected. "SUAW showed me that 90 minutes weekly maintained my connection to research, preventing the massive restart costs after long breaks."

Habits Dimension: The social accountability transformed writing from obligation to identity-affirming practice. "SUAW sessions became how I express my scholarly identity, not just what I produce," Sarah explained. "This subtle shift made writing intrinsically rewarding again rather than another task to complete."

Case Study 4: New Staff Member Building Connection

Dr. Miguel Ortiz joined the education faculty as a lecturer, moving interstate for the position. Facing both professional establishment pressure and social isolation, he joined the faculty's SUAW group during his first month.

Mindful Awareness Dimension: The focused writing periods helped Miguel recognize his tendency to use writing as escape from transition anxiety. "In SUAW sessions, I noticed how my topic choice reflected emotional state," he reported. "This awareness helped me distinguish between productive writing and avoidance behavior."

Self-Compassion Dimension: The community normalized the challenges of establishing new research while teaching. "Seeing established colleagues also juggling these demands helped me set realistic expectations," Miguel noted. "I stopped viewing struggle as personal failure and recognized it as inherent to academic life."

Empowerment Dimension: The autonomous structure allowed Miguel to balance immediate teaching demands with long-term research goals. "Having space to choose my focus each session—sometimes lesson planning, sometimes research—reduced the conflict between these roles," he explained. "This integration helped me develop coherent professional identity."

Time Dimension: The regular sessions provided temporal landmarks during a period of transition. "SUAW created structure when everything else felt chaotic," Miguel reflected. "Knowing Tuesday afternoons were for writing with colleagues gave me stable reference point each week."

Habits Dimension: The group's consistent practices facilitated Miguel's integration into departmental culture. "Learning the department's writing rhythms through SUAW fast-tracked my sense of belonging," he said. "The shared rituals around writing created connection when I knew few people."

Each of these cases illustrates how SUAW transforms writing from potential stressor to self-care activity by creating conditions where mindful awareness, self-compassion, empowerment, time mastery, and habit formation flourish without explicit instruction. The relationality of self-care is embodied in ways that work across individual and collective wellbeing, supporting the development of healthy ecosystems – something we will explore further in the next section of the chapter.

SUAW as a Relational Ecosystem of Care

Beyond individual dimensions, SUAW exemplifies an "ecosystem of care" rather than merely a community or individual practice. This ecosystem approach positions SUAW within a networked understanding of self-care that is inherently relational (Giddens, 1986; Bondi, 2005; Lemon, 2021). While traditional approaches to academic writing often emphasise isolation and individual achievement, SUAW creates a relational space that acknowledges the interconnectedness of individual wellbeing with collective experience – specifically interdependence and reciprocity; diversity and inclusion; and regenerative capacity and collective resources.

Central to understanding SUAW as a relational ecosystem is recognising the mutual interdependence between participants. Unlike traditional writing environments where writers work in isolation, SUAW creates what might be termed "relational productivity"—where each participant's presence and focus simultaneously supports their own writing and contributes to others' progress through what Hatfield et al. (1994) termed "emotional contagion". This reciprocal exchange creates what Fredrickson (2013) identifies as "upward spirals" – where positive emotional experiences generate resources that benefit both individuals and the collective. This interdependence doesn't require direct interaction, creating what organizational psychologists call "parallel play" – side-by-side activity that supports without demanding interaction (Burkus, 2017). As Lemon (2021) notes, relational self-care acknowledges that "we care for self in order to care for others." In SUAW, this manifests as participants simultaneously tend to their own writing needs while creating supportive conditions for others.

Effective ecosystems require diversity. SUAW acknowledges that "some writers need absolute quiet while others thrive with gentle background noise, that some find their flow in early morning sessions while others come alive at twilight" (Lemon, 2024, p. 52). This diversity strengthens the ecosystem's resilience – its capacity to maintain function despite disturbances – by accommodating various working styles, disciplinary backgrounds, and career stages. The inclusive nature of SUAW sessions creates what sociologists term "weak ties" – connections between individuals from different backgrounds and disciplines that often prove more valuable for idea generation and professional development than "strong ties" within established networks. By bringing together writers across hierarchical boundaries, SUAW creates relational connections that challenge traditional academic power structures, embodying what Lemon (2021) describes as "care that flows across I, we, and us."

Perhaps most significantly, SUAW creates "regenerative writing spaces" (Lemon, 2024b) – environments where participants leave with more energy than they arrived with, countering academia's often depleting effect. This regenerative quality emerges through balanced reciprocity: each participant contributes presence and focus while receiving community support, creating sustainable exchange patterns that build rather than deplete resources. This capacity connects to the idea of "collective resource building" (Fredrickson, 2001), which demonstrates how positive emotional experiences in community contexts expand both individual and shared resources. By creating conditions for what Csíkszentmihályi (2009) identified as flow – complete absorption in optimally challenging activities – SUAW sessions generate positive emotional states that accumulate over time into psychological resources that benefit both individuals and the community.

The relational ecosystem approach to SUAW aligns with emerging perspectives that position wellbeing as socially situated rather than individually determined. As Lemon (2021) notes, "self-care is not an individual act—it's a collective act. We must all take care of each other" (p. 241). SUAW embodies this perspective by creating writing contexts where individual wellbeing and productivity arise from and contribute to collective flourishing.

Permission-Giving as Relational Practice: From Individual to Collective Permission

Academic cultures typically operate through what sociologists call "permission-withholding" dynamics – where evaluation, critique, and judgment represent default interaction modes (Bourdieu, 1988). SUAW inverts this dynamic through collective permission-giving – creating relational spaces where imperfection, struggle, and process receive explicit validation. Permission involves both external sanctioning and internal authorization to engage in activities otherwise constrained by social norms or psychological barriers. In academic contexts, writing often becomes burdened by perfectionism, impostor syndrome, and evaluation anxiety – creating what psychologists term "paralysis by analysis" (Baumeister & Heatherton, 1996). What distinguishes SUAW's approach is its shift from individual to collective permission-giving. Rather than positioning permission as something individuals must generate internally against cultural resistance, SUAW creates relational contexts where permission becomes a shared resource – generated, maintained, and distributed through collective practice; thus we are embodying a relationality, where "we care for self in order to care for others" (Lemon, 2024, p. 52).

This collective permission manifests in several ways:

1 **Explicit permission** – The name "Shut Up & Write!" paradoxically gives permission to write without talking about writing (often a procrastination form).
2 **Implicit permission** – Others' visible writing process without perfection implicitly permits one's own imperfect writing.
3 **Self-permission** – Participants internalize these permissions, developing what Lemon (2024) calls "self-dialogue scripts" that support rather than sabotage writing.
4 **Relational permission** – The collective acknowledgment that writing struggle is universal creates what Neff (2011) terms "common humanity" – recognition that challenges are shared rather than evidence of personal inadequacy.

By creating spaces where permission flows between and among participants rather than being granted from authority figures, SUAW challenges traditional hierarchical academic structures, embodying what Lemon (2021) describes as networked rather than individualistic approaches to wellbeing. This permission-giving practice gradually transforms internal monologues from what cognitive psychologists call "evaluative self-talk" (judging output quality) to "process self-talk" (focusing on the writing experience itself). This shift connects directly to self-compassion research, which demonstrates that self-critical evaluation significantly impairs performance while self-compassionate approaches enhance both wellbeing and achievement (Neff et al., 2007).

What makes SUAW unique is that this transformation occurs through relational exchange rather than isolated practice. Participants witness others' writing processes, hear colleagues normalize struggles during breaks, and absorb alternative narratives about academic writing that counter perfectionistic cultural messaging. This collective permission-giving addresses what Slemon et al. (2021) identify as a significant gap in self-care literature: approaches that recognize the socially situated nature of wellbeing practices rather than positioning them as purely individual responsibilities.

While SUAW operates primarily at grassroots level, its implications for institutional change deserve examination through a relational lens. As Santos (2016) argues, preparing alternatives to dominant institutions often proves more effective than directly opposing them. SUAW represents what organizational theorists call "prefigurative intervention" – embodying the future it seeks to create rather than merely advocating for change. SUAW sessions represent what organizational theorists term "pockets of good practice" – localized innovations that can catalyse broader cultural change through relational networks. Through several mechanisms, SUAW challenges institutional norms around both writing and wellbeing:

1 **Visibility** – SUAW makes writing visible as social practice rather than mysterious solitary activity, demystifying academia's core work.
2 **Normalization** – Regular sessions normalize both struggles and joys of writing, countering silence around writing difficulties.
3 **Community Building** – Cross-disciplinary SUAW groups create connections spanning traditional institutional silos, fostering new collaborations.
4 **Relational Networks** – SUAW creates what Rogers (2003) termed "diffusion networks" – social connections that transmit new practices through demonstration and social proof.

What distinguishes SUAW from individualistic approaches to institutional change is its focus on creating relational alternatives rather than individual resistance. By establishing writing as communal rather than solitary practice, SUAW challenges fundamental assumptions about academic work while simultaneously creating supportive environments for that work to flourish. There is a **reimagining of academic wellbeing as relational practice**. Most significantly, SUAW challenges the institutional separation of productivity and wellbeing, demonstrating that these goals can be integrated rather than competing. This aligns with growing critique of self-care as an overly individualized response to structural problems (Gill & Orgad, 2022; Slemon et al., 2021). By providing a concrete, accessible model of communal academic practice that simultaneously enhances productivity and wellbeing, SUAW offers practical response to what

Gill and Orgad (2022) identify as "positivity complex" – individualistic approaches that obscure structural factors while requiring personal responsibility for systemic challenges. Instead, SUAW embodies what Lemon (2021) describes as relational care "that moves across I, we, and us to support wellbeing."

Relational Identity Transformation through SUAW: From Individual Role to Relational Identity

Regular SUAW participation facilitates profound identity shifts connecting to wellbeing literacy development – how individuals comprehend, compose, and intentionally employ wellbeing-related language in relational contexts (Oades et al., 2021). This transformation manifests through several mechanisms that extend beyond individual identity to collective and relational identity formation. SUAW participation catalyses what social psychologists term "identity integration" – where the role of "writer" transitions from external requirement to internalized self-concept. However, unlike purely individualistic identity formation, SUAW creates what might be termed "relational writer identity" – a sense of self that exists not in isolation but in relationship with other writers. This transformation occurs through:

1 **Social reinforcement** – Others' recognition strengthens writer identity through what sociologists call "reflected appraisal".
2 **Consistent communal practice** – Regular participation in a writing community creates behavioural consistency shaping self-perception through self-perception theory mechanisms (Bem, 1972).
3 **Community membership** – Belonging to a writing community confers what sociologists term "role legitimacy" – the sense of rightfully occupying a writer identity.
4 **Relational positioning** – Identity forms not just as individual writer but as member of writing community with shared experiences and values.

Research by Flores and Day (2006) on identity formation demonstrates how practice contexts significantly influence professional identity development. Similarly, studies on communities of practice show that identity formation happens through legitimate peripheral participation in community activities (Lave & Wenger, 1991) – precisely what SUAW facilitates for emerging academic writers.

Beyond professional identity, SUAW fosters wellbeing literacy—"the capability of comprehending and composing wellbeing languages, sensitive to contexts, used intentionally to maintain or improve the wellbeing of oneself or others" (Oades et al., 2021, p. 3). What distinguishes SUAW's contribution is that this literacy develops in relational rather than individual context. Participants develop:

1 **Shared vocabulary** – Terms for different writing states, barriers, and strategies that create common language for discussing wellbeing.

2 **Collective comprehension** – Understanding connections between writing practices and wellbeing outcomes through shared experience.
3 **Relational composition** – Ability to articulate writing experiences and needs in ways that connect with others' experiences.
4 **Contextual sensitivity** – Recognition of how different environments affect writing wellbeing, developed through contrast between SUAW and traditional academic spaces.

This literacy development addresses what Lemon (2024a) identifies as crucial for sustainable self-care: building "a wellbeing literacy [that] is about meeting yourself each day, learning who you really are and continuing to be present with your needs" (p. 51).

Particularly significant is how this literacy development occurs not in isolation but through relational exchanges that acknowledge interconnection. As participants develop language for articulating their own writing experiences, they simultaneously develop the capacity to recognize and respond to others' needs – embodying care that flows across self and others (Lemon, 2021). This mutual development contrasts sharply with individualistic approaches to wellbeing literacy that position development as purely internal process disconnected from community contexts.

Conclusion: SUAW as Integrated Relational Wellbeing Practice

Viewing SUAW through the lens of a five-dimensional self-care framework (Lemon, 2024a) reveals how this seemingly simple practice embodies sophisticated wellbeing principles within a relational context. SUAW demonstrates that academic productivity need not come at wellbeing's expense – indeed, sustainable productivity emerges from wellbeing practices that address both individual needs and structural challenges. Considering the place of how mindful awareness, self-compassion, empowerment, time, and habits manifest within SUAW creates what positive psychologists call "upward spirals" – virtuous cycles where improved wellbeing enhances productivity, which in turn supports wellbeing (Fredrickson, 2013). This integration offers a promising response to academia's wellbeing crisis, providing a practical model for writing communities that nurture both scholarly output and psychological flourishing. Moreover, conceptualising SUAW as an ecosystem of care, permission-giving practice, institutional change catalyst, and identity transformation vehicle moves beyond individualistic self-care frameworks to embrace more relational understanding of academic self-care that is systems based and is an act that moves across I, we, and us to support wellbeing. As Schulz et al. (2022) argue, "self-care is not an individual act—it's a collective act. We must all take care of each other" (p. 241). SUAW exemplifies this collective approach, creating regenerative writing spaces where writers sustain each other through mutual presence and shared purpose.

The relational approach to self-care embodied by SUAW offers several advantages over individualistic models:

1. **Distribution of responsibility** – By positioning wellbeing as communal rather than an individual concern, SUAW addresses what Gill and Orgad (2022) identify as a problematic tendency to individualize responses to structural challenges.
2. **Sustainable resource generation** – Relational practices create what Fredrickson (2013) terms "collective positivity resonance" – emotional resources that benefit both individuals and communities in self-sustaining cycles.
3. **Systemic impact** – By changing writing practices at the communal rather than individual level, SUAW creates potential for broader institutional transformation.
4. **Identity reinforcement** – Relational contexts provide stronger identity reinforcement than individual practice alone, as identities form and solidify through social recognition (Lave & Wenger, 1991).
5. **Wellbeing literacy development** – Shared language and understanding around wellbeing emerges through collective practice, creating what Oades et al. (2021) identify as a contextually sensitive capability for maintaining wellbeing.

By integrating productivity and wellbeing through relational practice, SUAW offers a model for academic communities seeking to address both the mental health crisis in academia and the intensifying productivity demands of contemporary higher education. As writing constitutes core academic practice, transforming how we write together may prove a powerful catalyst for reimagining academic culture more broadly – moving from isolated competition toward communities of mutual care and shared flourishing.

References

Baumeister, R. F., & Heatherton, T. F. (1996). Self-regulation failure: An overview. *Psychological Inquiry*, *7*(1), 1–15. https://doi.org/10.1207/s15327965pli0701_1

Bem, D. J. (1972). Self-perception theory. In L. Berkowitz (Ed.), *Advances in experimental social psychology* (Vol. 6, pp. 1–62). Academic Press.

Bondi, L. (2005). Making connections and thinking through emotions: between geography and psychotherapy. *Transactions of the Institute of British Geographers*, *30*(4), 433–448.

Bourdieu, P. (1988). *Homo academicus*. Stanford University Press.

Brewer, J. A. (2021). *Unwinding anxiety: New science shows how to break the cycles of worry and fear to heal your mind*. Avery.

Brown, K. W., & Ryan, R. M. (2003). The benefits of being present: Mindfulness and its role in psychological well-being. *Journal of Personality and Social Psychology*, *84*(4), 822–848. https://doi.org/10.1037/0022-3514.84.4.822

Burkus, D. (2017). *Under new management: How leading organizations are upending business as usual*. Mariner Books.

Clear, J. (2018). *Atomic habits: An easy & proven way to build good habits & break bad ones*. Penguin.

Csíkszentmihályi, M. (2009). *Flow: The psychology of optimal experience*. Harper & Row.

Duhigg, C. (2012). *The power of habit: Why we do what we do in life and business*. Random House.

Edmondson, A. (1999). Psychological safety and learning behavior in work teams. *Administrative Science Quarterly*, *44*(2), 350–383. https://doi.org/10.2307/2666999

Flores, M. A., & Day, C. (2006). Contexts which shape and reshape new teachers' identities: A multi-perspective study. *Teaching and Teacher Education*, *22*(2), 219–232. https://doi.org/10.1016/j.tate.2005.09.002

Fong, M., & Loi, N. M. (2016). The mediating role of self-compassion in student psychological health. *Australian Psychologist*, *51*(6), 431–441. https://doi.org/10.1111/ap.12185

Fredrickson, B. L. (2001). The role of positive emotions in positive psychology: The broaden-and-build theory of positive emotions. *American Psychologist*, *56*(3), 218–226. https://doi.org/10.1037/0003-066X.56.3.218

Fredrickson, B. L. (2013). Positive emotions broaden and build. *Advances in Experimental Social Psychology*, *47*, 1–53. https://doi.org/10.1016/B978-0-12-407236-7.00001-2

Garland, E. L., Farb, N. A., Goldin, P. R., & Fredrickson, B. L. (2015). Mindfulness broadens awareness and builds eudaimonic meaning: A process model of mindful positive emotion regulation. *Psychological Inquiry*, *26*(4), 293–314. https://doi.org/10.1080/1047840X.2015.1064294

Giddens, A. (1986) *The Constitution of Society. Outline of the Theory of Structuration*. 2nd Edition, University of California Press, Berkeley.

Gill, R., & Orgad, S. S. (2022). Get unstuck: Pandemic positivity imperatives and self-care for women. *Cultural Politics*, *18*(1), 44–63. https://doi.org/10.1215/17432197-9516926

Grant, A. (2017). *Originals: How non-conformists move the world*. Penguin.

Hatfield, E., Cacioppo, J. T., & Rapson, R. L. (1994). *Emotional contagion*. Cambridge University Press.

Hülsheger, U. R., Feinholdt, A., & Nübold, A. (2015). A low-dose mindfulness intervention and recovery from work: Effects on psychological detachment, sleep quality, and sleep duration. *Journal of Occupational and Organizational Psychology*, *88*(3), 464–489. https://doi.org/10.1111/joop.12115

International Self-Care Foundation. (2019). *What is self-care?* http://isfglobal.org/what-is-self-care/

Kabat-Zinn, J. (2003). Mindfulness-based interventions in context: Past, present, and future. *Clinical Psychology: Science and Practice*, *10*(2), 144–156. https://doi.org/10.1093/clipsy.bpg016

Lave, J., & Wenger, E. (1991). *Situated learning: Legitimate peripheral participation*. Cambridge University Press.

Lemon, N. (2021). Holding the space: A teacher educator's poetic representations of pre-service teachers acts of self-care. In M. P. Hall & A. K. Brault (Eds.), *Academia from the inside* (pp. 169–193). Palgrave Macmillan. https://doi.org/10.1007/978-3-030-83895-9_8

Lemon, N. (2024a). *The 'how' of self-care for teachers: Building your wellbeing toolbox*. Routledge.

Lemon, N. (2024b, December 19). Where wellbeing science meets writing: The magic that is SUAW! *The Wellbeing Whisperer*. https://www.exploreandcreateco.com/the-wellbeing-whisperer/2024/12/19/where-wellbeing-science-meets-writing

MacBeth, A., & Gumley, A. (2012). Exploring compassion: A meta-analysis of the association between self-compassion and psychopathology. *Clinical Psychology Review*, *32*(6), 545–552. https://doi.org/10.1016/j.cpr.2012.06.003

Magyar-Moe, J. L. (2014). *Therapist's guide to positive psychological interventions*. Academic Press.

Mason, J. (2002). *Researching your own practice: The discipline of noticing*. Routledge.

Mewburn, I., Osborne, L., & Caldwell, G. (2014). Shut up & write! Some thoughts on communities of academic practice. *Journal of Academic Language and Learning*, *8*(3), 49–57.

Murray, R. (2015). *Writing in social spaces: A social processes approach to academic writing*. Routledge.
Narasimhan, M., Allotey, P., & Hardon, A. (2019). Self care interventions to advance health and wellbeing: A conceptual framework to inform normative guidance. *BMJ*, *365*, l688. https://doi.org/10.1136/bmj.l688
Neal, D. T., Wood, W., & Drolet, A. (2012). How do people adhere to goals when willpower is low? The profits (and pitfalls) of strong habits. *Journal of Personality and Social Psychology*, *104*(6), 959–975. https://doi.org/10.1037/a0032626
Neff, K. D. (2003). Self-compassion: An alternative conceptualization of a healthy attitude toward oneself. *Self and Identity*, *2*(2), 85–101. https://doi.org/10.1080/15298860309032
Neff, K. D. (2011). *Self-compassion: The proven power of being kind to yourself*. William Morrow.
Neff, K. D., Kirkpatrick, K. L., & Rude, S. S. (2007). Self-compassion and adaptive psychological functioning. *Journal of Research in Personality*, *41*(1), 139–154. https://doi.org/10.1016/j.jrp.2006.03.004
Oades, L. G., Ozturk, C., Hou, H., & Slemp, G. R. (2021). Wellbeing literacy: A language-use capability relevant to wellbeing outcomes of positive psychology interventions. *The Journal of Positive Psychology*, *15*(5), 696–700. https://doi.org/10.1080/17439760.2020.1789711
Papen, U., & Thériault, V. (2018). Writing retreats as a milestone in the development of PhD students' sense of self as academic writers. *Studies in Continuing Education*, *40*(2), 166–180. https://doi.org/10.1080/0158037X.2017.1396973
Parks, A. C., & Biswas-Diener, R. (2013). Positive interventions: Past, present, and future. In T. B. Kashdan & J. Ciarrochi (Eds.), *Mindfulness, acceptance, and positive psychology: The seven foundations of well-being* (pp. 140–165). Context Press.
Rogers, E. M. (2003). *Diffusion of innovations* (5th ed.). Free Press.
Ryan, R. M., & Deci, E. L. (2000). Self-determination theory and the facilitation of intrinsic motivation, social development, and well-being. *American Psychologist*, *55*(1), 68–78. https://doi.org/10.1037/0003-066X.55.1.68
Santos, B. D. S. (2016). *Epistemologies of the south: Justice against epistemicide*. Routledge.
Schulz, P., Kreft, A. K., Touquet, H., & Martin, S. (2022). Who cares? Self-care for gender-based violence researchers — Beyond bubble baths and chocolate pralines. *Qualitative Research*, *23*(5), 1461–1480. https://doi.org/10.1177/14687941221087868
Shapiro, S. L., Carlson, L. E., Astin, J. A., & Freedman, B. (2006). Mechanisms of mindfulness. *Journal of Clinical Psychology*, *62*(3), 373–386. https://doi.org/10.1002/jclp.20237
Sheldon, K. M., & Elliot, A. J. (1999). Goal striving, need satisfaction, and longitudinal well-being: The self-concordance model. *Journal of Personality and Social Psychology*, *76*(3), 482–497. https://doi.org/10.1037/0022-3514.76.3.482
Slemon, A., Jenkins, E. K., & Bailey, E. (2021). Enhancing conceptual clarity of self-care for nursing students: A scoping review. *Nurse Education in Practice*, *55*, 103178. https://doi.org/10.1016/j.nepr.2021.103178
Sword, H. (2017). *Air & light & time & space: How successful academics write*. Harvard University Press.
Wood, W., & Neal, D. T. (2007). A new look at habits and the habit-goal interface. *Psychological Review*, *114*(4), 843–863. https://doi.org/10.1037/0033-295X.114.4.843
Zacher, H., Brailsford, H. A., & Parker, S. L. (2014). Micro-breaks matter: A diary study on the effects of energy management strategies on occupational well-being. *Journal of Vocational Behavior*, *85*(3), 287–297. https://doi.org/10.1016/j.jvb.2014.08.005

2 "It's About Accountability More Than Community"

Embedding Co-Working within Graduate Research Training

Rebecca Howe, Claire Akhbari, Bianca Williams, and Eleanor Benson

Introduction

SUAW has been regularly deployed in academic settings since its inception. Indeed, these sessions are now regarded as value-adds offered by universities (and others) to supplement graduate research degrees, as they help students write and cultivate a sense of community in what is often an isolating learning experience (Khoo, 2016; Mewburn et al., 2014). With research training as context, this chapter reflects on four years of hosting SUAW as an embedded component of the Australian Centre's Interdisciplinary Graduate Research Program in Indigenous Settler Relations (the Grad Program). Highlighting three key Grad Program activities —the orientation and welcome event, mid-year writing retreat, and annual student feedback—we consider how SUAW, as intentionally stepped out through this program structure, supports students to disrupt colonial relations.

Designed as a cohort approach, the Grad Program is open to any graduate researcher undertaking research related to Indigenous settler relations in Australia and the world. Program activities are enriched by the diverse projects and contributions of the students. SUAW is embedded in the Grad Program schedule as a stepped process. Monthly online co-working sessions flow into a three-day mid-year hybrid writing retreat and connect to an extended five-day residential retreat at the end of the year. The combination of online, hybrid, and in-person group writing has allowed students to participate from across the continent and overseas. The recurrence of these co-working sessions complements other Grad Program activities, including masterclasses, workshops, a research symposium, and a critical reading group. By providing space for knowledge acquisition, co-working, and discussion, the Grad Program also creates opportunities to practise reflexivity, accountability, and collaboration. We have heard from students how it enriches their graduate study experience and have seen the cohort forming lasting and generative relationships.

The Grad Program was developed as part of the Indigenous Settler Relations Collaboration (ISRC), which was co-founded as a research unit in 2018 by Torres Strait Islander Associate Professor Sana Nakata and White settler Professor Sarah Maddison. At the heart of the ISRC's approach was understanding that "Indigenous-settler relations [are] an integral part of the fabric of Australia [and] central and foundational to the politics of this continent" (Nakata & Maddison, 2020, p. 2). Central to this project was resisting (re)producing the inherently oppressive conditions of settler colonialism as inevitable, immutable, and omnipotent in the hope of facilitating more just possibilities (Maddison & Nakata, 2020). The Grad Program was launched in 2021, as the ISRC was transforming from a faculty research unit into the Australian Centre, a university research centre. The re-launched Australian Centre (2025) concentrates research on the settler state, its culture, institutions, sovereignty, and identities. Indigenous settler relations remains a key focus of the Centre, with the Grad Program a central part of the research training undertaken. In 2021, the ISRC launched the Graduate Research Program with an inaugural cohort of 40 students. Since then, participation has steadily increased, drawing from a broader range of disciplines, institutions, and locations. Most graduate researchers in the Program are non-Indigenous, a prominent reminder of the ongoing need for institutions to invest in Indigenous scholars and scholarship.

When developing the Grad Program, we drew upon research (Pihama et al., 2019) that identified the generic higher degree by research upskilling sessions, of which SUAW often forms a central component, as unfit for purpose. This is because of participants' unique positions, lived experiences, and the focus of their work, as well as the broader settler colonial context of so-called Australia and working in institutions that are sites of the reproduction of colonial logics (Rowe & Tuck, 2017). Drawing on the work of Michelle Trudgett (2014) and inspired by the Te Kupenga o MAI (Māori and Indigenous) (Pihama et al., 2019) and Supporting Aboriginal Graduate Enhancement (SAGE) (Pidgeon et al., 2014) programs, the Grad Program is based on and promotes Indigenous doctoral pedagogy as best practice for all students. Crucial for the majority non-Indigenous participants, this includes maintaining a focus on settler responsibility and justice for First Nations, seeking to be in relation with, and of service to, Indigenous peoples and sovereignties. For Indigenous participants, the program fosters accountability through various means, with SUAW as a key approach. As one student reflected, ideas are introduced and gradually become "lived and embedded" in both thought and practice. This is especially evident in long-term participants, who sustain the program's principles beyond academia. Rather than simply adopting techniques, the program encourages deeper engagement with the politics of Indigenous doctoral pedagogy and its broader research implications.

SUAW is unique in the Grad Program because it is a practical extension of Strakosch's (2019) argument that the technical is political. An imperative to understand technical practices as "a central site where foundational political relationships are asserted and contested" (p. 3) opens space for attending to "the ongoing nature of colonisation [and] the persistence of Indigenous sovereignty" (p. 119). To think with Strakosch (2019) about the political in this broad sense involves resisting the idea that there are isolated techniques that we can impart to make research students better academic objects. We are aware that doing this results in training that lacks criticality around the colonial nature of knowledge production (Bodkin-Andrews et al., 2019) and produces narrow specialisation (Williams & Lee, 1999) and a dehumanised study experience that is shallow in its skilling (Beasy et al., 2019). Instead, the Grad Program recognises students' subjectivity and their often-fraught place within the colonial institution. The foundational understandings of the ISRC and the Australian Centre means that we would have certainly been reinscribing colonial relations if we had not structured the Grad Program's SUAW with an anti-colonial and non-colonial ethos.

Embedding SUAW sessions into the program structure as an intentionally stepped process creates opportunities for students to disrupt the normative modes of relating that colonial institutions implicitly encourage. SUAW sessions in the Grad Program are student-led and coordinated with care and intentionality in relation to the broader program structure. Fostering accountability in order to avoid reproducing colonial harm requires a cognisance of the ways we relate, and are in relation, to one another. Students are oriented to this notion in the welcome sessions. Relationships, as peers and co-workers, are built through the mid-year writing retreat and other activities. Finally, annual student feedback enables opportunity for critical reflection and makes explicit the relational obligations of the ISRC/Australian Centre and the University more broadly. In the SUAW sessions themselves, there is a standard format that starts with greetings and sharing writing goals and concludes with a reflection on achievements. Participants are intentionally prompted to express their preferences for the length of breaks between Pomodoro cycles, the timer to use, whether to have cameras on, the option to chat, and reminders to take breaks from the computer. Relationality evolves over time, while accountability is established through negotiation and mutual agreement on how to be together. In this way, SUAW sessions in the Grad Program are a key site where students are supported to be cognisant of their positionality and attendant relational obligations, and to construct the space with care and reciprocity.

As with the Grad Program, this chapter emerges from and occurs as an ongoing Indigenous settler relations practice. Our collective work, comprising White settlers and Indigenous scholars, requires a careful examination of position and privilege. As we attempt to define our collective identity, the act of naming the 'we' becomes fraught with questions—who counts, who is named, and who is left out? As we navigate power imbalances in our praxis, we have found it increasingly difficult to articulate these complexities. Terms like partnerships, collaborations, and alliances are often used to describe relationships between Indigenous peoples and settlers, but these terms tend to gloss over the deeper struggles of working within contested, colonised spaces. Through our various roles at the ISRC and Australian Centre (past and present), we draw on lessons from writers, theorists, activists and community practitioners whose responses to power imbalances teach us about working in ways that do not reproduce colonising dynamics (Kwaymullina, 2016; Land, 2015; The

Red Nation, 2021). Ultimately, our reflective practice demands an honest engagement with the contradictions inherent in collaboration across difference, particularly in a context of disputed sovereignty.

We write as part of the work we do, which seeks to individually reject and collectively dismantle the personal and structural privilege gained from foundational and ongoing genocide and dispossession. We are also conscious of the tension inherent in doing critical, anti-colonial work within and directed at sites of colonial reproduction such as the University of Melbourne. From this experience, we initially planned to document the use of SUAW in the Grad Program process as a resource. But by asking how SUAW contributes to work that disrupts settler colonial relations and processes, we began to appreciate how often critical work in the academy goes unrecorded and unaccounted for. Producing a record of our work was quickly realised as something with the potential for people to open up and examine, and perhaps to adapt according to their context.

This chapter is an unfolding story of accountability created through an intentionally stepped process of embedding co-working. The narrative follows the Exquisite Corpse method as a form of collective inquiry into the subversive (Gooding, 1991). First, there are the Grad Program welcoming sessions, which serve as both an orientation and a prompt for students to contribute to a supportive criticality in their graduate research experience. Second, we introduce an Exquisite Corpse artwork created at a mid-year writing retreat and explore how it has come to inform how we understand the collective and iterative ways we work and contribute to the whole that makes up the Grad Program. Third is a selection from the annual feedback from students who share their experiences of engaging in SUAW as a practice of accountability which attempts to support them in disrupting the colonial relations of the University and elsewhere. In the final section, we open it out and detail some prompts that may help others to think deeply about where SUAW is used and what the sessions can accomplish.

Unfold 1: Grad Program Welcome Sessions

The Grad Program welcome sessions mark the first fold in this story of accountability and community. They orient students to the Program and provide structured time for making self-introductions and connections. During these sessions, the principles of engagement are presented as the Program's supporting framework. These principles are adapted from Sisters Uncut (2018), Abolitionist Futures (n.d.), Principles of Universal Design via Imagining Abolition (2021), and the Safer Spaces guidelines from the Border Abolition (2021) conference. We thank these collectives for their labour, care, and thought as we join this long tradition of building accountability into relations.

Working as a set of prompts, these principles are rooted in the recognition that oppression is widespread and socially entrenched and that we live in a world characterised by material and epistemological violence that is foundational to and reproduced in societal institutions. We make this supporting framework clear at the outset because people all respond to harmful experiences differently. We clarify that these resources are available to guide us in the ongoing, self-directed, and personal work of accountability, reflection, and repair.

The Grad Program supports accountability through these principles of engagement. For example, the principles highlight that what is created together in the Grad Program is an imperfect space. A point made at the welcome sessions is that making mistakes is not as much of an issue as not *knowing* about mistakes. This understanding obliges listening, noticing, and critical reflection. In these ways, creating a culturally safe-enough space requires relationships. In a program that is centred on Indigenous settler relations, it means asking what it is to be in relation and understanding the settler colonial systems and structures which shape these dynamics. Another point conveyed to students is that there is choice and agency in this. Made particularly clear is the expectation that First Nations students join to enrich their graduate experience, not to prove who they are, and especially not to help settlers along on their learning/healing journey.

Creating a safe-enough space for dialogue and relationality is essential because we live in a settler colonial state that is inherently violent. Asserting this underlines that while some students may study this violence, for others it also forms part of an inherited and living experience. As the Centre's former Deputy Director (2022–2025), Julia Hurst, calls on us to remember and keep remembering: For Indigenous scholars, this is not theory, it is lived (Hurst & Read, 2022). Decter and Taunton (2022) argue that in initiatives like the Grad Program, "there is a *balance* of working independently and collaboratively, of stepping forward to embrace the responsibility of affecting one's spheres of influence and stepping back to decentre colonial whiteness" (p. 95, emphasis added). In our various roles at the Centre, we are articulating, facilitating, and practising these principles of engagement.

The welcome sessions orient students to the relational ethics of the Grad Program as a set of prompts for action. In the following section, we discuss how incorporating SUAW sessions into the program schedule provides opportunities to practise accountability, with the principles of engagement serving as a framework for deepening critical engagement and guiding the ongoing responses of individuals in a collective seeking to disrupt colonial relations.

Unfold 2: Mid-Year Writing Retreat

The Grad Program's mid-year writing retreat marks the second fold in this story. Held in July, this three-day SUAW retreat occurs while other Program activities pause for the semester break. The Pomodoro Technique organises the writing time, while afternoon discussions of work-in-progress help build intellectual intimacy through peer feedback. Following participants' requests for activities in their breaks, a suggestion was made to play the Exquisite Corpse drawing game.

"It's About Accountability More Than Community" 25

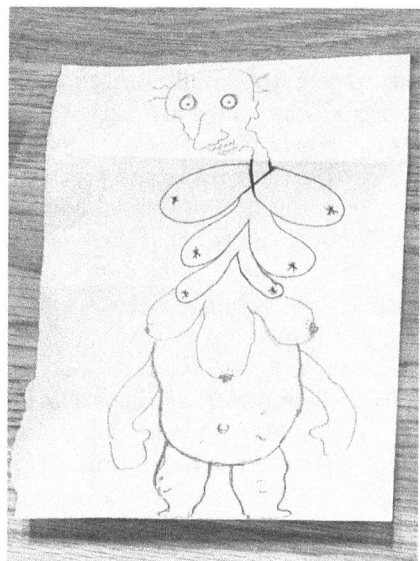

Image 2.1 Collective artworks created during the 2022 retreat.

Students take turns drawing a section of a body, folding the paper down and passing it to the next person, with only a glimpse of the drawing showing past the fold. Image 2.1 shows one of these collective artworks created during the 2022 retreat. On the left is a section with the pen ready for the next participant. On the right is the finished composition, which participants unfolded to delighted surprise and laughter.

Exquisite Corpse relates to this accountability story as both the artwork and the Grad Program are collective projects at different scales. Intentional parameters hold the collectivity together, while people contribute uniquely to the composition and the Program. As each person draws a different body part and participates in various activities, the results are often surprising. The collectivity continues to unfold with people contributing and responding without a predefined outcome.

Implementing SUAW as a stepped process means that the regular sessions lead students up to the intensive 3-day mid-year retreat, which, in turn, builds momentum for the 5-day end-of-year retreat. This is part of the intentional parameters that seek to emulate the positive factors in graduate students' experience that are illustrated in the literature, including the importance of relationship building (Schulz et al., 2019; Pidgeon et al., 2014), the creation of inclusive spaces that enhance interpersonal communication and relationship building (Fredericks & Lee Brien, 2014), the importance of developing a community of practice (Hutchings et al., 2018), and the opportunity to meet fellow graduate students in the context of a support structure that challenges students to be accountable to the goals they set for themselves (Pidgeon et al., 2014).

Scheduling regular SUAWs punctuated by writing retreats is about more than maintaining accessibility and building momentum. It offers an opportunity to go beyond traditional and limited notions of graduate research accountability as only being answerable to ethics committees and supervisors. Students having spaces to practise expands the kinds of accountability on offer. When we say that there is space to *practise*, we are referring to repetition, an exercise of a skill to interrupt prescribed and entrenched patterns of relating to build proficiency. The fact that these are not the sorts of relationships or skills typically valued or measured in graduate research program development reminds us that the university system is violent in that it is not set up for people to succeed, work collaboratively, or disrupt colonial relations.

Describing the Exquisite Corpse as a form of collective artwork created during the mid-year writing retreat and a mode of inquiry has helped us identify how SUAW provides opportunities for practice. Now, we turn from the supportive framework and the structuring of activities to the experiences of students in the Program. We suggest that SUAW can be used to support challenging traditional understandings of where and how to implement accountability in a graduate research training context.

Unfold 3: Annual Grad Program Feedback

The final fold in this story concerns the annual feedback survey of the Grad Program participants, which is launched after the end-of-year writing retreat. We share this feedback to show how students experience the attempt to weave accountability into each part of the Graduate Program.

SUAW sessions are the second most popular Grad Program activity, with student comments indicating a deepening of the connections fostered through co-working and conversation.

> There is such a variety of people in the program. It's just so interesting and inspiring to kind of hear what everyone's doing.
>
> The opportunity to connect with and work alongside others working in a similar area, including in the shut up and write sessions
>
> I only attended one [SUAW] at the end of the year because I was unsure and not confident in some of the large groups. I really enjoyed the group and look forward to this year's sessions.
>
> I loved meeting the other students, especially when we initiated an [additional] ongoing online SUAW.

The opportunity SUAW provided was for students to be together as they were thinking through and applying their knowledge in their writing. We found responses that highlight the value of peer review in the sense of discussing each other's work informally and formally. For example, reflecting on an experience of feeling safe to ask questions in both workshops and SUAW sessions, a student said, "I gained knowledge and skills in forming a critical lens". Additional comments include:

> SUAWs create focus and accountability, it opened invitations to join other groups.
>
> The eye-opening aspects of being a white researcher meant that my approach is now much slower and considered, which I think it is imperative – so the only obstacle to this is the institutional clock ticking. The obstacles have been that there were challenges to my thinking that are hard to undo within the university setting but I agree are important …

Like the unfolding of the full image at the end of the Exquisite Corpse game, the skills, mutuality, invitations, and changed thinking appear as surprising and self-reinforcing results of participation in SUAWs.

There are also different sorts of experiences and responses, including important feedback in the survey about cultural safety. In response to a question asking if there was anything that might have increased their participation, a student responded: "Confidence". Elaborating that "I could not gauge my cultural safety in Zoom sessions … Maybe this year will be different". Providing opportunities to practise another form of accountability in the Grad Program SUAW context is important. But what this feedback shows is that there is still more to be done in the Program and how high the stakes are. A crucial reminder (for some of us) is that "understanding one's relationships to Indigenous sovereignties and colonial occupation provides a foundation from which white settlers can engage as active accomplices and also brings the imperative of accountability into sharp focus" (Decter & Taunton, 2023, p. 248). First Nations students continue to re-enrol in subsequent offerings of the Program. The opportunities for accountability are thus reciprocal and multi-directional.

Feedback shows that the Program and the embedded SUAW sessions are having some positive impact as students create their own Exquisite Corpse experiences of the Program through the folding and unfolding of their ideas in an expansive collective form of accountability.

> I really value the ISRC for the exposure to the most relevant thinking and writing and contextualization of this within the academy.
>
> [The Program has] expanded my thinking beyond my own research project, and made me think about the connections between my work and contemporary research practices.
>
> … most importantly I've really valued being connected in with a group of people who share similar values and a supportive ethos. I haven't found that anywhere within my faculty really.
>
> It was good to see non-indigenous people wanting to understand themselves better, the colonial structures and impacts that do not rest.
>
> An evident culture of support and rigour at the Australian Centre.

I don't come across many graduate research students who have the capacity to engage on these issues. In the course of conversation with several people I have recommended the program though, so it really depends on what I understand about other students' research and intent.

Through SUAW, the Grad Program is providing opportunities to practise another form of accountability. In turn, participants are providing the Australian Centre with opportunities for accountability.

Opening Out SUAW as an Intentional Stepped Process

As we have unfolded this accountability story in three parts, we now open it all out to discuss how SUAW might be used in ways that support the difficult work of disrupting colonial relations. Building accountability is a core component of Indigenous settler relations. Our use of SUAW occurs in a space of tension, and there is much to unpack in resisting (re)producing the inherently oppressive conditions of settler colonialism. The context of this work pushes us to consider the underlying politics of graduate research training, undertake an honest accounting of the University, return to guiding values, and put all our thinking and talking into action. These are four steps that we have undertaken that might be applied to other contexts.

Consider the Underlying Politics

It is important to recognise that the Grad Program is one example of the many experiences of the inherent tension in doing critical or anti-colonial work within and to a colonial institution that those involved in the ISRC and the Australian Centre have experienced since their inception. As with all other activities that have formed part of the work done, we continue to think deeply about the politics of the seemingly technical aspect of the Program's offerings, including SUAW. Improved student wellbeing may well be an outcome, but by acknowledging students' subjectivity, the Grad Program is able to ask how accountability and relationality might operate differently for participating students. We share these reflections in this chapter as part of our commitment to accountability in our various roles in coordination, management, and facilitation.

An Honest Accounting

Our experience has led us to understand it is not enough to simply organise SUAW sessions for students. Rather, programming requires deep consideration of the processes and the places that we are embedded in. Of course, this is not without risk, both organisationally and ethically. The University has policies that we are bound to and procedures that we are restricted by. Further, by saying that we are structuring the Grad Program's SUAW with an anti-colonial and non-colonial ethos, we risk creating a misperception of autonomy from the University. This is not the case. Although we engage with and are guided by critical Indigenous, radical, abolitionist scholarship and other scholars, we are *of* the institution, and in fact, this is often the strength of our contribution.

(Re)turn to Guiding Values

As such, we return to the guiding relational principles to check that we are working in alignment with our values of a place-based ethic, reflexivity, and reciprocity, including in the context of SUAW sessions. These are not static ideals, but active commitments that shape how SUAW is conceived and delivered. At this stage, we pause to ask critical questions: Does this offering recognise and respond to its location on Indigenous lands? How are we positioning ourselves within this work, and are we inadvertently reproducing the logics of the White possessive? (Moreton-Robinson, 2015). We also reflect on the Centre's position: What is gained through its association with particular scholars, knowledges, or practices? And importantly, is that engagement reciprocal, or extractive? These questions are central to ensuring that the process is not only productive, but principled. Returning to these values ensures that SUAW remains grounded in ethical practice and accountable to the places and relationships it is part of.

Step Up, Take Action

We can never avoid the inherent tension produced in our work. We can, however, enact our ethics through practice, which is to say that:

- Irrespective of whether it is delivered in a university context or not, all SUAW would benefit from considering the colonial conditions of the writing and the wellbeing it is being set up to support.
- There is a wealth of publicly available analyses and methodologies that inform the work. This chapter's references is a selection of those we use and recommend.
- Frankly, there is no excuse not to engage in this depth of analysis and translate it into action.

Conclusion

The Grad Program has an anti-colonial ethos that encourages criticality, including in the writing process and in undertaking a graduate research degree. There is a politics involved in the delivery that students—First Nations students and those on the fringes of their faculties and disciplines—do not find in other parts of the University. We have used an Exquisite Corpse artwork to illustrate the embedded accountability in our Program's design and delivery. This method and the Grad Program are collective practices shaped by intentional parameters. We see the layers of accountability created through co-working as an integral part of the Program philosophy, which aims to address the increasing desire for resources and spaces to understand and interrupt the coloniality of the University (Grande, 2020). A focus on accountability also helps us examine the practices of designing, facilitating, and sustaining SUAW. In opening up these practices to scrutiny, we also share our critical perspective on the role of co-working sessions in research training, which supports students' disruptions of colonial processes in knowledge production.

References

Abolitionist Futures (n.d.). About Us. *Abolitionist Futures.* https://abolitionistfutures.com/about-us

Beasy, K., Emery, S., & Crawford, J. (2019). Drowning in the shallows: An Australian study of the PhD experience of wellbeing. *Teaching in Higher Education, 26*(4), 602–618. https://doi.org/10.1080/13562517.2019.1669014

Bodkin-Andrews, G., Page, S., & Trudgett, M. (2019). Working towards accountability in embedding indigenous studies: Evidence from an indigenous graduate attribute evaluation instrument. *Australian Journal of Education, 63*(2), 232–260. https://doi.org/10.1177/0004944119863927

Border Abolition. (2021). *Border Abolition 2021 (conference proceedings).* Border Abolition Organising Committee. https://borderviolence.eu/app/uploads/BorderAbolition2021_ConferenceProgram.pdf

Decter, L., & Taunton, C. (2022). Embodying decolonial methodology: Building and sustaining critical relationality in the cultural sector. In E. Morton (Ed.), *Unsettling Canadian Art History* (pp. 87–111). McGill - Queen's Press.

Decter, L., & Taunton, C. (2023). An ethic of decolonial questioning: Exercising the quadruple turn in the arts and culture sector. In H. Igloliorte & C. Taunton (Eds.), *The Routledge Companion to Indigenous Art Histories in the United States and Canada* (pp. 247–260). Routledge. https://doi.org/10.4324/9781003014256-28

Fredericks, B., & Lee Brien, D. (2014). I have pen, book and food; Now, let's write: Indigenizing a postgraduate writing workshop. *AlterNative: An International Journal of Indigenous Peoples, 10*(4), 422–433. https://doi.org/10.1177/117718011401000408

Gooding, M. (1991). *A Book of Surrealist Games.* Redstone Press.

Grande, S. (2020, October 21). The Endemics of Pandemics at the Settler University [Video]. *YouTube.* https://youtu.be/_nN0Tpkv_uA?si=Lb1rVv4W1PyhiZb6

Hurst, J., & Read, P. (2022). Walking proudly out of step: Reversing genocide. In P. Ashton & P. Hamilton (Eds.), *The Australian History Industry* (p. 146). Australian Scholarly Publishing Ltd.

Hutchings, K., Bodle, K., & Miller, A. (2018). Opportunities and resilience: Enablers to address barriers for Aboriginal and Torres Strait Islander people to commence and complete higher degree research programs. *Australian Aboriginal Studies* (2), 29–49.

Imagining Abolition (2021). *Principles of Universal Design for Presentations.* Imagining Abolition: Beyond Prisons, Wars, and Borders. https://sites.google.com/view/imagining-abolition/home/universaldesign?authuser=0

Khoo, T. (2016, 23 February). Shut up and write – so hot right now (Part 1). *The Research Whisperer.* https://researchwhisperer.org/2016/02/23/suaw1/

Kwaymullina, A. (2016, 14 November). Guest Post: Ambelin Kwaymullina: Thoughts on Being an Ally of Indigenous Writers. *Justine Larbalestier.* https://justinelarbalestier.com/blog/2016/11/14/guest-post-ambelin-kwaymullina-thoughts-on-being-an-ally-of-indigenous-writers/

Land, C. (2015). *Decolonizing Solidarity: Dilemmas and Directions for Supporters of Indigenous Struggles.* Zed Books Ltd.
Maddison, S., & Nakata, S. (2020). Introduction: Questioning indigenous-settler relations: Reconciliation, recognition, responsibility. In S. Maddison & S. Nakata (Eds.), *Questioning Indigenous-Settler Relations: Interdisciplinary Perspectives* (pp. 1–13). https://link.springer.com/chapter/10.1007/978-981-13-9205-4_1
Mewburn, I., Osborne, L., & Caldwell, G. (2014). Shut up and write! Some surprising uses of cafes and crowds in doctoral writing. In C. Aitchison & C. Guerin (Eds.), *Writing Groups for Doctoral Education and Beyond: Innovations in Theory and practice.* Routledge.
Moreton-Robinson, A. (2015). The White Possessive: Property, power, and Indigenous sovereignty. University of Minnesota Press.
Nakata, S., & Maddison, S. (2020). Working through the problems: Negotiating friendship, producing results. *Griffith Review*, (67).
Pidgeon, M., Archibald, J., & Hawkey, C. (2014). Relationships matter: Supporting Aboriginal graduate students in British Columbia, Canada. *Canadian Journal of Higher Education*, 44(1), 1–21. https://doi.org/10.47678/cjhe.v44i1.2311
Pihama, L., Lee-Morgan, J., Smith, L. T., Tiakiwai, S. J., & Seed-Pihama, J. (2019). MAI Te Kupenga: Supporting Māori and Indigenous doctoral scholars within higher education. *AlterNative: An International Journal of Indigenous Peoples*, 15(1), 52–61. https://doi.org/10.1177/1177180119828065
Rowe, A. C., & Tuck, E. (2017). Settler colonialism and cultural studies: Ongoing settlement, cultural production, and resistance. *Cultural Studies↔Critical Methodologies*, 17(1), 3–13. https://doi.org/10.1177/1532708616653693
Schulz, S., Vass, G., Moodie, N., & Kennedy, T. (2019). Critical race and whiteness studies: What has been, what might be. *Critical Race and Whiteness Studies*, 1(1), 1–7. https://acrawsa.org.au/wp-content/uploads/2019/06/CRAWS-Inaugural-Editorial_2019.pdf
Sisters Uncut (2018). Safer Spaces Policy. *Sisters Uncut.* https://www.sistersuncut.org/saferspaces/
Strakosch, E. (2019). The technical is political: settler colonialism and the Australian indigenous policy system. *Australian Journal of Political Science*, 54(1), 114–130. https://doi.org/10.1080/10361146.2018.1555230
The Australian Centre. (2025). *Graduate Research.* The University of Melbourne. https://arts.unimelb.edu.au/australiancentre#updated-graduate-research
The Red Nation. (2021). *The Red Deal: Indigenous Action to Save Our Earth.* Common Notions.
Trudgett, M. (2014). Supervision provided to Indigenous Australian doctoral students: a black and white issue. *Higher Education Research & Development*, 33(5), 1035–1048. https://doi.org/10.1080/07294360.2014.890576
Williams, C., & Lee, A. (1999). Forged in fire: Narratives of trauma in PhD supervision pedagogy. *Southern Review: Communication, Politics & Culture*, 32(1), 6–26.

3 Writing in Company
Looking at the Screen, Looking at Each Other

Cally Guerin

Introduction

Writing a doctoral thesis can be a lonely, isolating process, particularly if regarded as an activity to be conducted alone behind closed doors. To mitigate this loneliness, many different forms of writing groups have been introduced by universities and doctoral scholars. SUAW–style groups are now ubiquitous across the world of doctoral writing and have repeatedly been demonstrated to improve the overall wellbeing of participants (see, for example, Aitchison, 2009; Aitchison & Guerin, 2014; Beasy et al., 2020; Costello et al., 2024; Déri & Tremblay-Wragg, 2022).

This chapter reports on a "Writing in Company" version of SUAW, detailing the process and the reasoning behind the specific choices for this model at an Australian university. The standard SUAW structure has been modified over time to suit the emerging needs of the doctoral cohort and also those of the facilitator. When these sessions ceased after several years of operation, as the facilitator I was surprised by the response from long- and short-term participants, provoking reflection on what works and why for this particular model. My aim in this narrative is to use my personal observations to inform broader conclusions about an effective SUAW model.

Writing in Company – Emergence of the Model

In my roles as a researcher developer at several Australian universities, I've experimented with different models of writing groups for a number of years (Aitchison & Guerin, 2014; Guerin et al., 2013; Guerin & Aitchison, 2023). In a recent iteration, I established weekly online writing groups using Zoom, following the SUAW model. These sessions had been a feature of our local university-wide Academic Writing Month (AcWriMo – http://www.phd2published.com/acwri-2/acbowrimo/about/) activities in 2021 and participants expressed a wish to continue the sessions beyond the end of November and into the new year to maintain their momentum from AcWriMo. I had some writing projects I needed to complete, so maintaining this structure seemed a

Writing in Company 33

Image 3.1 The sense of companionship and connection is captured in a screenshot of the Zoom participants – a grid of squares with faces all directed towards us as the writers look at their documents appearing on their screens.

helpful way to ensure I carved out time from my other work responsibilities to get my own writing done too. These "Writing in Company" sessions created an effective alignment between the demands of my job as a researcher developer providing opportunities for PhD candidates across all schools in the university and my own research writing commitments.

We continued to meet online for Writing in Company sessions on an ad hoc basis for another 2.5 years – fitting the sessions into and around our busy work lives to keep the thread of writing productivity alive. Following the rapid switch to online teaching in 2020, doctoral candidates were attuned to meeting on Zoom and working from their own desks. I nominated a two-hour period at least once a week (sometimes more, depending on the urgency of my publication deadlines and other work demands, occasionally even creating mini writing retreats with daily sessions) and circulated the Zoom link to the ever-growing list of subscribers. Participants were welcome to attend as suited their own schedules and responsibilities. It was not a regular timeslot – my job didn't work that way – which meant that some days were ideal for some members, and other days were better for different individuals. It became a fluid interdisciplinary group of PhD candidates from across the institution who were all at different stages of their candidature. New participants asked to be added to the list having heard about the writing sessions from existing members, from my mentioning of the group in workshops, or they had read about it on our unit's website. The 85 list members in June 2024 attended with varying regularity, some coming along for most sessions, others joining in only now and then. I tidied up the list every six months, confirming who wanted to remain on the list and removing those who hadn't attended at all. Surprisingly, those who attended only sporadically still wanted to be on the list, despite my asking if they'd prefer not to be bothered by the invitation emails. Each session ended up with between 10 and 15 attendees each time – to me this seemed small enough to feel personal, large enough to feel part of a broader university community.

Over time, I started to notice how much I personally looked forward to the sessions, and found myself thanking participants for their company at the end of each writing period. Their presence and productive energy were contributing something very positive to my own job satisfaction and sense of a researcher identity – plus, I was getting some writing done. While my tasks weren't always research writing for publication, it was focused time at my computer getting on with whatever jobs needed to be done.

When I finished at that university in mid-2024 to move onto a new position in another university, I announced that these sessions wouldn't be running anymore. I was surprised by the number of effusive thank you notes that Writing in Company participants sent me, many of which were copied to the whole group email list, and others that were sent privately. Of course this was flattering, but it also made me pause and consider what it was about these sessions that seemed to have hit the mark in ways that some of my carefully thought-out, highly research-informed workshops had not succeeded in. This chapter is my reflection on trying to understand what made this model of SUAW work so effectively for the participants and also for me.

Benefits of Doctoral Writing Groups

The benefits of participation in doctoral writing groups have been well documented (see, for example, Aitchison & Guerin, 2014, forthcoming; Déri & Tremblay-Wragg, 2022; Guerin et al., 2013; Guerin & Aitchison, 2023; Kozar & Lum, 2015; Maher et al., 2008). These benefits include learning how to produce research writing that communicates effectively within the expectations of disciplinary discourses; how to provide constructive feedback as a peer reviewer; how to carve out time and space to write; and how to establish productive writing habits.

Increasingly, this literature has focused more directly on the role that writing groups can play in the wellbeing of participants (Beasy et al., 2020; Pretorius, Macaulay & Cahusac de Caux, 2019; Wilson & Cutri, 2019). Attention is drawn to the sense of community and affirmation of a researcher identity that comes from working with doctoral peers over a period of time, building trust and forming relationships that emphasise belonging and connection. These benefits are common to most SUAW groups, and part of what has repeatedly been shown to be successful in these groups.

Wellbeing of Writing Companions

Like other SUAW models described in this volume, the Writing in Company model promotes wellbeing in multiple ways through caring for the physical, emotional, and psychological dimensions of research writers. In particular, physical wellbeing is cared for by allowing writers to work online from their usual workspace which is more likely to have been ergonomically adapted to suit them and their individual requirements than a classroom desk or café table; a break halfway through includes a guided stretch to keep bodies mobile. Emotional and psychological wellbeing are supported through the creation of a collegial, collaborative community where writers can feel a sense of belonging to a care-full scholarly community.

Gravett's (2023, p.1) notion of wellbeing as enhanced by "connections, mattering, and relationality" resonate strongly here. These three concepts are intertwined in the Writing in Company model, pivoting on the idea of "mattering" in terms of being both important and having a material dimension. The group and the activity clearly matter to participants: it's important enough to impel them to show up, to write together, and to support each other's efforts to advance their research – they keep on turning up. By taking their engagement in this activity seriously, group members reinforce each other's confidence that their research matters, that it is important and valuable. We see an ethics of care operating between members based on "mutuality and responsibility" (Sultana, 2022, p.2; Costello et al., 2024). The material matter through which they come together is the faces on their computer screen, the physical location of the images of their writing companions. Clicking the Zoom link is what links them into this community – the digital connection becomes invested with the extra meaning of connection to like-minded peers.

Relationality in this space is thus twofold: group members perceive themselves in relation to others, identifying their similarities and differences, and finding a place within the network of scholars; they also relate to each other, sharing experiences, celebrating triumphs, and commiserating over disappointments. They recognise that everyone has good and bad days, ups and downs, and not all days or all stages of research writing are equally productive. Key to the group is kindness and acceptance that each individual is at a different point on their writing journey.

I see the role of the facilitator in the Writing in Company model is thus to be welcoming and accepting of all who turn up, regardless of their writing stage or the size of their plan. The job is to hold participants in a safe space that is non-judgmental and inclusive; it's necessary to be accepting of those whose complicated lives mean they turn up late or need to leave early.

In this way, a light touch, caring space can be activated.

In this model, the facilitator needs to ensure that the focus remains on what participants actually get done during the session as a positive achievement that takes them a step closer to their endgame. The job is not to be a counsellor inviting writers to bare their soul to the group; rather, the writing group can be a respectful audience who appreciates from lived experience the effort it takes to communicate complex ideas persuasively, meeting the requirements of different readers in a range of contexts (academic, general public, government policy, professional). The session is a place to announce triumphs big and small, knowing they will be received with kindness: this audience understands just how much intellectual effort is required to complete a successful ethics application (or to write a difficult email to a supervisor or co-author). We are here to take each other seriously, not to brush off each other's concerns, nor to diminish the emotional, mental, and even physical challenges being confronted. Importantly, this is a compassionate space, not a competitive one.

On top of the physical, emotional, and psychological wellbeing, there is one further dimension of wellbeing that is supported by the Writing in Company model: the satisfying intellectual accomplishment experienced during the writing sessions. This achievement is enhanced via strategic developmental prompts in response to announced writing tasks. As well as offering structure for the writing week, the Writing in Company model provides targeted writing development in a timely manner.

This mix of physical, emotional, psychological, and intellectual wellbeing is no small thing: it strongly reinforces participants' identity as researchers. In this space they are demonstrating to themselves and to their peers that they are capable of succeeding as researchers at the same time they are being welcomed into the research community of writing companions.

Wellbeing of the Facilitator

The participants' success also feeds into the facilitator's own wellbeing – an aspect of SUAW wellbeing that I had not previously appreciated and is rarely mentioned in research into doctoral education. Given the reportedly high levels of stress and mental health concerns and the distinct lack of wellbeing amongst academic staff worldwide (Nicholls et al., 2022; Urbina-Garcia, 2020), this is not a minor issue.

Firstly, there is (of course) satisfaction in opening out a space where these new researchers have positive experiences, and in knowing that I've done something useful to advance their research and make progress towards completing their degree. Creating an encouraging environment where new researchers get a chance to thrive is immensely satisfying. Although "thriving" is not easily measured objectively (in a university climate that seeks to measure everything), Writing in Company makes an undeniable contribution towards helping participants feel good about achieving their goals. This contribution to others' wellbeing is deeply satisfying as a teacher.

Secondly, the Writing in Company model also reinforces my own identity as a writing expert who has been teaching, researching, and publishing on doctoral writing since 2008. Stating writing goals at the outset of each meeting provides opportunities for the facilitator to offer useful advice on whatever aspect of research writing participants are focusing on. Working with this receptive audience is immensely validating. The advice can be targeted towards the current task, providing personalised guidance that is "just in time, just enough, and just for me" (Rosenberg, 2001). Although the focus is on personalised feedback, others in the group are also likely to bump up against similar situations in the near future, and they too benefit from hearing the suggestions and storing links to resources.

Gravett (2023), taking up Schwarz's (2019) views on relational pedagogy, reminds us that "one good interaction between individual teachers and students can be all that matters" (p.31). While this pedagogical attitude is often focused on what makes for student success, there is also validation for the teacher in such interactions when that guidance is enthusiastically received. Writing in Company builds this into repeated iterations over multiple sessions, enhancing the facilitator's sense of intellectual wellbeing as a valuable asset in the Writing in Company relational network.

Participants appear to perceive this as a care-full place, but as an academic developer I certainly want to resist being perceived as one of "the kind ladies in writing support" (as my colleague Susan Mowbray once described it in a disappointed tone). Rather, my aim is to provide something more intellectually stimulating and substantial than just a nice pat on the back, empty praise and "well done, dear!". Genuine care is much more complex and nuanced.

Burton (2021) warns us against the dangers of being naïve about how "kindness" can be used to maintain structural inequalities in the contemporary, neoliberal university, where each person is treated as being responsible for their own individual success or failure. Sure, it feels good to make encouraging, accepting noises and create a space where everyone is focused on being positive. But it's important to remember that small, personalised instances of kindness can actually bolster rather dismantle institutional power structures, encouraging us to cope with difficult situations that are not of our own making, nor in our own interests. It is necessary to consider how our own actions play into these effects.

Nevertheless, participants have arrived in the session committed to doing some research writing. While there might be complex debates outside of this space about how and why they interact with the broader academy, here we are focused on the task in hand. We can bear witness to each other's struggles and triumphs in research writing. Such validation could be interpreted as encouraging people to remain in an unhealthy environment; or it could be understood as connecting into an ethics of care (Gravett, 2023).

Although we might distrust the neoliberal university enterprise, I do believe that the actual content of doctoral research continues to have great value. These writers are working on important topics that are potentially widely beneficial. It's not just career advancement for the individual that we are encouraging in facilitating SUAW sessions – it's work that contributes to knowledge that leads us towards a fairer and more just society; that improves lives in multiple ways from health to education, from law to the natural environment; that influences big-picture policy through feasible answers to complex questions. Writing groups can create a space to facilitate researchers crafting their message for the audiences who need to hear it.

Researcher developers share much in common with supervisors in their need to manage their energy and motivation in providing doctoral education.

Just as supervisors need to engage with their own self-care, it is also necessary for researcher developers to pay attention to what sustains them and renews their energy for the work (Lemon, Harju-Luukkainen & Garvis, 2022). In my opinion, those responsible for providing programs to develop postgraduate researchers ought to model the behaviours, attitudes, and dispositions they are encouraging in others. High-quality pedagogical interactions are engaging for supervisors, potentially operating as a "buffer against burnout" (Tikkanen et al., 2024); I believe that much the same can be claimed for researcher developers.

The Writing in Company Model: Practical Details

The elements that contribute to the effectiveness of the Writing in Company model include: the online mode; a structured timeframe; announcement and review of goals; movement and stretching; and learning about one's own capacities. The basic outline of this model has previously been introduced elsewhere (Guerin & Aitchison, 2023; Aitchison & Guerin, forthcoming).

Mode

Online sessions have numerous advantages for both participants and facilitators. Everyone can work in a familiar setting, in a workspace where their usual equipment and materials are available, and usually more comfortable than a café or classroom arrangement. Many writers will already be at their usual workplace, and clicking on the link requires no extra time to travel to the session. This comfort and efficiency are particularly welcomed by those who are obliged to fit their studies around multiple work and family responsibilities.

And, of course, online sessions mean that PhD candidates who live and work off-campus can work alongside their peers onscreen. Remote candidates frequently report feeling isolated from the institution and have limited opportunities to establish connections with the research community. Online writing groups create a space where geographic location and time zone are at least partially overcome. The sessions do require a relatively stable internet connection; in some remote communities this can be much harder to access than in urban areas (but experience has demonstrated it can also be an issue in the middle of large cities!).

Online writing sessions are far less stressful for the organiser, too. There is no requirement for room bookings; no extra travel time to ensure you as the organiser are on time to greet participants, nor find an unfamiliar room on the other side of campus; no need to organise catering nor to clean up after the session. Staff wellbeing is often overlooked in the focus on student wellbeing conversations, and this is one way facilitators can exercise self-care choices to make their own work lives a little simpler.

During the writing sprints, wherever possible participants are encouraged to keep cameras on but microphones off, thus "fostering a sense of accountability, validation, and camaraderie" (Costello et al., 2024, p.4). Of course, there are all sorts of situations in which this is not suitable, including those where internet bandwidth struggles to maintain a reliable connection when using video. However, seeing others working at their desk feels like being in company, and the gentle "surveillance" of being seen by colleagues helps modify behaviour and resist distractions. We ask ourselves: Have I honoured the agreement to stick with the writing until the bell rings? Or did I allow myself to leave the desk for some possibly legitimate but non-urgent task (e.g., check and answer an email, freshen up the teapot, slip out for a bathroom break)? Clearly, this self-monitoring is not intended to be at all punitive – all participants are adults who will make choices that are appropriate for their own circumstances – but it can help resist temptation and continue working on the nominated task. While the Zoom SUAW doesn't have the encouraging sound of keyboards clack-clacking as writers pump out the words, the presence of peers' faces in the corner of the screen seems to have a similar effect.

Timeframe

The optimal timing for this group has emerged as two 50-minute sprints with a 10-minute break in between (which is used as 5 minutes to get up and move around, followed by a 5-minute guided stretch for those who wish to join in). Although the classic "pomodoro" sprints are 25 minutes (Cirillo, 2018), I have found that 50 minutes seems to work better for the majority of research writers. True, some may have a dip in concentration around halfway through, but staying at the desk and pushing through allows many to maintain their train of thought and push deeper into their intellectual explorations.

Insisting on the 10-minute break in the middle, however, has also proven to be effective to refresh mind and body for longer periods of concentration (see, for example, Kim et al., 2017). Notably, the enforced breaks can be very beneficial to those who are inclined towards "time blindness" and hyperfocus.

We found it useful to adhere closely to the start and stop times of the structured writing sprints. Latecomers can be acknowledged via the chat so that others are not disturbed; similarly, those who have to leave early for various commitments note their writing output in the chat but slip off without disrupting others. Thus, all are welcome to join in as they can, in recognition of the busy, challenging lives doctoral writers manage in the background.

Announce Goals

The first 10 minutes of the session are used for participants to announce their writing goals for the session. Being aware of this expectation encourages preparation in advance, resulting in more efficient use of the time. Lots of the thinking and decision-making occurs in the lead-up to the session, so that valuable writing time isn't used up remembering where the text is up to or locating articles to be read.

Writing goals for each session are entered into the Zoom chat as a record to refer back to. Participants are encouraged to be very specific in nominating these goals. Instead of saying they are "working on Chapter 3", they identify which paragraphs will be written in the session; instead of saying they are "editing", they identify the purpose of that editing is to clarify the argument flow or to reduce the word count; instead of saying they are "responding to reviewer comments", they identify which comments will be tackled in the session. Some writers choose to nominate a word count goal for the session, which can also be highly motivating as a tangible output.

Identifying specific goals also creates conditions where the facilitator with expertise in teaching research writing can add value to the session, offering simple tips and advice or referring writers to useful resources. This feedback can be delivered verbally with brief comments if the group is not too big (sticking to the agreed start time is crucial – this is not the place for long-winded waffle). Since participants often need to write similar sections or genres, the guidance is broadly applicable, even if not focused on the specific task nominated for the session. For example, simple writing prompts to structure an abstract can remind the whole group of this approach for the next time they are writing that genre; when a writing companion announces they are "restructuring" their chapter, sharing a link to the website explaining the reverse outline process is helpful for others later on.

Physical Stretch

The short break midway through the two-hour writing block is used to encourage some physical movement. The facilitator interrupts participants, reminding them that this is the time to get up and move around, dash to the bathroom or freshen up their hot drinks, and look into the distance instead of focusing on the screen in front of them.

Five minutes are then devoted to a basic stretch of neck and shoulders lead by the facilitator. If the facilitator is not confident about running this element, there are numerous five-minute videos of "desk yoga" and stretches for office workers available free on YouTube, for example. Facilitators can play the video and share their screen with participants. Caring for the physical wellbeing of the group contributes to the overall sense of everyone being looked after, as well as the obvious benefits of loosening up the body.

Reflection on Achievement

The final phase of the Writing in Company model invites participants to observe their progress for the session. They look back to their nominated writing task and assess whether they reached their goal, once again typing their response into the Zoom chat. They are encouraged to notice what went well for them during the session and also to consider what their next step (or next task or focus) ought to be. By breaking down the tasks into specific chunks, writers notice what they have actually accomplished, rather than constantly focusing on what they haven't done yet. Negative thinking that "I haven't completed this chapter" is replaced by "I have finished this section of the chapter".

Benchmarking

Finally, there are advantages in hearing about what other research writers expect to complete in a writing session, and where they focus their attention. There are very few opportunities in doctoral studies to benchmark one's own progress and output expectations against peers (Guerin & Aitchison, 2023). Publicly announcing goals and reporting on achievement offers one means for the group to measure themselves against roughly similar counterparts.

Conclusion

The model outlined in this chapter won't suit all research writers, of course. Some are uncomfortable working in close proximity to others, or in following the constraints in starting and stopping according to an externally imposed schedule. Some want to work longer, others need to break more frequently. My intention here is to report on a model that has worked well for many in the Australian context of doctoral studies, in the hope that others might also find it is an effective rhythm for them too. In explaining my background reasoning, I want to indicate that this pedagogy is not random; rather, it grows out of years of experimenting and adapting the original concept of SUAW. Most importantly, by sharing this model, I reflect on how Writing in Company can significantly contribute to the wellbeing not only of the participants, but also the facilitators.

Acknowledgements

A special thank you to all the wonderfully positive, productive doctoral candidates who have joined me in writing groups at the University of Adelaide, Australian National University, and La Trobe University. The most recent writers at La Trobe University kindly agreed to be photographed for this chapter.

References

Aitchison, C. (2009). Writing groups for doctoral education. *Studies in Higher Education*, *34*(8), 905–916. https://doi.org/10.1080/03075070902785580
Aitchison, C., & Guerin, C. (Eds). (2014). Writing groups, pedagogy, theory and practice: An introduction. *Writing groups for doctoral education and beyond*. Routledge.
Aitchison, C. & Guerin, C. (forthcoming). The enduring magic of writing groups: Reflections on practices and theoretical understandings. In E. Moreno Mosquera (Ed.), *Training research writers in Latin America*. WAC Clearinghouse.

Beasy, K., Emery, S., Dyer, L., Coleman, B., Bywaters, D., Garrad, T., … Jahangiri, S. (2020). Writing together to foster wellbeing: Doctoral writing groups as spaces of wellbeing. *Higher Education Research & Development*, *39*(6), 1091–1105. https://doi.org/10.1080/07294360.2020.1713732

Burton, S. (2021). Solidarity, now! Care, collegiality, and comprehending the power relations of "academic kindness" in the neoliberal academy. *Performance Paradigm*, 16, 20–39. https://openaccess.city.ac.uk/id/eprint/26939/

Cirillo, F. (2018). *The pomodoro technique: The life-changing time-management system.* Virgin. https://www.pomodorotechnique.com/

Costello, M., Nyanjom, J., Bailey, S., & Ireson, D. (2024). Care in the academy: How our online writing group transformed into a caring community. *International Journal of Educational Research*, *127*, 102441. https://doi.org/10.1016/j.ijer.2024.102441

Déri, C. E., & Tremblay-Wragg, É. (2022). Academic writing groups in higher education: History and state of play. *International Journal of Higher Education*, *11*(1), 85–99. https://doi.org/10.5430/ijhe.v11n1p85

Gravett, K. (2023). *Relational pedagogies: Connections and mattering in higher education.* Bloomsbury Publishing.

Guerin, C., & Aitchison, C. (2023). Finding confidence in writing: Doctoral writing groups. In: D. L. Elliot, S. S. E. Bengtsen, K. Guccione (eds) *Developing researcher independence through the hidden curriculum*. Palgrave Macmillan, Cham. https://doi.org/10.1007/978-3-031-42875-3_13

Guerin, C., Xafis, V., Doda, D. V., Gillam, M. H., Larg, A. J., Luckner, H., … & Xu, C. (2013). Diversity in collaborative research communities: A multicultural, multidisciplinary thesis writing group in public health. *Studies in Continuing Education*, *35*(1), 65–81. https://doi.org/10.1080/0158037X.2012.684375

Kim, S., Park, Y., & Niu, Q. (2017). Micro-break activities at work to recover from daily work demands. *Journal of Organizational Behavior*, *38*(1), 28–44. https://doi.org/10.1002/job.2109

Kozar, O., & Lum, J. F. (2015). Online doctoral writing groups: Do facilitators or communication modes make a difference?. *Quality in Higher Education*, *21*(1), 38–51. https://doi.org/10.1080/13538322.2015.1032003

Lemon, N., Harju-Luukkainen, H. & Garvis, S. (2022). Learning with and from one another: Valuing self-care as a part of the higher-degree research student and supervisor relationship. In S. Obradovi-Ratkovi, et al., (Eds.), *Supporting student and faculty wellbeing in graduate education: Teaching, learning, policy, and praxis*. Taylor & Francis. https://doi.org/10.4324/9781003268185-13

Maher, D., Seaton, L., McMullen, C., Fitzgerald, T., Otsuji, E., & Lee, A. (2008). "Becoming and being writers": The experiences of doctoral students in writing groups. *Studies in Continuing Education*, *30*(3), 263–275. https://doi.org/10.1080/07294360.2020.1713732

Nicholls, H., Nicholls, M., Tekin, S., Lamb, D., Billings, J. (2022). The impact of working in academia on researchers' mental health and well-being: A systematic review and qualitative meta-synthesis. *PLoS ONE* 17(5): e0268890. https://doi.org/10.1371/journal.pone.0268890

Pretorius, L., Macaulay, L. & Cahusac de Caux B. (Eds.), (2019). *Wellbeing in doctoral education: Insights and guidance from the student experience*. Springer. https://doi.org/10.1007/978-981-13-9302-0_12

Rosenberg, M. J. (2001). *E-Learning: Strategies for delivering knowledge in the digital age*. McGraw Hill.

Schwarz, H. L. (2019). *Connected teaching: Relationship, power, and mattering in higher education*. Stylus.

Sultana, F. (2022). Resplendent care-full climate revolutions. *Political Geography*, 99 (1), 102785. https://doi.org/10.1016/j.polgeo.2022.102785

Tikkanen, L., Ketonen, E., Toom, A., & Pyhältö, K. (2024). PhD candidates' and supervisors' wellbeing and experiences of supervision. *Higher Education*, 1–19. https://doi.org/10.1007/s10734-024-01385-w

Urbina-Garcia, A. (2020). What do we know about university academics' mental health? A systematic literature review. *Stress and Health*, 36(5), 563–585. https://doi.org/10.1002/smi.2956

Wilson, S., & Cutri, J. (2019). Chapter 7: Negating isolation and imposter syndrome through writing as product and as process: The impact of collegiate writing networks during a doctoral programme. In L. Pretorius, L. Macaulay, & B. Cahusac de Caux (Eds.), *Wellbeing in doctoral education: Insights and guidance from the student experience*. Springer.

Section 2
SUAW as a Tool for Academic Development and Wellbeing

4 Expanding a Creative Writing Practice to Foster Connection, Wellbeing, and Engagement across Multiple Disciplines

Kristyn Harman, Lucy Christopher, Caylee Tierney, Philippa Moore, Stephanie Richey, and Mandy Pink

Introduction

Our chapter explores challenges and opportunities arising from the authors' context of working within a distributed regional university with staff and students located across several campuses in Lutruwita/Tasmania. The authors noticed how the COVID-19 pandemic led to physical isolation yet gave rise to flourishing online writing communities. Following a return to physical campuses, University of Tasmania (UTAS) students and staff continued to experience isolation. Within the creative writing discipline, senior lecturer Lucy Christopher launched the Creative Writing (CreW) Club in 2023, a regular online writing session to foster connection and wellbeing and to support the development of creative outputs within the university.

We explore how and why the successful CreW Club model was scaled up and adapted to foster an engaged online writing community across multiple disciplines at UTAS. The CreW Club model was itself adapted from other successful fora, most notably the London Writers' Salon (LWS) (n.d.). Our decision to adapt CreW Club to a 'November Write In' in 2023 similarly drew on NaNoWriMo, the novel writing month challenge conceived in San Francisco in 1999 (National Novel Writing Month, n.d.).

We examine the inspiration and goals that underpinned our 'November Write In', which comprised weekday 50-minute online gatherings run as researcher development throughout November 2023 and November 2024. Recognising the distributed nature of our campuses, and aiming to provide a level playing field in regard to access, we consciously adopted Zoom as our platform on which to host these gatherings. Academics and Higher Degree Research candidates across multiple disciplines, as well as professional staff, were invited to join daily or as available, for a session run by self-selected peer hosts. In 2023, participants ranged from 10 to 28 (with 36 distinct attendees), and in 2024 sessions comprised 10 to 19 participants (with an average of 15, and 44 distinct attendees).

These sessions aimed to reconnect colleagues, to provide time in which to write companionably, and to boost wellbeing and productivity. Sessions were deliberately scheduled at the beginning of each working day at a time that

DOI: 10.4324/9781003633334-6

followed school drop offs for those for whom that was a consideration and, inspired by the London Writers' Salon as well as our own hopes for these sessions, were structured as follows with a run sheet provided for hosts to follow:

- Host welcome, acknowledgement of Country, and inspiring quote
- Intention setting in the Zoom chat (mainly 2023)
- Focused 'writing' time ideally with cameras on
- Gentle drawing back together
- Reporting in the Zoom chat with the host encouraging a few participants to share progress verbally (with chat or emoji reactions)
- Recording individual word count/progress in a shared spreadsheet.

The chapter draws on the November Write In experience to examine, from personal and professional perspectives, SUAW in relation to belonging, community, and motivation/support/encouragement. We offer our reflections as participants from perspectives including academic, PhD candidate, professional staff, and host. We conclude by highlighting how, in 2023, our online Write In reignited community following the COVID-19 pandemic and then, in 2024, pivoted to provide a safe and collegial space during a challenging time of workplace change.

Visual Narrative

Image 4.1 represents some of the quantitative achievements of the 2023 and 2024 November Write Ins. While quantitative achievements are not the only measure of success from the sessions, these outcomes provide a sense of how the November Write Ins fostered connection, wellbeing, and engagement by bringing colleagues together to write while also increasing productivity.

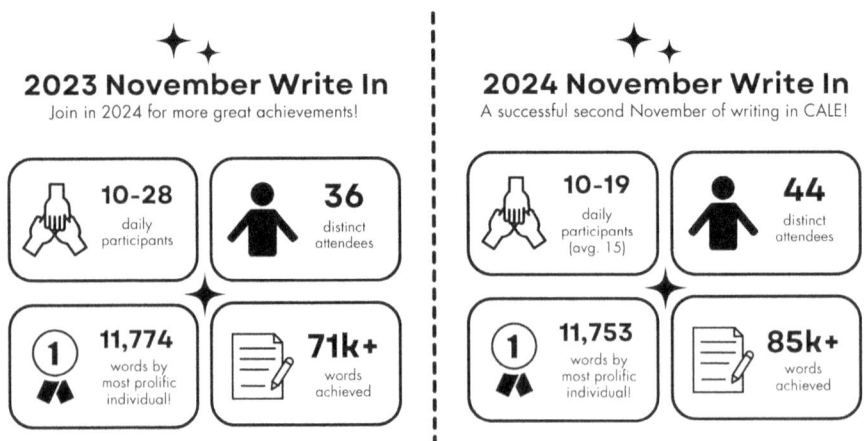

Image 4.1 Achievements from our SUAW.

Literature Review

Numerous scholars have emphasised the "growing demand" globally "for academics to increase their publication output" (Olszewska & Lock, 2016, p. 132). Writing groups are widely viewed as providing a means of doing so. As Déri et al. (2021) point out, writing groups formed "on the basis of intellectual traditions" (p. 85) date back to at least the Middle Ages, so they are hardly an innovation. Such groups have, however, evolved over time, diversifying to meet the ever-changing needs of participants. Interestingly, Déri et al. (2021) found that writing groups predominate in the social sciences and humanities, two areas key to our own research and writing context.

In our chapter, we centre wellbeing through consideration of our case study's success in fostering connection, companionability, and renewed belonging across a multi-disciplinary group of geographically dispersed participants. In doing so, we draw particularly on Wilmot and McKenna's (2018) work on writing groups as transformative spaces, building on the earlier work of Aitchison (2009). Our reflections and analysis include an examination of key structures and features of the November Write In that generated a supportive and motivational environment, encouraged holding space for the fragility of writing at the beginning of the day, and inspired intentional goal setting.

Carr and Becker (2017) highlighted the evidence-based need to create "a supportive venue for academics, struggling with finding enough time to write" (para. 1). They elaborated several types of writing approaches, with 'snack writing' being most closely aligned with our initiative. Following *Times Higher Education*'s description of 'snack writing' (following Olga Wojtas), Carr and Becker (2017) described this as "the act of 'working in small bursts' for periods varying from 30 to 90 minutes with no distractions" (para. 7). They explicated a "strict set of rules" considered "essential" (para. 13) to the success of snack writing sessions, many of which were common to our approach. These include starting and ending on time, engaging in writing (or nothing) for the entirety of the session, and avoiding distractions (such as checking emails). Writers come prepared to be immersed in, and to trust in, the process (Carr & Becker, 2017).

Wilmot (2016) has explained how the "ongoing massification and democratisation" (p. 257) of higher education internationally has led to increasingly diverse cohorts of postgraduate students in a context of increased pressure to publish more and higher quality work. Writing groups can be useful in helping to develop students' academic writing capabilities and in supporting productivity. Such groups, however, tend to be horizontally aligned. That is, when designed to support postgraduate cohorts, they "typically only include students and a facilitator" to "provide a non-threatening space" (Wilmot, 2016, p. 258). Our SUAW group diverged from this model by including professional colleagues writing alongside academic colleagues drawn from a range of disciplinary backgrounds and career stages, ranging from postgraduate candidates to tenured professors. We discuss our rationale for adopting this approach and reflect on its utility in our chapter.

Author Reflections

Lucy Christopher (Academic Staff, Creative Writing)

I began CreW Club in 2023 to build and support the College's creative writing community. Arriving from Bath Spa University – a world leader in fostering and supporting creative writing methodologies, pedagogies, and creative research outputs – I realised creative writing had a lesser profile at UTAS. However, UTAS had creative writing academics and alumni who were multi-award winning and best-selling writers across multiple genres and audiences: a significant pedigree for any university. I also noticed a small but enthusiastic bunch of creative writing PhD and undergraduate students. I was keen to capitalise on, and nurture, this significant creative writing talent, while providing space and accountability for the creative process.

Anyone engaged in creative practice at UTAS is welcome to attend CreW Club, the idea being, as is common across creative writing communities, that we are equal in how we engage in *process*, and we all have something to learn from each other. In 2023, CreW Club met fortnightly for an hour online, beginning by sharing recent practice and by setting writing intentions. I read an inspirational quote, then we wrote silently with cameras on for 50 minutes. Towards the end of the session, we shared progress, thoughts, and encouragement. There were a few loose 'rules': 1) We write creatively, or we do nothing – no other task is allowed; 2) We keep cameras on and write together in silence; and 3) We encourage each other's progress.

Our November Write In came from a conversation with the then Associate Dean of Research Performance when she shared her hopes of growing a research community both nurturing and productive. I mentioned the success of CreW Club, and how it emerged from creative practice methodology forged by writing communities across the world. Perhaps cheekily in a room full of more traditional academics, I also told her one could do worse than turn to the methodology of creative writing research to simultaneously build wellbeing *and* research outputs. My first suggestion for the Write In was to engage academics in creative praxis or, at least, the beginning 'big picture' imagining work of new research projects.

I suggested academics engage in creative praxis because the discipline of creative writing is all about phenomenological process, where "the process is as important as the outcome" (Avieson, 2008). By nurturing process, we nurture output, which then, in turn, nurtures process again – think of the famous lithograph by Escher, which shows two hands drawing each other. There is an obvious, simple benefit for wellbeing – by focusing on process we take the pressure off output, and we engage in curious play.

There are also other benefits. Reading creative writing research or reading fiction gives readers new understandings about the world, creates opportunities for deep thinking and reflection, and allows the brain to access a state of relaxation (Shaffer et al., 2019). Reading fiction also increases readers' empathy and facilitates engagement with the world (Stansfield & Bunce, 2014). I would argue, backed by my own decades of observing developing writers, that the *practice of writing* does all this even more strongly. Writing fiction encourages empathy through deep imagination, and engaging in the focus that comes with writing forces the brain into a more deeply engaged cognitive state than we usually experience. Beyond this deeper engagement with subject material, a regular writing practice has been shown to improve memory, creativity, and verbal capacities, and numerous studies have shown writing improves mood, decreases stress, and improves general wellbeing (Baikie & Wilhelm, 2005; Habens, 2018).

Although most participants were not engaged in creative practice research in the November Write In, our chapter discusses the many benefits that resulted from this daily writing practice. If I were to help run this project again, I would encourage participants to be even more creative – to engage in playful, generative, and imaginative activities rather than analytical ones. Or, even better, I would suggest devoting 2 hours to a Write In: the first hour playful, generative, and imaginative and the second applying this to current research, whether creative or traditional.

Kristyn Harman (Academic Staff, History)

My interest was piqued when my College promoted daily online writing sessions throughout November 2023. I had limited prior experience of joining writing communities online. However, prior to working from home during the pandemic, I had happily joined an in-person writing group that turned my typically unproductive Friday afternoons into productive writing time. Boosted by the quiet companionship of others, I was inspired to immerse myself in writing an article that was later published. I also discovered a sense of collegiality and wellbeing from these in-person writing sessions being bookended by people sharing their intentions and outcomes in deeply honest ways.

As well as bringing my own intentions to the 2023 November Write In, I was motivated to attend as the then Associate Head of Research in the School of Humanities. I value the practice of leading by example, so found it important to be a good role model. Participating in our Write Ins helped me feel that I was supporting colleagues who put time and effort into planning, and skills into convening, the sessions.

I attended 16 of the 22 working days on which the group met. If I had another commitment, it was with regret that I missed our Write In session. Surprisingly, I quickly met my initial writing goal. This led to my setting three further writing goals, all of which I achieved. These were all history-related projects. While I write in the non-fiction genre, I nevertheless find writing to be a deeply creative process. Previously I had learned how dedicating a regular amount of time to writing daily worked wonders, yet without the support and collegiality of a wider group, it was all too easy to let this practice slip. As Olszewska and Lock (2016) have pointed out, finding time for writing is a key challenge academics aiming for publications face. Our mutual commitment to meeting was invaluable to me in 'showing up' and being present. Learning more about various colleagues' writing goals was also a welcome reminder of the broad sweep of academic work that requires thought, planning, research, and writing.

As the end of the Australian academic year approached, it was with a mix of satisfaction and relief that I reflected on our College's Write In. It felt both personally and professionally satisfying to have connected virtually with so many colleagues over our weeks of working alongside each other. I also experienced a deep sense of relief at having crossed so many things off my to-do list as we headed towards the summer break. It felt a little luxurious to have completed written work far ahead of a deadline.

My sense of connection to colleagues and my writing practice motivated me to sign up to the November 2024 Write In, despite having taken on a senior leadership role that allows less time for writing. Having observed our skilful hosts running sessions the previous year, I realised that I had been engaged in experiential learning and gained the confidence and, I hoped, competence to join the roster of hosts, even opting to host our inaugural session on 1 November. One of the key challenges I faced when hosting a session (I hosted 5) was to keep a discreet eye on the clock so as not to fail in my duty to gently remind colleagues when our writing time was ending.

Caylee Tierney (Professional Staff, Research Officer)

I took part in the 2023 and 2024 November Write Ins as an organiser, a participant, and an occasional host. I am the only person who joined for every session in 2023 and every session in 2024 (one other person joined for every session in 2023). This included days that, as a part-time employee, were not workdays.

My deep engagement with the November Write Ins is likely attributable to my sense of these as a space where I belonged. The 2024 sessions were particularly valuable to my wellbeing in the workplace, as in that period, my research administration role was proposed as surplus to operational requirements. The November Write In and the impact I saw it having on other participants proved a vital reminder of the value of my work.

Unsurprisingly, those of us who joined every session lay claim to the highest individual word counts of over 11,000 words in 2023 and 2024 respectively. Perhaps as unsurprisingly given the state of academic workloads in Australia (Khan & Siriwardhane, 2021; Miller, 2019; Ross et al., 2024), both individuals who were able to carve out the time to attend daily were employed substantively as professional staff. While word production is not everything, these results indicate that consistently showing up bears fruit.

With my view over the entirety of the Write Ins, I saw various measures of success – some participants recorded the words they cut, others had less quantitative goals/intentions and achievements including editing work. My consistent presence in the sessions also gave me a strong sense of the benefits other participants were receiving. Themes that shone through include connection (especially feeling less lonely in writing and in facing challenges), encouragement within the group, and peer problem solving.

Particularly fresh in my mind is a comment from a postgraduate student about coming to the sessions and witnessing those further advanced in their careers sharing challenges with writing. The student found it heartening to see that their struggles did not mean they were doing something wrong and that they were not alone in having difficulty. This moment demonstrates the value of gathering such a diverse group of researchers together despite perceived disadvantages of doing so (Skarupski & Foucher, 2018; Wilmot, 2016).

Two factors I consider key to the success of the Write Ins are the cohort of hosts and the largely consistent structure of the sessions (on writing group structure, see Costello et al., 2024; Skarupski & Foucher, 2018). The consistent structure was especially important with varying hosts, and for a Write In that ran every weekday, having a cohort of hosts served as an antidote to the sessions becoming monotonous. I organised the hosts in 2024 and was conscious of having all five Schools under the College represented to reflect the variety of participants we encouraged to join. We achieved this and also recruited a postgraduate student host to reflect the differing career stages of participants.

Philippa Moore (PhD Candidate, History and Creative Writing)

I participated in the 2023 and 2024 November Write Ins with my own writing projects (usually the latest draft of the creative component of my PhD) and as an occasional host. In 2024, I also hosted the CreW Club while Lucy Christopher was on leave. Prior to this, I had participated in SUAW sessions run by the university's student union, TUSA, for postgraduate students across all disciplines. In 2021, these comprised weekly 2-hour Zoom sessions which by 2022 had expanded to three 2-hour weekly sessions. Most weeks, I attended all sessions. I was the only creative writing postgraduate in the group but was intrigued to see that the free writing practice I associated with my own research area had productive application for those writing theses in science, law, education, and other disciplines.

The TUSA SUAW sessions were crucial in helping form my academic identity due to the COVID-19 pandemic restrictions. I was about 8 months into my candidature when campuses closed, conferences were cancelled, and interactions shifted online. It has been well-documented that the socio-cultural practices within universities have a significant impact on the development of identity and sense of community and agency among postgraduate students (Pretorius & Macaulay, 2021; Rangarajan & Daneshfar, 2023; Smart, 2014). With these practices suspended indefinitely, I struggled in how to continue to progress. As Rangarajan and Daneshfar (2023) discuss, "a PhD student's sense of belonging, self-esteem, and self-efficacy are tied to their sense of identity" (p. 39) and for much of 2020 I feared this was quite fragile: I was navigating a river in a canoe without a paddle.

This situation was by no means unique to me – it was the case for every other postgraduate student in the world and even in so-called 'normal' times, it is "not unusual for doctoral students to experience a range of challenges while pursuing their degree" (Grant-Skiba, 2023, p. 88). TUSA's sessions boosted my confidence by providing a space to regularly share my research and progress with peers. My solid experience of these online sessions as a participant meant that when the concept was adopted by my College in 2023, I believed I could meaningfully contribute. I was delighted when Lucy Christopher began a creative writing-focused SUAW group (CreW), and even more so when the College Write Ins were announced. From my perspective, these had the effect of uniting us after several uncertain years. It also helped me network more within the College.

Whether it was as a participant in the College Write Ins where I could be as active or silent as I chose, or as the facilitator of CreW in 2024, where a more high-octane presence was necessary, I really enjoyed being a part of the group. Not every session was immensely fruitful but the process of continually showing up always resulted in forward movement overall. That was an important lesson I took into my final months before thesis submission. Kamler and Thomson (2007) argue that doctoral writing is "text work *and* [emphasis added] identity work" (p. 168) and I found this to be the case for my PhD journey. The Write Ins and CreW were a vital part of the experience, both in getting words written and in helping form a stronger sense of myself as a creative scholar and practitioner.

Stephanie Richey (Academic Staff, Education)

In the 2023 November Write In, I chose to work on multiple small research tasks, such as editing or an ethics application. In retrospect, I wished I had chosen a project in the writing stage so I could see my daily word count and feel a sense of progress and achievement. The Write In duration seemed like a challenge, as I was more familiar with a 2-hour SUAW. The belief that more time is needed is a commonly reported writing block (Skarupski & Foucher, 2018). However, I found that the accountability of joining the November Write In encouraged me to begin working on a task immediately, and where possible, I used the time as a springboard to continue after the session.

The key outcome of my participation in 2023 was fostering a sense of connection to the overarching College, which I had previously been lacking due to working on the regional campus. Joining the November Write In provided a tangible insight into the range of disciplines within the College, allowing me to put faces to names I had previously seen in College communications, and learn of colleagues' research and writing areas. Being a host enabled verbal conversation with participants, which promoted a stronger sense of connection. When not hosting, connection was also found through engagement in the chat space at the end of the session, during which we celebrated each other's achievements with replies or emoji reactions. I also got to know colleagues from their hosting. This increased sense of connection from the 2023 Write In fostered my wellbeing.

For 2024, I deliberately chose two projects at the writing stage. This meant I increased my word count each day and visually saw the progress, leading to a greater sense of achievement during the second Write In. Adding to the word count on writing outputs provided a deep sense of accomplishment, especially in the two instances where I wrote over 500 words. This confirmed my reflection from 2023 that working on projects in the writing stage would be more fulfilling and aligned with a shift in my personal practice to using SUAW sessions for distinct 'output creation' tasks – for example a journal article to share new knowledge, rather than a research task such as an ethics application. This philosophical shift in how I use my time in SUAW created a better sense of purpose and achievement, leading to increased wellbeing as an academic with tension between high workload and publication pressure – a common cause of stress identified by Ross et al. (2024). Joining a dedicated SUAW group, which the November Write In offered daily, provided strong accountability to attend and set a clear writing intention for the session, leading to increased productivity, connection, and wellbeing.

Mandy Pink (Professional Staff, Research Program Manager)

As a research administrator, my motivation for attending the Write In sessions in 2023 and 2024 was to monitor how they might function as a tool for building a supportive environment and catalyst for interdisciplinary endeavours among researchers who are geographically dislocated. I observed that growing familiarity among participants and the scheduled debrief at the end of each session enabled a sharing of research content and exchange about overlapping topics. I will explore how this might be progressed through topic themes in future Write Ins. In 2024, anxious with job uncertainty, it was deeply calming to start the day with shared purpose at the Write Ins. The sessions removed me from downbeat corridor conversations, and I faced tasks I had been avoiding. The group positivity was infectious.

Final Thoughts

The creative writing discipline's core methodologies were successfully adapted to suit our multi-disciplinary group and participants' varying goals and intentions. Session hosts provided heartfelt and engaged acknowledgements of Country, recognising the peoples on whose lands we were meeting, and paying respects to the many generations of knowledge sharers who cared for, and who continue to care for, Country. Features such as the inspirational quotes adapted smoothly to serve as a gentle, welcoming, and inclusive element of the Write In that doubled as writing prompts to guide uncertain participants into their work via free, unconscious writing. Participants noted the importance of the collective as a means through which to hold themselves accountable (to the self). We were inspired to 'show up'.

Consistent with Wilmot and McKenna's findings (2018), we discovered how our November Write Ins fostered ways of learning about the writing process, with a particular strength being the vertical composition of our cohort. Writers learned from each other through sharing their experiences openly, trials as well as triumphs, thus normalising some of the challenges faced when seeking to share work through publication. Our collective experience assisted in socialising a postgraduate candidate to academe (Déri et al., 2021), while increasing a sense of belonging, particularly for academic colleagues physically located at our smaller, regional campuses. Our professional colleague who at times participated during unpaid hours found value in the camaraderie offered through our sessions as she worked on writing projects related to her recently completed doctoral studies.

The November Write Ins extended beyond a simple tool to improve productivity (Olszewska & Lock, 2016), being utilised to build a vibrant cross-disciplinary writing community within which participants expressed curiosity about their colleagues' research, responded positively to the open sharing enabled through the trust built by hosts, practiced self-care, and expressed enhanced senses of belonging and wellbeing.

Conclusion

The November Write Ins fostered connection, wellbeing, and engagement for us as participants across several disciplines, career stages, and campuses, and, in our experience, for other participants. In 2023, the Write In created a space for connection between diverse groups of colleagues, expanding networks and the visibility of research throughout the College. In 2024, the Write In community supported wellbeing during the uncertainty of institutional change. Participants engaged with and embraced the sharing built into the Write In structure, which was pivotal to both years' success and specific value in terms of wellbeing, belonging, and community. Without such enthusiastic participation and the diversity of participants – undeniably a strength – the November Write Ins would not have been the same positive, collegial experience that we will remember them as, and which will likely motivate us to engage in future writing groups to enhance our individual and collective senses of wellbeing.

References

Aitchison, C. (2009). Research writing groups. In J. Higgs, D. Horsfall & S. Grace (Eds.), *Writing qualitative research on practice* (pp. 253–263). Sense.

Avieson, B. (2008). Writing – A methodology for the new millennium. *Text, 12*(2), 1–11. https://doi.org/10.52086/001c.31693

Baikie, K. A., & Wilhelm, K. (2005). Emotional and physical health benefits of expressive writing. *Advances in Psychiatric Treatment, 11*(5), 338–346. https://doi.org/10.1192/apt.11.5.338

Carr, C., & Becker, T. (2017). *A report on the shut up and write HERG writing retreat at Dartington Hall, Jan 2017, and an argument for writing retreats at the University of Luxembourg*. https://hdl.handle.net/10993/35138

Costello, M., Nyanjom, J., Bailey, S., & Ireson, D. (2024). Care in the academy: How our online writing group transformed into a caring community. *International Journal of Educational Research*, *127*, Article 102441. https://doi.org/10.1016/j.ijer.2024.102441

Déri, C. E., Tremblay-Wragg, É., & Mathieu-Chartier, S. (2021). Academic writing groups in higher education: History and state of play. *International Journal of Higher Education*, *11*(1), 85–99. https://doi.org/10.5430/ijhe.v11n1p85

Grant-Skiba, D. (2023). My PhD saved my sanity and my life. In L. Pretorius, B. Cahusac de Caux & L. Macaulay (Eds.), *Research and teaching in a pandemic world: The challenges of establishing academic identities during times of crisis* (pp. 87–103). Springer Nature Singapore.

Habens, A. (2018). Ink:Well – Writing for wellbeing on the 'Hero's Journey'. *Writing in Practice*, *4*. https://www.nawe.co.uk/DB/current-wip-edition-2/articles/inkwell-writing-for-wellbeing-on-the-heros-journey.html

Kamler, B., & Thomson, P. (2007). Rethinking doctoral writing as text work and identity work. In B. Somekh & T. A. Schwandt (Eds.), *Knowledge production: Research work in interesting times* (pp. 166–179). Routledge. https://doi.org/10.4324/9780203609156

Khan, T., & Siriwardhane, P. (2021). Barriers to career progression in the higher education sector: Perceptions of Australian academics. *Sustainability*, *13*(11), Article 6255. https://doi.org/10.3390/su13116255

London Writers' Salon. (n.d.). *About us*. https://londonwriterssalon.com/#about

Miller, J. (2019). Where does the time go? An academic workload case study at an Australian university. *Journal of Higher Education Policy and Management*, *41*(6), 633–645. https://doi.org/10.1080/1360080X.2019.1635328

National Novel Writing Month. (n.d.). *History*. Internet Archive. https://web.archive.org/web/20180910110811/https://nanowrimo.org/history#expand

Olszewska, K., & Lock, J. (2016). Examining success and sustainability of academic writing: A case study of two writing-group models. *Canadian Journal of Higher Education*, *46*(4), 132–145. https://doi.org/10.47678/cjhe.v46i4.186346

Pretorius, L., & Macaulay, L. (2021). Notions of human capital and academic identity in the PhD: Narratives of the disempowered. *Journal of Higher Education*, *92*(4), 623–647. https://doi.org/10.1080/00221546.2020.1854605

Rangarajan, R., & Daneshfar, S. (2023). Processing uncertainty during COVID-19: A collaborative autoethnography of two stranded international PhD students. In L. Pretorius, B. Cahusac de Caux & L. Macaulay (Eds.), *Research and teaching in a pandemic world: The challenges of establishing academic identities during times of crisis* (pp. 623–647). Springer Nature Singapore.

Ross, P. M., Scanes, E., & Locke, W. (2024). Stress adaptation and resilience of academics in higher education. *Asia Pacific Education Review*, *25*, 829–849. https://doi.org/10.1007/s12564-023-09829-1

Shaffer, V. A., Bohanek, J., Focella, E. S., Horstman, H., & Saffran, L. (2019). Encouraging perspective taking: Using narrative writing to induce empathy for others engaging in negative health behaviors. *PloS One*, *14*(10), Article 0224046. https://doi.org/10.1371/journal.pone.0224046

Skarupski, K. A., & Foucher, K. C. (2018). Writing accountability groups (WAGs): A tool to help junior faculty members build sustainable writing habits. *Journal of Faculty Development*, *32*(3), 47–54. https://link.gale.com/apps/doc/A626042506/AONE

Smart, F. (2014). Poetic transcription: An option in supporting the early career academic? *Journal of Perspectives in Applied Academic Practice*, *2*(3), 66–70. https://jpaap.napier.ac.uk/index.php/JPAAP/article/view/114

Stansfield, J., & Bunce, L. (2014). The relationship between empathy and reading fiction: Separate roles for cognitive and affective components. *Journal of European Psychology Students*, 5(3), 9–18. https://doi.org/10.5334/jeps.ca

Wilmot, K. (2016). Designing writing groups to support postgraduate students' academic writing: A case study from a South African university. *Innovations in Education and Teaching International*, 55(3), 257–265. https://doi.org/10.1080/14703297.2016.1238775

Wilmot, K., & McKenna, S. (2018). Writing groups as transformative spaces. *Higher Education Research & Development*, 37(4), 868–882. https://doi.org/10.1080/07294360.2018.1450361

5 The Power of Writing in Community
Fostering Wellbeing and Self-efficacy among Postgraduate Researchers

Sarah Kneen, Padma Inala, Lily Pearson, Nicola Tomlinson, and Charlotte Evans

Introduction

Student mental health and wellbeing is an increasing concern for universities. Research and interventions have been encouraging; however, these have been largely focused on undergraduates' needs (Canham-Spence et al., 2025). The national Postgraduate Research Experience Survey (Slight, 2017) reported widespread low levels of wellbeing amongst postgraduate researchers (PGRs). At the University of Manchester, as in other higher education institutions in England, PGRs are a cohort which falls outside of "staff" or "student" training and support, facing unique challenges and requiring their own tailored offer (Metcalfe et al., 2020). Upon reviewing existing researcher development provision at the University, disparate offerings were identified across faculties, resulting in inequitable access to PGR–level critical writing and wellbeing support. PGR feedback from existing Library skills workshops also called for support in developing writing efficacy and confidence. Accordingly, the Library sought to review research into challenges facing PGRs and potential means of addressing them, to which we could actively contribute as a centralised support service at the University.

The literature suggests ongoing concern about the mental health and wellbeing of PGRs, with Levecque et al. (2017) finding that PGRs were at substantially higher risk of developing common psychiatric disorders such as depression than other groups of university students. PGRs consistently report that doing a PhD is a stressful experience at some stage (Metcalfe et al., 2018). Working in isolation is a key factor impacting PGR wellbeing, particularly for those on fieldwork or remote campuses and for international PGRs who may struggle with reduced access to friends and family (Metcalfe et al., 2018). An academic environment characterised by expectations of high achievement and high workloads can trigger imposter syndrome—understood broadly as "an overwhelming feeling of being an intellectual fraud despite evidence to the contrary" (Cisco, 2020, p. 200). However, PGRs report that they are often unwilling to talk about their wellbeing issues or seek help, for fear of the impact this might have on their career or perception of their progress (Metcalfe et al., 2018).

DOI: 10.4324/9781003633334-7

Since the COVID-19 lockdowns, studies have pointed to a "desire for informal contact with colleagues and the peer support this provides" to mitigate such mental health challenges (Jackman et al., 2022, p. 710).

The process of writing up research is a key factor contributing to researcher anxiety and stress. Barriers to writing include time constraints, competing priorities with administrative and teaching duties (Jackson, 2009; Kornhaber et al., 2016), lack of motivation, sense of competition among peers, isolation, and fear of failure (Johnston et al., 2014; McGrail et al., 2006). PGRs have also been found to be susceptible to developing negative concepts of their writing abilities, which can impact on their progression (Litalien and Guay, 2015). These barriers compound those already faced by disadvantaged communities, such as neurodivergent individuals, who may struggle "getting ready to start a task, starting a task, staying on task and completing a task" (Eagle, Baltaxe-Admony & Ringland, 2024, p. 11). Writing a substantial thesis is a core component of the completion of a doctoral degree in the UK and plays an essential role in the process that Amell et al. (2022, pp. 260–1) term researcher "becoming": a ritual transformation by which PGRs become independent researchers. Therefore, addressing the affective implications of sustained academic writing at PGR level is essential for supporting researchers' wellbeing during this process.

Writing in community has been found to provide numerous benefits to the wellbeing of PGRs and academic researchers more generally (Moore, 2003; Wilson & Cutri, 2019). Wilson and Cutri (2019, p. 64) highlight a growing body of research that illustrates the impact of practising academic writing in community on several modulators of PGR wellbeing, including "anxiety, isolation, and self-sabotaging behaviours". Writing retreats in particular have been found to develop PGRs' writing self-efficacy—understood as a writer's beliefs surrounding their writing abilities and resources (Mitchell et al., 2017, p. 206)—posited as a key factor in supporting PGRs' wellbeing surrounding writing (Vincent et al., 2021). Reasons for the potency of writing in community include providing a source of motivation (Murray, 2013), peer support in the form of shared struggles and celebrations, and a means of making visible the writing process, as opposed to the final product (Wilson & Cutri, 2019). Scheduling regular writing time, collegial support, and writing retreats have been found to be enablers to writing in community (Johnston et al., 2014; Kornhaber et al., 2016). In particular, studies have reported PGRs' positive experiences of attending and establishing community writing groups using the Shut Up & Write! (SUAW) model as a means of mitigating isolation and other barriers to writing (Wilson & Cutri, 2019). PGRs have identified benefits such as increased motivation, a "feeling of solidarity", accountability for achieving a predetermined goal, and the opportunity for mutual support that led to feeling "successful and valued" (Wilson & Cutri, 2019). Although these results are primarily anecdotal and may not apply to all PGRs, this evidence suggests the range of benefits SUAW may offer in support of PGRs' affective and output-focused experiences of writing.

Providing the conditions for this writing community within a university library has unique advantages. Library staff have been described as "third space professional[s]" (Whitchurch, 2008) within higher education, who can provide academic support within the University while not being responsible for directly assessing learners' work (White & Webster, 2023, p. 4). Learners may confide in staff about their learning experience (and life circumstances impacting upon it) in ways that they are unprepared to share with academic staff responsible for marking their assessments (White & Webster, 2023, p. 4). Third-space professionals can harness the advantages of their liminal positionality when facilitating writing in community in order to emancipate postgraduate researchers and promote self-efficacy.

This chapter will outline how, through collaboration with researchers and student partners, using the SUAW model in writing support for researchers at the Library has helped to boost PGR writing skills, wellbeing, and sense of belonging. Finally, it will explore the limitations encountered in implementing the SUAW model in this context, as well as potential future considerations.

Community Writing Support at the University of Manchester Library

In 2018, we added SUAW sessions and writing retreats to the Library's My Research Essentials programme. The design of these sessions aimed to create a supportive cross-disciplinary community of researchers; improve the self-efficacy of those researchers by introducing them to writing, wellbeing and productivity strategies; and foster partnerships between and with researchers in the ongoing development of the support. These aims serve a core value of learning development practice (Webster, 2019)—learner "emancipation"—as we sought to ultimately empower session attendees with the skills and confidence to curate their independent writing practice and advocate for their own wellbeing.

The writing retreats and SUAW sessions use the same core pedagogical model which informs the majority of our teaching activities at the Library. This model is constructivist and facilitative, positioning staff not as "experts" who "transmit" knowledge to learners but as facilitators of the learning process, to which all make a unique and valued contribution (Blake & Illingworth, 2015). Facilitators of writing retreats and SUAW work alongside attendees, sharing their goals, personal strategies, and progress during breaks. This open partnership is designed to foster a sense of equality and contrasts with the culture of "academia", regularly experienced as exclusionary (Islam et al., 2024; Lynam et al., 2024) and found to induce feelings of imposter syndrome among PGRs (Morris, 2021). Morris (2021, p. 141) found direct links between PGRs' sense of belonging and wellbeing, with belonging being supported by "equal treatment as peers in an academic setting" and their contributions being valued.

Another cornerstone of our team's approach is working in partnership with students as co-creators (Grayson et al., 2018; Blake et al., 2020), and our Library Student Team (a group of paid student-staff members, including PGRs) are embedded at every stage of the development and delivery of our sessions. They collaborate on the design by helping to write workshop plans and supportive blogs, providing invaluable insight into the PGR experience—with one team member, Lily, co-authoring this chapter! They also co-deliver sessions, as well as welcoming, registering, and making hot drinks (during on-campus sessions) for attendees. Their work creates a supportive peer environment, contributing to learner emancipation and several facilitators of belonging outlined by Morris: "identification with other learners" and "recognition of postgraduates as an important constituent of the university" (2021, p. 141). It may also help to break what Browne and Moffett (2014, p. 234) call the "culture of silence" about the inherent uncertainty and emotional challenges of research, as Butler-Rees and Robinson (2020) note the importance of peer-support spaces where PGRs can talk openly about these challenges.

Our SUAW sessions are two hours long and take place every two weeks, alternating between online and on-campus formats. They make use of the Pomodoro technique, shown to promote concentration and flow during writing (Cirillo, 2019), including three concentrated writing blocks of 30 minutes with two 10–minute breaks. Their structured, regular format was designed to support PGRs in building positive writing habits and to combat isolation through writing in community.

The writing retreats are full-day events which take place several times per semester in Library training rooms. Each retreat begins with a short (20–minute) interactive workshop exploring different wellbeing, writing, or productivity research and strategies. The rest of the day is split between concentrated writing blocks which vary in length and breaks in which attendees reflect using structured prompts or share their progress and challenges with peers. The focus on reflective practice and goal setting helps PGRs to recognise their existing skills and abilities, and their role as the "expert" in their own wellbeing. PGRs are encouraged not to see each other as competition, but as partners constructing learning together, sharing strategies for the benefit of all. A complimentary lunch and optional wellbeing walk reinforce the essential link between maintaining wellbeing and productive writing practice.

A survey is emailed to attendees after all of our writing support sessions, which has an average response rate of 14% at the time of writing. Respondents rate the quality of the content, structure, and session facilitators, and comment on supportive elements as well as areas for improvement. We invite ad hoc feedback during all sessions, and in December 2024, we asked writing retreat attendees to create a visual representation of the impact the retreats have had on their wellbeing. The results section that follows will explore the extent to which our aims are reflected in the feedback collected.

Results

As of December 2024, over a thousand individuals had engaged with our community writing sessions, representing 1,634 total attendances. Attendees were predominantly PGRs (90%), alongside some staff, post-doctorate researchers, master's students, and undergraduates. Repeat attendees were frequent, with 55% attending more than one session and 24 attendees attending 11 or more!

Quantitative feedback indicates that over 97% of survey respondents rated the sessions as engaging and useful, and the content and structure as excellent or good. Writing retreat respondents reported being slightly more likely to "incorporate what they had learned into their work", perhaps due to the additional time given in retreats for learners to reflect on insights and set goals. In the following, qualitative feedback responses have been analysed in line with our aims of supporting PGR wellbeing through community and writer self-efficacy, along with our core value of learner emancipation.

Wellbeing through Community

A sense of "communal endeavour" came through in the majority of survey responses. Respondents enjoyed the "sense of camaraderie that comes with everyone sitting in a room writing together", noting that it was "nice to see a few regulars" with whom attendees began to network. Respondents found it valuable to have the "opportunity to chat with people [with] similar experiences", including Library Student Team and staff members who have also completed a PhD, appreciating the "personal insights and experiences" that they can offer rather than the traditional teacher–student power dynamic. Respondents indicated the importance of having a dedicated space where they felt valued and cared for, highlighting "the nice warm feeling of being supported by the university in my research endeavours". This reflects Morris' finding that a sense of being valued members of the university community is essential to PGRs' belonging and wellbeing (2021, p. 141). Factors which seemed to create this feeling of being valued were the "approachable and friendly" facilitators and the complimentary refreshments which made "it feel like such a welcome space". Enjoyment of the writing process and motivation to write in community was reported, and respondents said that the sessions helped to reinforce their "professional identity as researchers/writers" by working alongside fellow writers, rather than in isolation.

Image 5.1, created by Beck Heslop, a regular attendee at our writing sessions, shows a representation of two people working—one at home alone and one at a writing retreat. The person working alone appears distracted and overwhelmed by doubts and negative thoughts, disrupting the writing process. In contrast, the person at the writing retreat is smiling alongside others, making "good progress" and focused on their ideas having "outsourced decisions and willpower". Reflective drawings from other attendees reinforced this idea of writing in community as a powerful enabler of motivation; one made comparisons to "being at the gym with a gym partner—they keep you going for longer". Another drawing depicted the attendee's PhD journey from overwhelm, loneliness, and demotivation to productivity, community, and smiling faces having discovered the retreats, to finally feeling optimistic having

BECK HESLOP, 2nd writing retreat (+ many shut up and writes)

Image 5.1 An attendee's reflective drawing of what the writing retreat means to them (Heslop, 2024).

completed their thesis and started their own writing group. These drawings offer a compelling insight into the value of community writing sessions in supporting both productivity and wellbeing for a range of individuals.

Self-Efficacy and Writing

Respondents reported that they enjoyed the highly structured nature and atmosphere of the sessions, as it helped them feel more motivated and productive and more able to set much-needed boundaries between "writing time" and their work and home life. One researcher highlighted that the "atmosphere created by the structure … really helped me focus and I was much more productive as a result. It also helps me stay *present* and not get distracted." Respondents mentioned that the sessions enabled them to publish more work in a shorter period than they had previously managed. Alongside increased productivity, researchers collectively benefited from the "ability to share ideas about productivity and helpful strategies", and input from peers and facilitators who often signposted relevant resources. Respondents appreciated that they were "reinforcing those writing habits we all know we should cultivate", and shared that the sessions helped to reduce their anxiety and stress around writing, boosting their confidence. Feedback indicated that structured writing in community was crucial to engendering more positive emotional responses to writing, creating greater self-efficacy, as researchers commented that the sessions "… helped me relax when I was feeling very overwhelmed" and made it "easier to tackle bigger/scarier tasks. I was making edits based on comments from my supervisor which I often put off due to nerves."

Emancipation

In support of our core value of fostering emancipation, respondents reported feeling motivated to change their own writing practice and empowered to apply aspects of the sessions to their day-to-day practice. Examples include using the Pomodoro technique in their own time, and practising goal setting and reflection. A preference for seeking opportunities to work alongside others was also evident; several respondents commented that they intended to recreate the conditions to take social breaks from writing with others, whether virtually or in person. Many respondents reported being inspired to establish their own SUAWs and writing retreats with peers following the same framework, with one attendee sharing that they had won funding to host their own residential writing retreat using our open-access workshop materials. Respondents also reported making connections, swapping contact details, and building writing networks with fellow attendees who they later maintained contact with.

Respondents appreciated that we listened to and incorporated their ideas for the sessions, such as adapting the length of writing blocks in the writing retreats to account for energy levels and having longer breaks to facilitate deeper conversation. We made changes to our refreshments to "make it zero waste" and allowed attendees to feed into refreshment and lunch choices. Our commitment to co-creation and building upon feedback reflects the close partnership between our attendees, the Library Student Team and staff, which can arguably contribute not only to wellbeing and belonging, but also PGR emancipation—the sense that this is "their space" which they feel safe in and empowered to shape to suit them.

Discussion and Future Directions

Creating support that is equitable, accessible, and inclusive is at the heart of the Library's skills and development provision and enables everyone to participate in, and gain a sense of belonging to, the community (Blake & Illingworth, 2015; Library for Educators, 2020). The SUAW sessions and writing retreats incorporate much of this good practice, and the many positive comments received from attendees suggest we have been successful to some degree in achieving this when providing writing support for PGRs. However, we acknowledge the limitations of this feedback, which represents the views of only a small proportion of attendees. Thus far we have also been unable to collect feedback from those who do not attend sessions, who might be experiencing barriers to attendance and engagement.

Feedback received via other Library training programmes has been helpful in assessing areas for improvement. For example, feedback from members of the Disabled PGRs' Forum suggests many of their members struggle to access our on-campus sessions due to the timing of workshops, a fear of coming to campus due to health concerns, and the inaccessibility of campus. Concerns from neurodivergent members of the group include finding the group work, group discussions, and prescribed breaks in in-person sessions difficult to navigate. Therefore, one of our intentions is to consider how we might remove barriers to attendance and improve access and engagement with our writing sessions.

The Library does offer online SUAW sessions; however, the writing retreats are only held in person, meaning most of our writing sessions are in a physical space. Increased understanding of the barriers faced by some groups would enable us to plan accommodations to improve access and inclusion at our sessions (Disabled Students UK, 2022), with the hope of enabling as many learners as possible to engage and feel a part of the community. We know that, whilst some individuals or groups may have a preference for online sessions, there are those who prefer the in-person sessions we provide, as evidenced from feedback we receive. Therefore, a more nuanced and considered approach is required, as online and on-campus settings both pose barriers and positives to wellbeing, and it isn't a case of "one size fits all" (Lee, 2022). One way in which we hope to address some of these issues is to work more closely in partnership with our disabled and neurodiverse community (and other communities) via well-established groups and forums at the University. These partnerships will hopefully facilitate fruitful conversations and opportunities for feedback from those not attending so we can gain a better understanding of why this is, what we can do to change it, and how best to adapt our sessions to be as inclusive and accessible as possible.

Another area for future consideration is how we might further encourage writer emancipation using reflection to help embed learning into their day-to-day practice. This was an area we identified in our feedback as most likely to have been achieved by writing retreat attendees, rather than those joining SUAWs, possibly owing to the scheduled reflection time the day-long events offer. Attendees at SUAW may be missing out on exploring writing strategies and goal setting due to limited time, with the focus of these sessions concentrated more on enabling productivity and social connection. One way to address this could be to utilise time outside of the sessions through asynchronous learning and activities. Using pre- and post-session blog posts would allow SUAW attendees to participate in more activities, discussion, or reflective prompts signposted via the posts. This is a model we have used previously to encourage community, connection, and learning for students during the COVID-19 pandemic, where a Study Together series was developed aimed at supporting the wider student body, focusing on activities to improve their academic skills (Aston et al., 2021).

One of the most important elements of the Study Together series was the creation of asynchronous materials to support the online sessions in the form of pre- and post-session blog posts, providing much-needed scaffolding for learning as well as care and socioemotional support (Bali, 2020). Creating similar blog posts for SUAW could be a way to encourage reflection, connection, and application of learning. It also could help demystify what to expect and the level of participation involved, alleviating any anxiety prospective participants might feel, especially if attending for the first time. Including links to useful topics, resources, or templates for writing strategies or goal setting would allow SUAW participants to engage in learning activities in a similar way to those at the writing retreats. The post-session blog posts could act as a session summary and reflection and help participants feel empowered to follow up on any discussion or learning points. In the same way as the pre-session blog posts, creating this detailed aftercare would help participants to feel supported and connected. Using this type of asynchronous support also allows information to be accessed by anyone regardless of whether they can attend the live sessions or not, making the information much more inclusive and accessible.

Ideas to further support self-efficacy include the creation of an informal, online community space where conversations and support could take place and continue asynchronously. Having such a space would allow anyone unable to attend in-person sessions to still contribute to, and benefit from, discussions and ideas, and to access help and support if needed. This would empower individuals to expand their existing networks by forming new connections and broaden the community as a whole. Where an online community space would be hosted, and how this would be facilitated, are issues to be considered, along with whether ownership of this should sit with the Library or elsewhere.

An online community space could also provide a catalyst for PGRs to set up their own SUAW sessions and supportive networks within their respective schools or more widely. There is often feedback calling for us to increase the frequency of our sessions; however, resource restrictions (space, staff, and financial) in the Library often prohibit this. Having PGRs host writing sessions themselves could be one way to further self-efficacy, whilst making the sessions more sustainable and addressing the call for more.

Conclusion

This chapter has demonstrated the value of writing in community to support the wellbeing and self-efficacy of postgraduate researchers. Positioning sessions within a centralised service provides a supportive structure for researchers to develop their own emancipatory writing practice, whilst co-creation of development and facilitation alongside student partners ensures an evolving service with student needs at the forefront. To best meet the needs of a diverse student body, services must engage in continuous reflection on feedback and proactive improvement. Readers looking to implement SUAW in similar contexts could follow a similar model to support learner wellbeing whilst remaining flexible and adapting to emerging developments and best practice.

References

Amell, B., Addison, M., Taylor, Y., & Breeze, M. (2022). Getting stuck, writing badly, and other curious impressions: Doctoral writing and imposter feelings. In M. Addison, M. Breeze & Y. Taylor (Eds.). *The Palgrave handbook of imposter syndrome in higher education* (pp. 259–276). Springer International Publishing. https://doi.org/10.1007/978-3-030-86570-2_16

Aston, S., Stevenson, M., & Inala, P. (2021). Facilitating connections and supporting a learning community: Together. *Journal of Learning Development in Higher Education*, (22). https://doi.org/10.47408/jldhe.vi22.765

Bali, M. (2020, May 28). *Pedagogy of care: COVID 19 edition*. Reflecting allowed. https://blog.mahabali.me/educational-technology-2/pedagogy-of-care-covid-19-edition/

Blake, J., & Illingworth, S. (2015). Interactive and interdisciplinary student work: A facilitative methodology to encourage lifelong learning. *Widening Participation and Lifelong Learning*, *17*(2), 108–118. https://doi.org/10.5456/WPLL.17.2SI.107

Blake, J. R. S., Aston, S., & Grayson, N. (2020). From the outside in: Bringing student engagement to the centre. *New Review of Academic Librarianship*, *26*(2–4), 419–432. https://doi.org/10.1080/13614533.2020.1777172

Browne, B., & Moffett, L. (2014). Finding your feet in the field: Critical reflections of early career researchers on field research in transitional societies. *Journal of Human Rights Practice*, *6*(2), 223–237. https://doi.org/10.1093/jhuman/huu013

Butler-Rees, A., & Robinson, N. (2020). Encountering precarity, uncertainty and everyday anxiety as part of the postgraduate research journey. *Emotion, Space and Society*, *37*, 100743. https://doi.org/10.1016/j.emospa.2020.100743

Canham-Spence, Y., Chapman, L., Creaton, J., Gower, O., & Strack, J. (2025). Doctoral student perspectives on mental health and wellbeing. In J. Creaton & O. Gower (Eds.), *Prioritising the mental health and wellbeing of doctoral researchers: Promoting healthy research cultures* (1st ed., Vol. 1, pp. 162–178). Routledge. https://doi.org/10.4324/9781003403210-10

Cirillo, F. (2019) *The Pomodoro technique*. https://www.pomodorotechnique.com/the-pomodoro-technique-book/

Cisco, J. (2020). Exploring the connection between impostor phenomenon and postgraduate students feeling academically-unprepared. *Higher Education Research and Development*, *39*(2), 200–214. https://doi.org/10.1080/07294360.2019.1676198

Disabled Students UK (2022). *Going back is not a choice*. https://disabledstudents.co.uk/not-a-choice/

Eagle, T., Baltaxe-Admony, L. B., & Ringland, K. E. (2024). "It was something I naturally found worked and heard about later": An investigation of body doubling with neurodivergent participants. *ACM Transactions on Accessible Computing*, *17*(3), 1–30. https://doi.org/10.1145/3689648

Grayson, N. J., Blake, J. and Stock, M. (2018) The co-creation of exam support: Students as partners in the research, planning, design and quality assurance of learning resources. *Journal of Educational Innovation, Partnership and Change*, *4*(1).

Heslop, B. (2024) *An attendees' reflective drawing of what the writing retreat means to them* [illustration]. The University of Manchester Library, Manchester.

Islam, M., Das, N., & Odaro, L. I. (2024). *Understanding and exploring the experiences of Black and Asian Postgraduate Research (PGR) students*. University of Southampton. https://www.southampton.ac.uk/~assets/doc/Black%20and%20Asian%20PGR%20Student%20Experience%20Report.pdf

Jackman, P. C., Sanderson, R., Haughey, T. J., Brett, C. E., White, N., Zile, A., Tyrrell, K., & Byrom, N. C. (2022). The impact of the first COVID-19 lockdown in the UK for doctoral and early career researchers. *Higher Education*, *84*(4), 705–722. https://doi.org/10.1007/s10734-021-00795-4

Jackson, D. (2009). Mentored residential writing retreats: A leadership strategy to develop skills and generate outcomes in writing for publication. *Nurse Education Today*, *29*(1), 9–15.

Johnston, J., Wilson, S., Rix, E., & Pit, S. W. (2014). Publish or perish: Strategies to help rural early career researchers increase publication output. *Rural and Remote Health*, *14*(3), 372–377.

Kornhaber, R., Cross, M., Betihavas, V., & Bridgman, H. (2016). The benefits and challenges of academic writing retreats: an integrative review. *Higher Education Research and Development*, *35*(6), 1210–1227. https://doi.org/10.1080/07294360.2016.1144572

Lee, J. (2022, April 15). Hyflex learning: What, why and how. *Times Higher Education*. https://www.timeshighereducation.com/campus/hyflex-learning-what-why-and-how

Levecque, K., Anseel, F., De Beuckelaer, A., Van der Heyden, J., & Gisle, L. (2017). Work organization and mental health problems in PhD students. *Research Policy*, *46*(4), 868–879. https://doi.org/10.1016/j.respol.2017.02.008

Library for Educators (2020, December 18). Virtual teaching and support. *Medium*. https://foreducators.medium.com/virtual-teaching-and-support-1be25054a7f

Litalien, D., & Guay, F. (2015). Dropout intentions in PhD studies: A comprehensive model based on interpersonal relationships and motivational resources. *Contemporary Educational Psychology*, *41*, 218–231. https://doi.org/10.1016/j.cedpsych.2015.03.004

Lynam, S., Lafarge, C., & Milani, R. M. (2024). Exploring the experiences of ethnic minority postgraduate researchers in the UK. *Educational Review (Birmingham)*, *76*(7), 1980–2000. https://doi.org/10.1080/00131911.2024.2316614

McGrail, M. R., Rickard, C. M., & Jones, R. (2006). Publish or perish: A systematic review of interventions to increase academic publication rates. *Higher Education Research and Development*, *25*(1), 19–35. https://doi.org/10.1080/07294360500453053

Metcalfe, J., Day, E., de Pury, J., & Dicks, A. (2020). *Supporting mental health and wellbeing for postgraduate research students: Programme evaluation*. Vitae. https://www.ukri.org/wp-content/uploads/2021/12/RE-141221-CatalystFundProgrammeEvaluation.pdf

Metcalfe, J., Wilson, S., Levecque, K. (2018). *Exploring wellbeing and mental health and associated support services for postgraduate researchers*. Vitae. https://www.ukri.org/wp-content/uploads/2018/05/RE_141221-MentalHealthReportFinal.pdf

Mitchell, K. M., Harrigan, T., Stefansson, T., & Setlack, H. (2017). Exploring self-efficacy and anxiety in first-year nursing students enrolled in a discipline-specific scholarly writing course. *Quality Advancement in Nursing*, *3*(1): 1–21. https://doi.org/10.17483/2368-6669.1084

Moore, S. (2003). Writers' retreats for academics: Exploring and increasing the motivation to write. *Journal of Further and Higher Education*, *27*(3), 333–342. https://doi.org/10.1080/0309877032000098734

Morris, C. (2021). "Peering through the window looking in": Postgraduate experiences of non-belonging and belonging in relation to mental health and wellbeing. *Studies in Graduate and Postdoctoral Education*, *12*(1), 131–144. https://doi.org/10.1108/SGPE-07-2020-0055

Murray, R. (2013). "It's not a hobby": Reconceptualizing the place of writing in academic work. *Higher Education*, *66*(1), 79–91. https://doi.org/10.1007/s10734-012-9591-7

Slight, C. (2017). *Postgraduate Research Experience Survey 2017: Experiences and personal outlook of postgraduate researchers*. Higher Education Academy. https://s3.eu-west-2.amazonaws.com/assets.creode.advancehe-document-manager/documents/hea/private/hub/download/pres_2017_report_0_1568037544.pdf

Vincent, C., Tremblay-Wragg, E., Déri, C., Plante, I. & Mathieu Chartier, S. (2021). How writing retreats represent an ideal opportunity to enhance PhD candidates' writing self-efficacy and self-regulation. *Teaching in Higher Education*, *28*(7), 1600–1619. https://doi.org/10.1080/13562517.2021.1918661

Webster, H. (2019, February 4). Emancipatory practice: The defining LD value? *rattus scholasticus*. https://rattusscholasticus.wordpress.com/2019/02/04/emancipatory-practice-the-defining-ld-value/

Whitchurch, C. (2008). Shifting identities and blurring boundaries: The emergence of third space professionals in UK Higher Education. *Higher Education Quarterly*, *62*(4), 377–396. https://doi.org/10.1111/j.1468-2273.2008.00387.x

White, S. & Webster, H. (2023). Hey you! They're calling you Tinkerbell! What are you going to do about it? *Journal of Learning Development in Higher Education*, *29*. https://doi.org/10.47408/jldhe.vi29.1120

Wilson, S. & Cutri, J. (2019). Negating isolation and imposter syndrome through writing as product and as process: The impact of collegiate writing networks during a doctoral programme. In L. Pretorius, L. Macaulay & B. Cahusac de Caux (Eds.), *Wellbeing in doctoral education* (1st ed., Vol. 1, pp. 59–76). Springer Nature Singapore.

6 Shared Goals, Collective Growth

Developing Shut Up & Write! Communities of Practice

Lyn Lavery and Rebecca George

Introduction

Shut Up & Write (SUAW) communities have emerged over recent years as an effective means for researchers and academic writers to manage the challenges of maintaining focus, productivity, and connection in the often isolating research environment. Initially designed as informal writing meetups, SUAW groups provide a structured yet flexible environment where researchers can work alongside peers in focused sessions, with opportunities for shared reflection and support. The value of SUAW groups extends beyond increased writing output; it fosters a sense of community and mutual accountability that helps members sustain motivation and overcome common research barriers.

While there is immense value in informal or ad-hoc SUAW sessions, this chapter argues that embedding SUAW within a wider community of practice (CoP) model can further extend the benefits. We explore how SUAW groups can operate within a CoP, to move beyond individual writing sessions and foster shared purpose, ongoing connection, and collective momentum. To illustrate this in practice, we provide a guide to developing and sustaining SUAW CoPs, using our community (Research Accelerator) as a case study to help others create thriving communities supporting productivity and wellbeing.

Communities of Practice

Wenger's (1998) concept of CoPs offers a valuable lens for understanding how groups of individuals build connections, share knowledge, and collaborate to enhance their expertise through shared practices. CoPs are defined by three core dimensions: a *domain* of shared interest, a *community* where relationships and mutual support develop, and a *practice* involving the collective resources and tools that members refine over time. Rather than being structured as formal instructional groups, CoPs facilitate learning through interaction and participation, with individual roles evolving over time from peripheral participants to core members. In research settings, CoPs can be crucial in overcoming isolation and fostering a sense of belonging and purpose. CoPs also help members

DOI: 10.4324/9781003633334-8

navigate challenges by drawing on collective wisdom and shared experiences, making them particularly relevant in initiatives such as SUAW communities, where researchers support each other to stay productive and motivated.

Digital communication has extended CoPs into virtual spaces, giving rise to virtual communities of practice (vCoPs) that support online collaboration and knowledge sharing (Bourhis et al., 2005). While vCoPs retain the foundational elements of domain, community, and practice (Wenger et al., 2009), they also face challenges in sustaining engagement and fostering meaningful connections across digital platforms. Nevertheless, vCoPs offer distinct advantages. By removing geographical and temporal barriers, they make participation more flexible and inclusive, allowing individuals from diverse locations and time zones to contribute at their own pace (Bourhis et al., 2005). This flexibility can enhance access to expertise, broaden perspectives, and support continuity in professional development, particularly for distributed or interdisciplinary groups.

The Case Study

Research Accelerator is a vCoP for researchers, established in New Zealand in 2020 in response to the COVID-19 pandemic. It has since grown into a global network, providing a vital space for connection and collaboration among researchers at various career stages. The community hosts an extensive library of resources including self-paced video courses, live training sessions, and personalised support, focusing on essential skills for data analysis and presenting research findings. Membership is open to any researchers interested in developing their research methods skills or connecting with others in the field. A small membership fee (in line with fees for joining professional associations) covers the costs of running the community. A key component of the Research Accelerator membership is regular SUAW sessions, the details of which are described throughout this chapter. The membership is further discussed in Roache et al. (2025) in relation to wellbeing, while the technological and social aspects are highlighted in Wood and Talmage (2025).

We are both involved in the day-to-day leadership of the community and bring slightly different perspectives. Lyn is the founder of Research Accelerator and remains the administrator of key aspects of the community. She has subsequently encouraged members to assume leadership roles to help sustain community momentum. Becky is one of those leaders, joining the community early in her doctoral research. Becky hosts regular SUAW sessions and contributes to the community social chat and communal resources. We both strongly believe in the life-changing influence this type of community can have on its members' scholarly development, personal insights, and career aspirations.

Quotes from a diverse range of members of the Research Accelerator community appear throughout the chapter. All quotes are from individual interviews with community members, transcribed verbatim but edited for readability. Interviews are sourced from a previous research project (Lavery, 2023) and re-used with permission.

Throughout this chapter, we use both CoP and vCoP terminology deliberately. When discussing the broader theoretical framework and principles that apply to all communities of practice, we use the abbreviation CoP. When referring specifically to virtual communities of practice (including our case study, Research Accelerator), we use the term vCoP to emphasise the digital context and its unique characteristics. This distinction is important as some aspects of community building remain consistent across both physical and virtual spaces, while others are uniquely shaped by the digital environment.

Steps to Developing a SUAW vCoP

Creating a thriving SUAW vCoP requires deliberate planning, a commitment to inclusivity, and the flexibility to adapt. Each evolutionary step reflects an iterative approach that is deeply rooted in shared values and sustained by collaborative effort. In this chapter, we propose a roadmap with practical steps for building a successful and sustainable SUAW vCoP.

Image 6.1 presents our proposed model. At the centre is SUAW participation, supported by the three foundational dimensions of a CoP: domain, community, and practice. These core elements are encircled by the key pillars of inclusivity, shared leadership, and adaptability to enable growth, resilience, and sustainability. In the remainder of this chapter, each step within this model will be described, evidenced, and illustrated by examples from Research Accelerator.

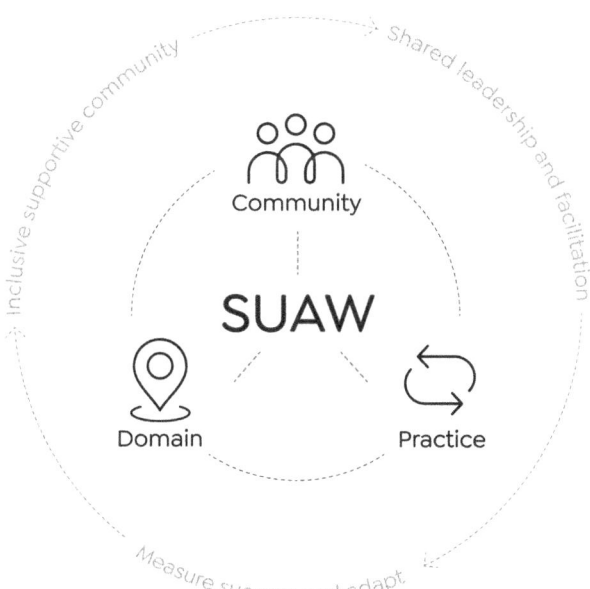

Image 6.1 Proposed model for SUAW vCoP development.

Step 1: Identify the Domain

A CoP begins with a shared *domain* of interest, which provides the foundation for connection and engagement among its members (Wenger, 1998). This domain represents more than a topic; it embodies a collective passion or purpose that draws individuals together. Whether the focus is on academic writing, teaching strategies, or a specialised area of research, the domain provides clarity and alignment, ensuring that all participants have a common understanding of their collective goals. This shared interest motivates individuals to engage, learn, and collaborate. By defining a clear domain, CoPs foster a sense of belonging and direction, offering a unifying purpose that sustains their activities over time.

In the case of Research Accelerator, the initial focus was on helping researchers build capacity in research methods, especially in data analysis and the use of tools such as NVivo and SPSS. During the early development stages, there was some debate about whether the domain should be broadened to encompass research methods more generally. After consultation with researcher development staff at several New Zealand tertiary institutions, it was decided that a narrower scope would be more appropriate, better addressing the specific needs of researchers and filling a gap in service delivery at the time. In retrospect, this deliberate narrowing of scope played a pivotal role in cultivating strong community bonds and enabling focused resource development. While the original emphasis on data analysis remains, Research Accelerator has since responded to member feedback by broadening its shared knowledge base to include resources on wellbeing, self-care, and productivity—recognising the need to support researchers balancing competing demands.

Step 2: Establish the Community

The concept of *community* is what transforms a shared interest into a thriving, collaborative group (Wenger, 1998). In a CoP, relationships begin to form through regular interaction, shared challenges, and early acts of mutual support. These connections are reinforced as members exchange insights, acknowledge each other's contributions, and start to recognise shared goals. As momentum builds, the group begins to shift from a collection of individuals to a connected community with a sense of shared purpose. This early relational groundwork is vital to establishing the trust and cohesion that will support deeper engagement over time (Wenger et al., 2002).

A key first step in establishing a community is identifying and engaging core members with the same interests or goals (Wenger et al., 2002). Recruitment strategies must align with the community's objectives and consider where potential members are located, for example, a particular institution, geographic region, or disciplinary knowledge base. Different domains require tailored outreach approaches, and it is important to determine how best to reach and communicate with prospective members. Potential avenues include professional networks, institutional email lists, social media, and academic interest groups.

Personal invitations are often the most effective means of attracting committed members (Yarris et al., 2019). Once a core group is established, encouraging members to extend invitations within their own networks can create a ripple effect that strengthens and diversifies the community. For example, as the Research Accelerator founder, Lyn initially reached out to participants from existing academic networks, leveraging email lists and social media to broaden reach. This approach secured an initial base of engaged members, who then helped to expand the community further by sharing their experiences with colleagues and peers.

Laying the groundwork for sustained engagement requires cultivating a culture of inclusion and shared responsibility from the outset. Founding members play a crucial role in modelling participation norms and fostering an atmosphere of openness. In Research Accelerator, this was established early through practices that encouraged active contribution, such as participating in sessions, engaging in discussions, and offering peer support. These early behaviours helped establish the community's values and set a rhythm that new members could quickly observe and adopt. While these early efforts lay the foundation, however, community growth and sustainability depend on the steps we explore next.

Step 3: Develop the Practice

The *practice* dimension of a CoP refers to the shared repertoire of tools, strategies, and knowledge that members develop and refine together (Wenger, 1998). This repertoire evolves over time and reflects the collective knowledge and expertise of members. It serves as a living repository of the community's learning, enabling members to draw on established practices while contributing new insights. This shared repertoire also helps establish the community's identity, encapsulating its unique way of approaching challenges and achieving goals.

Research Accelerator exemplifies this dimension with its accessible library of resources, all available through a central portal (Research Accelerator, 2025). Members frequently draw on these resources during SUAW sessions to address challenges or share insights, fostering ongoing knowledge exchange. For this chapter's focus on SUAW, rather than discussing the shared knowledge base more generally, we will discuss the *practice* of SUAW sessions and how these are structured to align with the community's evolving needs.

Scheduling, Session Structure, and Etiquette

Since its launch 4 years ago, the frequency of SUAW sessions in Research Accelerator has grown significantly. Initially starting with bi-monthly sessions, there are now a minimum of eight per week, running at least once daily (including weekends). Initially, we assumed the widely recognised SUAW term would resonate with members, but attendance was low. Feedback revealed that because the community domain was focused on data analysis, members did not always engage in writing and struggled to connect with the SUAW term. A simple name change to 'Shut Up & Research', better reflecting our vCoP's identity, led to a significant rise in attendance and increased demand for regular sessions.

Research Accelerator SUAW sessions are typically 3 hours in duration when held during the day and 2 hours in the evening. Within sessions, we run 50-minute timed work blocks with breaks. We initially used the widely popular Pomodoro Technique (Cirillo, 2018), which is based on 25-minute blocks, but based on member feedback, we expanded this to 50 minutes as members felt that they were just getting into the flow of their work when the timer interrupted them. Structured breaks are a core feature of our session format, providing time for rest and reset between work blocks. The relational value of these breaks is discussed further in Step 5.

For those considering setting up their own SUAW communities, we recommend an element of predictability and routine when scheduling sessions, which helps members prioritise their participation. Starting and finishing at specified times lets members know what to expect and helps them plan sessions into their daily timetables. This also helps them to protect their research and writing time from competing demands and gives the session credence within their daily activities: "*If I hadn't had the community, guaranteed, after half an hour, I would have been having a nap, or I would have been out in the garden, so I think it's absolutely fundamental to having finished* [my PhD] *by now*". In Research Accelerator, the routine of specified session times is balanced with flexibility, with members also supported to join mid-session, knowing that they can slip in and focus.

Etiquette for SUAW sessions is communicated clearly, so members know what to expect should they join mid-session and to ensure that the protected work time members value is not interrupted. This etiquette is part of the shared repertoire of knowledge and norms that are central to our community. For example, conversation is constructively managed by muting microphones during SUAW sessions and cameras remain active where appropriate to sustain connection and visual presence. While some SUAW groups do not actively encourage visual connection (e.g., Hammond et al., 2023) our members have found the visual presence of others a motivating and encouraging mechanism: "*Physically alone doesn't mean mentally or socially alone when you're online with somebody. Therefore, the value of a space* [or] *a platform…giving you visual cues that you are not alone is really powerful*". These shared routines represent more than just logistical arrangements; they reflect the community's values, support members' research identities, and help establish a collective sense of purpose.

Technology That Supports Engagement

Online platforms such as Zoom enable SUAW sessions to run anytime and anywhere and are becoming widely used by SUAW communities to enable members to engage (O'Dwyer et al., 2017). As one member noted, "*Regardless *of what people say about being online, you get to know each other quite well when you're in contact with each other often*". Research Accelerator's use of additional platforms such as Welo (a 24/7 virtual office space), WhatsApp, and its own dedicated website enables members to stay further connected regardless of geographic location. These tools also provide a sense of continuity, allowing members to engage with the community at their own pace: "[It] *is incredibly powerful to be in a space of your own choosing, where you have set up an environment that is conducive and motivating to your study and still be able to connect with others*".

In our experience, technology is most effective when it complements rather than complicates the vCoP's goals. Selecting user-friendly platforms and providing clear guidelines reduces participation barriers and fosters engagement. Additional key elements that we have found work well for hosting SUAW sessions within a vCoP include

- Clear, accessible, and regular communication of session details (including a calendar that integrates with members' schedules), which helps prioritise participation amid competing demands.
- Making good use of Zoom functionality during sessions, such as online chat, timer apps (to ensure timing visibility for all attendees), and breakout rooms for larger groups. The use of Zoom reactions and avatars can also add an element of fun and light-heartedness.

As the practice of SUAW sessions becomes more embedded, questions of sustainability naturally emerge. We suggest that shared leadership and facilitation are key to ensuring this sustainability, and we turn to these in the next step.

Step 4: Develop Shared Leadership and Facilitation

A CoP is an organic entity that enables members to participate, connect, grow, and contribute to leadership. Yarris et al. (2019) emphasise an apprenticeship model which allows members to transition from peripheral participation to active core membership at their own pace. Similarly, Rok (2009) highlights the importance of participative leadership as a mechanism for fostering ethical engagement, empowerment, and stakeholder ownership within a community. By embedding shared leadership principles, vCoPs can create sustainable engagement structures that prevent leadership burnout and maintain long-term momentum.

Within Research Accelerator, this participatory leadership model is evident in the use of member hosts for SUAW sessions. Hosts are carefully selected based on their emotional insight, open-mindedness, technical proficiency, and experience in group facilitation, ensuring they can read the room effectively and maintain a positive session dynamic. Typically, these hosts are senior or experienced community members who have observed and internalised the established expectations in action.

In contrast to rigid hierarchies, Yarris et al. (2019) emphasise the importance of enabling leadership structures within vCoPs, where members gradually assume more active roles based on their availability, interest, and expertise. Research Accelerator follows a similar principle, encouraging hosts to develop their own facilitation style while working within agreed-upon 'guardrails' which prioritise guidance over strict rules. These guardrails ensure that sessions maintain their focus on both relational connection and sustained productivity. Examples of guardrails from Research Accelerator include assigning specific hosts and the consistent use of a visible timer for SUAW sessions, to ensure they start and finish at designated times. While social breaks may vary in length, hosts are responsible for upholding the structure of focused work blocks.

We have found that a participatory leadership approach, guided by clear yet flexible structures, ensures that Research Accelerator remains resilient, inclusive, and member driven. By embedding active participation and shared leadership, the community reduces reliance on any single individual and fosters a strong sense of collective ownership, aligning with best practices (Wenger, 1998; Yarris et al., 2019; Rok, 2009). These leadership practices contribute to sustainability and the culture of belonging that defines the community.

Step 5: Create an Inclusive and Supportive Environment

A defining feature of Research Accelerator is the strong sense of connection and support that develops among members. One participant captured this with a powerful metaphor:

> We're all in this waka [Māori canoe] together. We're all in our own wakas, but everybody else in Research Accelerator is in that waka with you. So we metaphorically jump from waka to waka, but my perspective is that I'm in my waka, and everyone's with me on this, helping to paddle.

This relational spirit is at the heart of creating an inclusive and supportive environment within a SUAW vCoP. Mutual engagement allows members to participate actively, build relationships, and exchange ideas, creating a foundation for collaboration and shared learning (Wenger, 1998). This engagement is particularly important for navigating challenges inherent in academic life, such as balancing competing demands, managing progress, and maintaining productivity. A well-integrated vCoP facilitates knowledge sharing and provides emotional support, creating a space where members feel valued and empowered.

This is fostered within the Research Accelerator vCoP through the Māori concept of *whanaungatanga*, a sense of family connection, which emphasises relational ties that sustain its members both academically and personally. This includes a structured yet welcoming introduction to community norms, helping new members feel comfortable from the outset. As mentioned earlier, existing members play a key role in modelling inclusivity and encouraging participation, reinforcing a culture of trust and mutual support. As one member described:

> …initially I felt a little bit on the edge of it, but I felt very included and thoroughly welcomed. And then I felt I could start talking to people about things that I was experiencing and piggybacking off their knowledge. And that has been a game changer for me.

Wenger et al. (2002) highlight the importance of these social connections in sustaining CoPs, as they contribute to members' willingness to share experiences and engage deeply with one another.

Breaks as a Space for Inclusion and Peer Learning

One of the clearest examples of how Research Accelerator fosters connection is through the structure and use of breaks within SUAW sessions. The effectiveness of work-break cycles is well-documented (Biwer et al., 2023), although research on the role of breaks in fostering social connections is limited. We have found that breaks are crucial in strengthening relationships, as noted by this member: *"We connect as a community of practice, but this healthy approach to friendship, to social interaction… We all encourage each other with motivation and momentum"*.

We have both been members of other online groups where breaks were taken individually rather than on-screen with the group. This approach did not foster the same sense of connection or shared experience and, at times, created feelings of separation and distance. It left us feeling more isolated and ultimately deterred us from continuing with those groups. In our view, connection during breaks is fundamental to cultivating vCoP culture.

In addition to informal social interactions, these breaks often become spaces for meaningful peer interaction and academic dialogue. Questions and knowledge sharing are actively encouraged. A key feature of Research Accelerator's culture is the belief that there is no such thing as a stupid question, as one member noted:

> These experienced people are really good at what they're doing, and they understand it in a deep way. They don't make me feel silly, asking questions… I think this community enables you to be your authentic self and to be proud to be who you are, and everybody wants everybody else to succeed.

This creation of a safe space where participants can express themselves as learners, contributors, and mentors is crucial (Hammond & Lemon, 2024). Peer interaction is a vital mechanism through which members learn, as it allows them to oscillate between giving and receiving guidance depending on the task at hand. One participant reflected: "*It's okay to be a novice…you're not a novice at everything in life. You bring expertise… which is quite special to be able to be vulnerable and not feel like you're getting it right*". By allowing members to step into different roles, our vCoP facilitates skill development and a deep sense of belonging. The experience of this culture helps members transition from being novices to becoming scholars, strengthening their confidence and reinforcing their contributions to the wider community (Hammond & Lemon, 2024).

Reflective Learning, Identity, and Boundaries

Beyond immediate peer interaction, community participation also shapes how members see themselves as researchers and manage their work with confidence and clarity. Members frequently discuss progress, reflect on research stages, and share strategies for managing responsibilities. This collaborative process helps alleviate feelings of overwhelm, as one participant noted: "*It is just so powerful being alongside other researchers at whatever level and just seeing people doing research, doing the mahi [work], and seeing that it takes time, that it takes everyone time*".

A closely connected element of this support involves establishing and protecting boundaries around research and writing, an essential practice for maintaining both productivity and wellbeing (O'Dwyer et al., 2017; Sotiropoulou & Cranston, 2022). Research Accelerator members reinforce these boundaries by committing to scheduled SUAW sessions and developing and sharing strategies to defend their writing time from competing demands. As one member explained: "*…an ability to use* [SUAW] *as a boundary-setting system. It's a very useful tool… it's a mechanism to say, actually, these times are in the diary… immovable*".

In addition, Research Accelerator members often highlight the community's role in shaping researcher identity and self-perception. As one member noted: "*I have a stronger sense of self, ironically, because of the community. I know who I am and who I am not as a researcher. I know and recognise my strengths and weaknesses*". Hansen and Hamilton (2024) contend that relational participation in such groups fosters the development of research skills and scholarly confidence. They also suggest that peer reflection helps uncover the "intangibles of practice" (p.58), the emotions and unspoken elements of scholarly work. This process of collective reflection strengthens not only individual resilience but also the fabric of the vCoP itself.

Step 6: Measure Success and Adapt to Sustain the Community

Success in vCoPs is not a fixed outcome but an evolving process involving structural characteristics (Bourhis et al., 2005). Standard metrics alone cannot fully capture their impact, as vCoPs emphasise social connection, knowledge sharing, and active participation. Wenger et al. (2002) stress that long-term success depends on a community's ability to adapt to members' changing needs. We argue that this requires drawing on both quantitative and qualitative indicators.

Key quantitative indicators used within Research Accelerator include:

- **SUAW attendance trends** over time, including engagement patterns across different times of the day or week.
- **Activity levels** on platforms such as WhatsApp, online forums, and shared digital workspaces.
- **Membership data**, including new member numbers, retention rates, and international reach.
- **Leadership participation**, such as members volunteering to host sessions or contribute resources.
- **Engagement with shared resources**, such as template downloads, video library views, or discussion thread activity.

Qualitative insights are equally important for understanding the deeper impact of a vCoP. Research Accelerator incorporates the following approaches:

- **Regular member surveys** to assess satisfaction, perceived value, and areas for improvement.
- **Reflective interviews** with core members to explore experiences, challenges, and evolving needs.
- **Session feedback loops**, where hosts gather informal reflections during and after SUAW sessions.
- **Storytelling and testimonials** to capture the personal and academic impact of participation.

A successful CoP is not static; it must evolve continually to remain relevant and responsive to its members (Wenger et al., 2009). This means staying attuned to changing needs, expectations, and contexts, particularly as the academic environment shifts. Research Accelerator regularly adapts its SUAW offerings based on feedback gathered through both formal and informal channels. These adaptations are not one-off changes, but part of a continuous cycle of reflection and refinement that ensures the community remains vibrant, supportive, and member driven. In this way, evaluation is not an administrative exercise but a key mechanism for sustaining momentum and cultivating a sense of shared ownership and ongoing relevance.

Conclusion

Using Research Accelerator as a case study, this chapter outlined a series of practical steps to demonstrate how vCoPs can be developed to foster vibrant, collaborative spaces for mutual learning and support. While focused on a specific vCoP, the principles described can be adapted across institutional contexts and different types of researchers and writers. We acknowledge potential challenges for researchers with limited internet access, competing demands, or from diverse cultural backgrounds where collective writing practices may differ. Session timing, platform choice, and facilitation style may need adjustment depending on institutional culture, time zones, or career stage, yet the emphasis on inclusivity, responsiveness, and shared purpose remains constant.

We view our model as a relatively simple but effective means to not only support individual researchers but also address some of the systemic issues prevalent in research cultures. SUAW vCoPs require minimal institutional resources, and their collaborative nature directly counters the isolation and hyper-individualism often embedded in research environments. By emphasising shared goals, creating spaces for vulnerability, and validating the emotional aspects of scholarly work, these communities offer an alternative to productivity-driven research cultures that can undermine wellbeing. The model's focus on inclusivity and mutual support provides a microcosm of what healthier research environments might look like and offers a compelling blueprint for building sustainable, connected research communities.

References

Biwer, F., Wiradhany, W., Oude Egbrink, M. G. A., & de Bruin, A. B. H. (2023). Understanding effort regulation: Comparing 'Pomodoro' breaks and self-regulated breaks. *British Journal of Educational Psychology*, *93*(Suppl. 2), 353–367. https://doi.org/10.1111/bjep.12593

Bourhis, A., Dubé, L., & Jacob, R. (2005). The success of virtual communities of practice: The leadership factor. *The Electronic Journal of Knowledge Management*, *3*(1), 23–34. https://academic-publishing.org/index.php/ejkm/article/view/719/682

Cirillo, F. (2018). *The Pomodoro technique: The life-changing time-management system.* Virgin Digital.

Hammond, K., & Lemon, N. (Eds.). (2024). *Navigating tensions and transitions in higher education: Effective skills for maintaining wellbeing and self-care.* Routledge. https://doi.org/10.4324/9781032701349

Hammond, K., Trafford, J., Hassouna, A., Jowitt, L., Lees, A., Lucas, P., Power, N., & Stretton, C. (2023). "Ding!" Co-creating wellbeing in a Friday online research writing group. In N. Lemon (Ed.), *Reflections on valuing wellbeing in higher education: Reforming our acts of self-care* (pp. 159–177). Routledge.

Hansen, L., & Hamilton, D. (2024). Deciding not to die: On becoming an academic. In K. Hammond & N. Lemon (Eds.), *Navigating tensions and transitions in higher education: Effective skills for maintaining wellbeing and self-care* (pp. 55–66). Routledge. https://doi.org/10.4324/9781032701349

Lavery, L. (2023, September 28). Learning NVivo within an online community of practice: Better together? [Paper presentation]. *Lumivero Online Conference*.

O'Dwyer, S. T., McDonough, S. L., Jefferson, R., Goff, J. A., & Redman-MacLaren, M. (2017). Writing groups in the digital age: A case study analysis of shut up & write tuesdays. In A. Esposito (Ed.), *Research 2.0 and the impact of digital technologies on scholarly inquiry* (pp. 249–269). IGI Global Scientific Publishing. doi:10.4018/978-1-5225-0830-4.ch013

Research Accelerator. (2025). *Looking to accelerate your research?* https://www.researchaccelerator.nz

Roache, A., George, J., & Baker, L. M. (2025). Connection, momentum, and growth: Exploring the benefits and challenges of 'shut up & research' for researcher wellbeing. In N. Lemon, A. Bolzle, A. Santa Cruz, & R. Saunders (Eds.), *Shut up and write: Fostering wellbeing through collective writing practices*. Routledge.

Rok, B. (2009). Ethical context of the participative leadership model: Taking people into account. *Corporate Governance: The International Journal of Business in Society, 9*(4), 461–472. https://doi.org/10.1108/14720700910985007

Sotiropoulou, P., & Cranston, S. (2022). Critical friendship: An alternative, 'care-full' way to play the academic game. *Gender, Place & Culture, 30*(8), 1104–1125. https://doi.org/10.1080/0966369X.2022.2069684

Wenger, E. (1998). *Communities of practice: Learning, meaning, and identity*. Cambridge University Press. https://doi.org/10.1017/cbo9780511803932

Wenger, E., McDermott, R., & Snyder, W. (2002). *Cultivating communities of practice: A guide to managing knowledge*. Harvard Business School Press.

Wenger, E., White, N., & Smith, J. D. (2009). *Digital habitats: Stewarding technology for communities*. Cpsquare.

Wood, Y., & Talmage, A. (2025). Times to shut up, times to sing out: How technology fosters productivity and wellbeing. In N. Lemon, A. Bolzle, A. Santa Cruz, & R. Saunders (Eds.), *Shut up and write: Fostering wellbeing through collective writing practices*. Routledge.

Yarris, L. M., Chan, T. M., Gottlieb, M., & Juve, A. M. (2019). Finding your people in the digital age: Virtual communities of practice to promote education scholarship. *Journal of Graduate Medical Education, 11*(1), 1–5. https://doi.org/10.4300/JGME-D-18-01093.1

7 Pomodoro and ePortfolio
An Unlikely but Perfect Pair

Claire Bowmer and Dana Bui

Introduction

The purpose of this chapter is to hear what participants of a SAUW session think while attending in mostly silence. This SUAW session highlighted in this chapter is called Plan, Act, Reflect and ePortfolio (PARE). It aims to promote positive mental health outcomes in participants through inclusion, connection, and belonging by design. In the higher education context, there is a group referred to by Celia Whitchurch as third space professionals (2008, 2013), a cohort requiring strong resilience and self-identity (Thorpe & Partridge, 2024: Gordon & Whitchurch, 2010). There is a growing third space community in Australia (Mitchell et al., 2025). There is a sector where wellbeing is hidden (Lemon et al., 2024). Grant and Kennie find that

Image 7.1 SUAW for belonging by Claire Bowmer.

universities need to do more to support third space professionals as they transition from outside the sector to second careers (2024). This chapter provides vignettes of actual experiences on if and how the PARE supported them.

Gathering Stories

The narrative research method used is based on autoethnographic practices (Ellis & Adams, 2014). It was selected based on its effective application across the literature on reflective practice and wellbeing (Knightbridge, 2019). This qualitative approach is familiar in the educational setting and aligns with action research, which incorporates reflection at its core stage. Asking participants to reflect was apt for this group. Academics engage in reflective practice, especially when undertaking action research, where it is a key step (Bervian & Pansera-de-Araujo, 2020). The research was similar to a member survey and extension of the PARE activities. To accommodate reflection, there was an option to provide written comments or be part of a group conversation that was transcribed and reviewed.

Going around the circle to hear a range of perspectives is fitting, as the format of the PARE employs many conventions of learning circles, starting the session with a brief focus on positivity and defining it as a safe and confidential space. To reduce synthesis and maintain maximum integrity, the discussion is presented as follows, grouped by participant rather than thematically.

Framework for the Discussion Around Flourishing

A small group of facilitators discussed the pressing questions surrounding the support of wellbeing through ePortfolios, asking open ended questions on if the PARE helped build belonging or impacted wellbeing. This process highlighted a need for more wellbeing literacy discussion in the workplace, which is of importance in higher education (Dobele & Farrell, 2025). The questions explored the tension in higher education identified in the literature: while staff are expected to document their career achievements, there is limited support or guidance on how to do so (Manoharan, 2019: Ryan, 2013). The theoretical framework underpinning the inquiry was adapted from the workplace wellbeing research where identity purpose contributes to flourishing as a state of positive mental health (Molina-Sanchez et al., 2022). This borrows from the positive psychology in schools (Oades et al., 2021).

There are several reasons that a record of work contributions is critical for an individuals career and wellbeing growth. The documentation is required for securing future opportunities. Developing the reflexive skillset is invaluable, and the process advances job crafting and finding purpose in work (Molina-Sánchez et al., 2022). What is unknown are the stories of participants in the PARE. Although it was discussed by several guests on Create, Share and Engage, an ePortfolio-focused Podcast (Hoeppner, 2025), this chapter will provide insight into the relevance of PARE.

The PARE Community

The PARE community is organised around a writing practice rather than a professional association. This is a community across institutions in the adult education sector. Based in Australia, it draws participants from around the globe. The community grew organically from a series of events. PARE has hosted conferences, workshops, and an annual forum to foster ePortfolio practice. The PARE has continued since 2017, developed from a popular workshop at the ePortfolio forum. The continuation and momentum have been propelled by enthusiasts determined to continue the connections and support, which reflects the research of networks providing key connections in higher education (Ryttberg and Geschwind, 2019).

The Context of a Community for a Niche Type of Reflective

One reason this SUAW was surveyed about wellbeing is the unique genre. As a community, we believe that an ePortfolio is more about process and less about producing written outputs. A simple definition of ePortfolios is it is a reflective practice, a collation and annotation of learning artefacts (The Association for Authentic, Experiential,, and Evidence-Based Learning [AAEEBL], 2022; Slade et al., 2016; Polly et al., 2016). It can take the form of an unstructured journal through to a design showcase. For some practitioners, the outputs are merely social media tweets (Kassens, 2014). While the emphasis is on the process, it can also be private, have a limited audience, or be public. It is considered a support mechanism for learning and writing, for students through professionals. It proved beneficial during the stress and disruption of COVID-19. It was used by thesis students in Indonesia (Salim et al., 2021).

This is a practice that relies on regular writing, which a SUAW provides. This is not merely about building up written outputs but also reflections that benefit from being written in the present (Ustuk & Comoglu, (2021). Regular writing can lead to reflexive processes in the workplace and promotes lifelong learning, both promoted as key transferable skills for the future work landscape (Attwell, 2023). An example of this is in healthcare, where the critical reflective process is used to develop learning communities (Walker et al., 2013). The usefulness of the learning is in the immediacy of the reflection. Reflective practice is proposed as a tool for informing workplace research more broadly (Nilsson & Ellstrom, 2012). This connects with a literature review of career writing, which found themes of career insights and direction but also wellbeing and identity development (McNichol et al., 2024).

Reflective writing is adopted in fields including education and health. In education, reflection is considered active learning, which is promoted as part of constructivist theory (Rajan et al., 2025). Creating an ePortfolio of reflections is a familiar part of the journey to becoming a teacher (Bain, 2002). It is also used for assessing professional skills in medical science (Polly et al., 2016). It is intertwined with practicums and placements, and it is used in the workplace (Faller et al., 2020). Reflexiveness is considered a bottom-up rather than top-down strategy for development (Ustuk and Comoglu, 2021). Despite this demand for reflective writing, it is not often explicitly taught; there is little support (Ryan, 2013).

A SUAW Through the Lens of Workplace Wellbeing Initiatives

The focus on wellbeing is that we spend a large percentage of time at work and, for creatives, thinking about work. The benefits to institutions are that supporting wellbeing lead to more creative work as well as increasing outputs (Karanika-Murray et al. 2017).

People attend the PARE in their own time or within a work environment to create career and learning texts. It is unusual in that it is grassroots and independent, whereas workplace wellbeing initiatives are traditionally hosted by companies that recognise the issues caused by low levels of wellbeing (Danna & Griffin, 1999). Participants attending are in either academic or professional roles at universities or working in the EdTech, pathways educators, or vocational education sectors. This openness is deliberate and reflective of the consciously open nature of the group. This inclusion is important to third spacers (Whitchurch, 2025).

Third Spacers Need Community

A shift in recent years has been for professional staff to write not just industry blogs and technical guides but also to contribute to academic articles. This has led to professional staff bringing their perspectives to the scholarship of teaching and learning (Whitchurch, 2025). For many within the Technology Enhanced Learning sector, the commonality of the third space community is not in their role but in the polymathic nature of their work (Manoharan, 2019).

Mostly, the PARE community is made up of third spacers staff working in higher education across both professional and academic boundaries (Whitchurch, 2008: Caldwell, 2023). Recognition of the achievements of third spacers is an emerging area of research but has previously not been prioritised, which can lead third spacers to feel excluded and undervalued (Manoharan, 2019). There are tensions and a need for clarity in defining identity when working on the boundary of professional and academic work (Arumugam, 2024). However, through shared adversity comes connection and belonging (Whitchurch, 2025). This shared experience is needed to help third spacers to feel included, valued, and respected within the PARE community, which promotes wellbeing outcomes (Grant and Kennie, 2024).

Within the Landscape of Higher Education

Knowing where you stand and where your future lies in higher education is no longer optional. Higher education is markedly politicised and rapidly evolving to address the changing skill needs of future workforces (Whitchurch, 2008).

There is an enormous change in the current workforce, and responding to this can be challenging for wellbeing (Molina-Sánchez et al., 2022).

This also shifts the stressors on individuals' wellbeing; this is amplified by the restructures, and Australian universities are filled with reports of institutions facing financial uncertainty (Hare, 2025).

PARE serves a knowledge-based industry, however there are similarities in many professions; for career growth and promotion, individuals need to document and succinctly tell their stories of success. Higher education workers are a group that can particularly benefit from reflective practice (Grant and Kennie, 2024: Knightbridge, 2019). This context is not unique; initiatives in the workplace need to promote not just greater work engagement for productivity but also assist employees in avoiding workaholism (Molina-Sánchez et al., 2022), as third spacers are highly engaged and intrinsically motivated, so they risk falling into habits of workaholism (Grant and Kennie, 2024).

Structure of the PARE

The sessions are organised in Pomodoro style, so the facilitators set a 25-minute timer and then begin writing. The seasons start with setting the tone and sense of safety, which is the invitation to share positive news or updates right at the start. This is followed by the assurances that it is a confidential and supportive environment reminiscent of learning circles (Pranis, 2015). This is not a new practice and has much to learn from Indigenous communities' yarning circles (Mills et al., 2013). This is a legitimate form of qualitative research (Besserab and Ng'andu, 2010).

The participants are then encouraged to add their goals for the PARE season on an unassuming shared spreadsheet. This generates discussion, particularly on shared goals and identities. This discussion builds a sense of community during the first session, followed by a 5-minute break as a group to discuss our progress. Though brief, this break generates discussion, particularly in relation to goal achievement (or lack thereof), strategies for remaining focused, and the general ability to articulate ideas. This sharing of experiences, writing challenges, and goal achievement normalises the experience and allows for social connection during the breaks, reducing isolation and building a sense of connection. Goal setting and sharing ambitions is an established practice in development and higher education (Costa, 2017).

At the end of the session, there is a debrief. Here, the facilitators often make explicit connections between the participants by identifying commonalities and discussing the following steps to extend the productivity of the session.

The community provides a sounding board and source of research for implementing ePortfolio in courses institution wide and for individuals in ePortfolio practice. PARE provides a community touch-point for people with limited time, giving dedicated time to work and insights into peers' practices.

This is a collection of unfiltered accounts of the impact of a PARE and ePortfolio practice on participants' wellbeing and growth in the unique landscape of higher education.

Perspectives from the PARE Series

Vignette 1: Driving the Freelance Third Spacers

A pivotal volunteer in the PARE joins from the unique space of being an outsider on two fronts: a freelancer and in vocational education rather than the more predominant attendance from university staff. They describe the PARE as filling a gap, being different to most SUAWs in higher education:

> My experience was that these are generally focused on connecting a likeminded group of students or being a closed event for working on a particular paper, for example.

A big draw for them was accountability. Having more autonomy over your workday has both positive and negative impacts on the wellbeing of gig economy workers (Wan et al., 2024). This freelancer found:

> Saying my goals out loud made me more accountable. Being a facilitator pushed me to further commit to my writing goals, and I described it as energising and inspiring... I'm always so busy; I'm making myself some time, and then there are some other people in the room that help make me feel accountable for that.

As with many of the participants who shared, a key motivation is to informally mentor others and the practice of ePortfolios, which is often misunderstood. There is research to validate that this micro-advising and small mentoring interaction has a career-altering positive influence (Richardson et al., 2022). For new participants, this provides a deliberate safety net:

> I just give them some quick tips and tricks on how to get started and not feel like they have to take on this whole ePortfolio.

They go on to describe that new participants often report seeing polished websites but do not know that the practice can be in much simpler formats. The structure of the PARE that accommodates these side conversations would be the facilitator opening a breakout room for new participants.

Vignette 2: Avoiding the Void of Writing in the Third Space

The other end of the ePortfolio continuum is outward-facing writing (Batson et al., 2017). One participant shared the PARE provided, not just in time to write but also shifting their writing from an isolated activity.

> I started writing a blog and an ePortfolio... I felt like just another voice in a sea of loud voices. Then, I participated in my first PARE session.

> I found that I could connect with what everyone was talking about: their passions, struggles, and identities. This motivated me. I was still shouting into the void, but I was shouting with people, side by side.

They observed the facilitation and non-hierarchical nature of the group in a highly structured sector.

> In line with the challenges above, PARE's flat structure supports inclusion, connection and belonging… This lack of hierarchy allows for connection with little to no pre-defined hierarchy or status between us.

The open nature of the PARE can not be overstated in the context of higher education.

Vignette 3: High Expectations of a SUAW

An experienced ePortfolio and third spacers came with a history of participating in SUAWs. One of the reasons they came along and stayed to facilitate PARE is that they had previously experienced the boost of a SUAW on their output.

> I found Pomodoro productive when completing my own studies. I found some creative SUAW formats that involved writing on trains, destinations, and coffee shops.

That was the initial draw, and for the ePortfolios, there were some aspects of the format they found unconventional but suited their reasons for attending, which were both developing their own ePortfolio practice and connecting with the community. Connecting with the ePortfolios community was important, with it being a niche area.

They described how:

> My exposure to SUAW sessions came at a university, particularly focused on supporting PhDs. SUAWs are usually closed to a particular cohort or institution.

They reiterated the common theme among the group was to lift up others. They promoted the PARE as a way of giving back, recommending the sessions to colleagues working on accreditation portfolios such as CMALT Australasia and Advance HE. Clark notes that these are now open to third spacers (2021).

One aspect of the support is in providing accountability and motivation they find helpful for peers. They specifically highlighted that if the cameras stay on, the Pomodoro includes body doubling – simply having someone there doing the same thing – which can be an enabling mechanism for neurodiverse writers (Eagle et al., 2024). This suggestion of peer support has unique benefits in learning (Brock and Huber, 2017).

Vignette 4: Belonging for Third Spacers

Another participant, quite established in their career, provided insight into the motivations to attend.

> The accountability was a strong draw, as otherwise, you just don't do it, and if you are with other people, you hold yourself to account.

They highlight that it is allowing time for your own development and recognition of what you have already done. Their observation is that third spacers must make the choice to come along despite having so much going on. It is, in part, the frantic and high amount of activity they describe that makes an ePortfolio practice so critical. For context, the busyness they describe is partly due to the project-based format of much third space work and the behind-the-scenes nature of work that is done.

They identified an interesting contradiction with the draw to work alongside one another in developing such personal writing, which is the opposite of collaboration. However, there is a strong sense of belonging and community from the sharing aspects of the PARE; you make connections between what other people are doing and what you are working on.

> There is a level of support despite the challenge of each participant's portfolio practice and tool choice being incredibly varied. Everyone is working in a unique way, but there's an element of 'elbow support'.

Support is listed as one of the principles for digital ethics by the International Association for Authentic, Experiential, & Evidence-Based Learning (AAEEBL, 2022). Institutions heavily promote standard tools to enable support. However, students often resist this and want to have agency in tool choice (Slade et al., 2016).

Several of the participants who joined the conversation had traversed several institutions and roles and used ePortfolios to document freelance work. Defining your professional identity can be challenging in changing contexts; the ePortfolio is a tool for shifting those perceptions (Batson et al., 2017). They described the excitement of having new people come along as a sign that PARE is, in fact, open and inclusive.

> I always loved the fact, and I think that the belonging, and that when we saw people outside of their community join, that always used to make me like to go. I was so cool I'm like, Oh, there's another. There are other weird people. Attending provided a reminder to them that they were not alone and part of a whole community. They highlighted the contradiction of parallel writing.

As an ePortfolio is about the individual, there is the need for collaboration through this type of group as it isn't going to be a collaborative activity.

Participants elaborated that despite the vastly different portfolio practices, there was a sort of collaboration, and it was useful to see the overlaps and connections and similar takes on the same practice.

Vignette 5: Outside the Education Institutions

A more pronounced illustration of the undefined environment of third spacers is that of EdTech industry representatives and commercial consultants. There are additional challenges to being outside educational institutions. Although they engage with colleagues in universities in different capacities, incidental connections and mentoring can be missing. The EdTech professional who joined this conversation highlighted the concept of belonging and feeling included as an outsider as important.

> When I started joining these sessions because I'd been removed from being at a university and then moving to a different role and doing different things, I wanted to reconnect.

However, they shared that the reason it was the ePortfolio community that they chose to continue connection with is that they seem so open and willing to accept 'weird' people like them. They did not feel like outsiders. This acceptance could be in part a product of the variety of roles represented in the group, that it is forged around the connection of a shared reflective practice rather than professional identity.

The use of metaphors is every day in ePortfolios (Goh, 2019). Using a tree metaphor, one of the other participants eloquently put that the PARE sessions as being grounding resonated with them. They described spending time with the community and on their portfolio practice as,

> Your feet on the ground. You got the roots going through the ground.
> All those sorts of things, the recentering.

The connection they were working to maintain was not just with the community but with their own writing. Even attending and hearing others work during the sessions on portfolio projects for their institutions, they had to reassure themselves that their individual portfolio project was valid. They shared a novel strategy that others could adapt to keep connected with a writing practice. They found that even when there was too much going on to attend as planned, they made a note and set aside time in the evening to at least open their portfolio.

Potential Approaches Unearthed

The most transferable learning gathered from having these conversations is that it is inspiring to take a moment to reach out and listen to people in the

SUAW community. The format means there is not always space for feedback within sessions, so this is an opportunity to hear what is going on and the impact of the sessions. The perspectives shared here will feed back into the future of PARE sessions.

One approachis that PARE sessions strengthen this community's connections, by providing stepping stones between forums and other activities. These type of SUAW sessions could be wellbeing initiatives for industry networks. One benefit the participants celebrated was openness, connecting across institutions and streams.

A second approach, for individuals or even educational institutions looking to promote ePortfolio practice, SUAW could be added as a form of support to fill the void of teaching reflective practices in higher education (Ryan, 2013). However, it might be the independent and outside nature of this format that makes it a success, allowing participants to truly feel it is a confidential space.

A third approach is to accommodate the third spacers in your institution. Support for wellbeing and reflective practice could be one of the ways of getting the most out of third space experts, something that McIntosh and Nutt highlight as needing particular attention (2022).

A final approach is that it is a PARE is an example of a repeatable format for supporting creativity and individuality rather than requiring conformity in ePortfolios. Goal setting and keeping a running open record is a strong feature of the sessions.

Conclusion

Even if it is just introducing people in education to the language of wellbeing, a foundational step for articulating and managing wellbeing is having the terminology (Oades et al., 2022).

Sentiments that emerged will be familiar to SUAW attendees as accountability and community, such as the reoccurring comments about overcoming feelings of selfishness and being rewarded not just by producing words on the page but also developing strong writing habits. The wellbeing and more intangible community building and sense of camaraderie are invaluable. The sense of connection is vital for a niche writing community. The impact of sessions cannot be measured by output alone.

Unsurprisingly, practices that allow people to feel included, valued, and respected support good mental health outcomes. The large variety of roles, institutions, and industries supports connection through shared experiences. The impact of realising that as third spacer writers, you are not alone in your experiences, and this gives increased confidence to deal with day-to-day challenges.

Journalling and individual reflective writing that is incredibly varied in format and purpose is an uncommon candidate for Pomodoro sessions that have spanned over a decade. It is a support mechanism that requires regular writing, which in turn benefits from support.

Credit Statement

Sincere gratitude to the people who shared their stories and the contributor. Reviewing & Editing - Dana Bui 0009-0000-9072-9054. Writing - Review & Editing: Marlène Daicopoulos, Project administration: Allison Miller.

References

Arumugam, P. (2024). Negotiating the assumptions and identity tensions surrounding third space academics/professionals. In K. Heggart & M. Fatayer (Eds.), *Designing learning experiences for inclusivity and diversity: Advice for learning designers*. Sydney: UTS ePRESS. https://doi.org/10.5130/aal.d

Attwell, T. (2023). *Key transferable skills (resources for educators)*. RMIT University Library. https://rmit.pressbooks.pub/keytransferableskills/

Bain, J. D. (2002). *Reflecting on practice: Student teachers' perspectives*. Post Pressed.

Batson, T., Coleman, K. S., Chen, H. L., Watson, C. E., Rhodes, T. L., & Harver, A. (Eds.). (2017). *Field guide to ePortfolio*. Association of American Colleges and Universities.

Bervian, P. V., & Pansera-de-Araujo, M. C. (2020). The self-reflective community in the consolidation of teachers' knowledge through research education. *Góndola*, *15*(1), 118–134. https://doi.org/10.14483/23464712.14467

Besserab, D. & Ng'andu, B. (2010). Yarning about yarning as a legitimate method of Indigenous research. *International Journal of Critical Indigenous Studies*, *3*(1), 37–50. https://doi.org/10.5204/ijcis.v3i1.57

Brock, M. E., & Huber, H. B. (2017). Are peer support arrangements an evidence-based practice? A systematic review. *The Journal of Special Education*, *51*(3), 150–163. https://doi.org/10.1177/0022466917708184

Caldwell, J. (2023). [Rev. of The impact of the integrated practitioner: Studies in third space professionalism: edited by Emily McIntosh and Diane Nutt, Routledge, 2022]. *Perspectives: Policy and Practice in Higher Education*, *27*(1), 37–38. https://doi.org/10.1080/13603108.2022.2147239

Clark, D. (2021, May). Third space professionals and the challenge of CPD. *Advance HE*.https://www.advance-he.ac.uk/news-and-views/third-space-professionals-and-challenge-cpd

Costa, K. (2017). Forget goal setting—Try goal getting. *Women in Higher Education*, *26*(10), 13–19. https://doi.org/10.1002/whe.20492

Danna, K., & Griffin, R. W. (1999). Health and wellbeing in the workplace: A review and synthesis of the literature. *Journal of Management*, *25*, 357–384. https://doi.org/10.1016/S0149-2063(99)00006-9

Dobele, A. R., & Farrell, L. (2025). Positive wellbeing within workspaces. In *Supporting and promoting wellbeing in the higher education sector* (1st ed., Vol. 1, pp. 23–41). Routledge. https://doi.org/10.4324/9781003284772-4

Eagle, T., Baltaxe-Admony, L. B., & Ringland, K. E. (2024). "It was something I naturally found worked and heard about later": An investigation of body doubling with neurodivergent participants. *ACM Transactions on Accessible Computing* 17. https://doi.org/10.1145/3689648

Ellis, C., & Adams, T. E., (2014). The Purposes, Practices, and Principles of Autoethnographic Research, in Patricia Leavy (ed.), *The Oxford Handbook of Qualitative Research*, Oxford Library of Psychology. https://doi.org/10.1093/oxfordhb/9780199811755.013.004

Faller, P., Marsick, V., & Russell, C. (2020). Adapting action learning strategies to operationalize reflection in the workplace. *Advances in Developing Human Resources*, *22*(3), 291–307. https://doi.org/10.1177/1523422320927298

Goh, A. Y. S. (2019). Rethinking reflective practice in professional lifelong learning using learning metaphors. *Studies in Continuing Education*, *41*(1), 1–16. https://doi.org/10.1080/0158037X.2018.1474867

Gordon, G., & Whitchurch, C. (2010). *Academic and professional identities in higher education: the challenges of a diversifying workforce* (1st ed.). Routledge. https://doi.org/10.4324/9780203865255

Grant, J., Kennie, T., (2024) *The characteristics and career pathways of third-space research professionals in universities: Reflections from practice*. Higher Education Policy Institute. https://www.hepi.ac.uk/2024/08/08/the-characteristics-and-career-pathways-of-third-space-research-professionals-in-universities-reflections-from-practice-2/

Hare, J. (2025, April 17). University cuts: Jobs on the chopping block as unis face tough times. *Australian Financial Review*. https://www.afr.com/work-and-careers/education/thousands-of-jobs-face-the-axe-as-unis-slammed-again-20250417-p5lsfl

Hoeppner, K. (2025) Create. share. engage. *Mahara*. https://podcast.mahara.org/

Karanika-Murray, M., Hasson, H., von Thiele Schwarz, U., Richter, A., Cooper, C. L., & Leiter, M. P. (2017). Improving employee wellbeing through leadership development. In *The Routledge companion to wellbeing at work* (1st ed., pp. 332–344). Routledge. https://doi.org/10.4324/9781315665979-23

Kassens, A. L. (2014). Tweeting your way to improved #writing, #reflection, and #community. *The Journal of Economic Education*, *45*(2), 101–109. https://doi.org/10.1080/00220485.2014.889937

Knightbridge, L. (2019). Reflection-in-practice: A survey of Australian occupational therapists. *Australian Occupational Therapy Journal*, *66*(3), 337–346. https://doi.org/10.1111/1440-1630.12559

Lemon, N., Francis, J., & Baker, L. M. (2024). Well-being literacy in the academic landscape: Trioethnographic inquiry into scholarly writing. *Brock Education Journal*, *33*(1), 27–48. https://doi.org/10.26522/brocked.v33i1.1120

Manoharan, A. (2019). Creating connections: Polymathy and the value of third space professionals in higher education. *Perspectives: Policy and Practice in Higher Education*, *24*(2), 56–59. https://doi.org/10.1080/13603108.2019.1698475

McIntosh, E., Nutt, D., (2022) Blended professionals: How to make the most of 'third space' experts, *Times Higher Education*. https://www.timeshighereducation.com/campus/blended-professionals-how-make-most-third-space-experts

McNichol, A. K., Lengelle, R., & Poell, R. F. (2024). Career writing interventions for career learning: An integrative literature review. *British Journal of Guidance & Counselling*, *52*(6), 1151–1180. https://doi.org/10.1080/03069885.2024.2389845

Mills, K. A., Sunderland, N., & Davis-Warra, J. (2013). Yarning circles in the literacy classroom. *The Reading Teacher*, *67*(4), 285–289. https://doi.org/10.1002/trtr.1195

Mitchell, K., Dave, K., Hinze, M., & Tsirgialos, A. (2025). A narrative account of third space technology enhanced learning and teaching roles working in Australian higher education. *Journal of Learning Development in Higher Education*, *33*. https://doi.org/10.47408/jldhe.vi33.1272

Molina-Sánchez, H., Giorgi, G., Guajardo, D. C., & Ariza-Montes, A. (2022). Rethinking the subjective wellbeing for a new workplace scenario. *Sustainability*, *14*(8), 4581. https://doi.org/10.3390/su14084581

Nilsson, S. and Ellstrom, P. (2012) Employability and Talent Management: Challenges for HRD Practices. *European Journal of Training & Development*, *36*, 26–45. doi:10.1108/03090591211192610

Oades, L., Hou, H., Francis, J., Baker, L., & Huang, L. (2022). Well-being literacy: Language use as a way to contextualize the process of positive education. In K.-A. Allen, M. Furlong, D. Vella-Broderick, & S. Suldo (Eds.), *Handbook of positive psychology in schools: Supporting process and practice* (3rd ed.). Routledge. https://doi.org/10.4324/9781003013778-9

Oades, L., Taylor, J., Francis, J., & Baker, L. (2021). Wellbeing literacy as an emancipatory and transformative capability. In M. A. White & F. McCallum (Eds.), *Wellbeing and resilience education: COVID-19 and its impact on education* (1st ed.). Routledge. https://doi.org/10.4324/9781003134190-11

Polly, P., Vickery, R., Thai, T., Yang, J. L., Fath, T., Herbert, C., Jones, N., Lewis, T., Pather, N., Schibeci, S., & Cox, J. (2016). ePortfolios, assessment and professional skills in the medical sciences. In J. Rowley (Ed.), *ePortfolios in Australian Universities*, (pp. 47–64). Springer. doi:10.1007/978-981-10-1732-2_4

Pranis, K. (2015). Returning to the source. *Restorative justice*, *3*(3), 425–428. https://doi.org/10.1080/20504721.2015.1109364

Rajan, M., Herbert, C., & Polly, P. (2025). A synthetic review of learning theories, elements and virtual environment simulation types to improve learning within higher education. *Thinking Skills and Creativity*, *56*, doi:10.1016/j.tsc.2024.101732

Richardson, E. L., Oetjen, R., Oetjen, D., Gordon, J., Schroeder, L. H., Conklin, S., & Strawn, N. (2022). Micro-advising/mentoring: Small interactions can have broad career-altering impact on learner career progression. *The Journal of Health Administration Education*, *38*(4), 1001–1010.

Ryan, M. (2013). The pedagogical balancing act: Teaching reflection in higher education. *Teaching in Higher Education*, *18*(2), 144–155. doi:10.1080/13562517.2012.694104

Ryttberg, M., Geschwind, L. (2019) Professional support staff in higher education: networks and associations as sense givers. *Higher Education* 78, 1059–1074. https://doi.org/10.1007/s10734-019-00388-2

Salim, H., Susilawati, S., & Hanif, M. (2021). Reflective writing in the pandemic period: A university students' reflection. *Journal of Educational Technology and Online Learning*, *4*(1), 56–65. doi:10.31681/jetol.834129

Slade, C., Murfin, K., Trahar, P., & Rowley, J. (2016). A strategic approach to institution-wide implementation of ePortfolios. In *EPortfolios in Australian Universities* (pp. 173–189). Springer. https://doi.org/10.1007/978-981-10-1732-2_11

The Association for Authentic, Experiential, & Evidence-Based Learning [AAEEBL]. (2022). *Digital Ethics Principles in ePortfolios, version 3*. https://aaeebl.org/digital-ethics-principles-in-ePortfolios/support/

Thorpe, C., Partridge, H (2024). The third space in higher education: A scoping review. *Higher Education Policy*. https://doi.org/10.1057/s41307-024-00374-z

Ustuk, O., & Comoglu, I. (2021). Reflexive professional development in reflective practice: What lesson study can offer. *International Journal for Lesson and Learning Studies*, *10*(3), 260–273. https://doi.org/10.1108/IJLLS-12-2020-0092

Walker, R., Cooke, M., Henderson, A., & Creedy, D. K. (2013). Using a critical reflection process to create an effective learning community in the workplace. *Nurse Education Today*, *33*(5), 504–511. https://doi.org/10.1016/j.nedt.2012.03.001

Wan, Z., Zhang, L., Wang, L., & Zhang, F. (2024). Navigating autonomy: Unraveling the dual influence of job autonomy on workplace well-being in the gig economy. *Frontiers in Psychology*, *15*, 1369495. https://doi.org/10.3389/fpsyg.2024.1369495

Whitchurch, C. 2008. Shifting identities and blurring boundaries: The emergence of third space professionals in UK higher education." *Higher Education Quarterly* 62 (4): 377–396. doi:10.1111/j.1468-2273.2008.00387.x

Whitchurch, C. 2013. *Reconstructing identities in higher education: The rise of 'third space' professionals*. London, UK: Routledge. https://doi.org/10.4324/9780203098301

Whitchurch, C. (2025). Achieving inclusion: University staff working in third space between academic and professional spheres of activity. *Social Inclusion*, 14. https://doi.org/10.17645/si.9596

8 Community Support

Practical Strategies for Professional Self-Care and Wellbeing

Dewi Wahyu Mustikasari, Maslathif Dwi Purnomo, and Anugrah Imani

Introduction

We have seen our master students struggle to complete their master's degree because of the publication policy. Our graduate students who undertake their master's degree in English education must publish an academic writing paper in a national standardised indexing journal to be eligible to register the thesis examination. Unsurprisingly, the publication policy for graduate students in Indonesian higher education settings is getting more sophisticated because the requirements of school accreditation require documentation of graduate students' published manuscripts in international and/or national standardised indexing journals. Collaboration among universities is also highly recommended. Perfectionism and overexertion are valued to influence the culture of high expectations in the academia space. Academic success is associated with standards, achievements, and competitions (Grimmer, 2024). An Indonesian higher education context and its high expectation on the publication policy bring anxiety for graduate students and us, as well, as a part of the managerial positions in the institutional level. Academic success when completing a graduate study is often equated with meeting publication standards, promoting a perfectionist mindset that must be addressed.

After a period of time, our master's students completed their bachelor's degree and decided to continue their graduate study. The pressure to face higher education expectations may have different negative effects on each individual student. Going back to academia, especially after some time away, is a rocky journey for some individuals. Challenges arise during graduate study years. An isolated student experiences tension and the constant negotiation between personal and university expectations such as diasporic identities, pedagogical approaches, and different Western and Southeast Asian conceptions towards the identities of 'researcher, academic, and teacher' that influence the student learning process (Chin, 2024). Multiple identities shape the PhD journey, as individuals constantly negotiate these identities to manage their self-care and wellbeing (Wijetunga, 2025). Lived experiences in higher education involve a transitional process filled with personal challenges. It also demonstrates how individuals manage self-care and wellbeing during the transition (Hammond & Lemon, 2024).

DOI: 10.4324/9781003633334-10

We are academics who work at three public universities that are located in different provinces in Indonesia and have managerial responsibility in the graduate programmes in our organisations. We initiated an online community named the MoRA (Ministry of Religious Affairs) Academic Writing Club to support our students to manage their professional self-care and wellbeing while writing productively. Our organisations are supervised by MoRA; therefore, MoRA is used to name our community.

Academic development, self-care, and wellbeing have attracted considerable attention in higher education contexts. This chapter illustrates the Shut Up & Write! (SUAW) framework as a tool to develop the MoRA Academic Writing Club, an online writing community which facilitates academic development and understands authors' wellbeing during their professional self-care. The characteristics of the sessions are structured to connect our master's students to develop their sense of belongings and accomplishments in a collective agency. This chapter provides literature positionings towards professional self-care and wellbeing in the domain of community support. It shows challenges and success stories to support the online writing community. Strategies are also discussed for readers who wish to implement a similar approach for professional self-care and wellbeing to manage students' writing productivity.

Drawing from the SUAW framework (Lemon et al., 2025), we provide community support to cultivate the master's students' professional self-care and wellbeing by empowering individuals and nurturing a sense of belonging and creativity throughout their writing journeys. Self-care is "the ability of individuals, families, and communities to promote health, prevent disease, maintain health, and cope with illness or disability with or without the support of a health worker" (World Health Organization, 2023). In our conception, self-care includes collective support from three universities to help students maintain their physical and mental health while supporting their writing productivity and creativity. Promoting self-care is related to wellbeing. The World Health Organization defines wellbeing as follows:

> Wellbeing is a positive state experienced by individuals and societies. Similar to health, it is a resource for daily life and is determined by social, economic, and environmental conditions. Wellbeing encompasses quality of life and the ability of people and societies to contribute to the world with sense of meaning and purpose.
>
> (2021)

Developing an online community to accommodate students' wellbeing during the uncertain writing process reflects our effort to create a supportive environment with the purpose to improve student learning experiences in higher education.

The practical strategies are arranged based on the cores of SUAW. Writing is an iterative process which benefits from collective support from the community to minimise the pressure to publish an article and to stay focused on maintaining

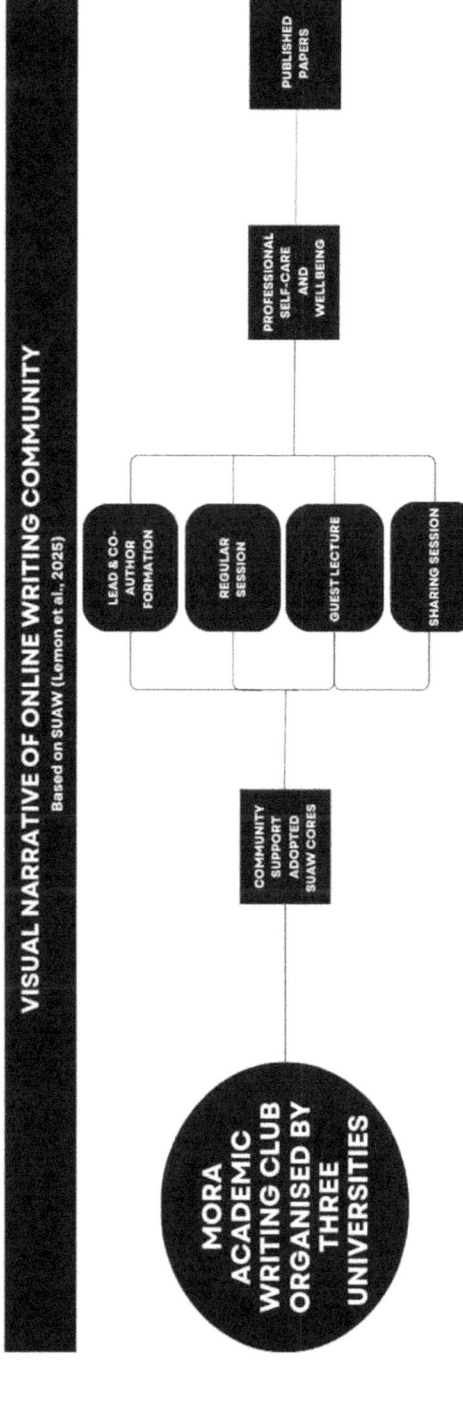

Image 8.1 Community support-based SUAW framework.

writing productivity in a structured environment. Master's students are encouraged to connect with students and academics from different universities to network and broaden their mindset to boost resilience and wellbeing.

The grand design of our online writing community was adapted from the SUAW core principles. Our goal was to provide a manageable and practical programme for our students, most of whom work as teachers. Most of them are self-funded and do not receive study-leave. However, institutional policies still classify them as full-time master's students. They are occupied with their routines as an employee to their organisations and engage to complete the master's programme. The core principles of SUAW emphasise connection, belonging, and accomplishment (Lemon et al., 2025). The community support of the MoRA Academic Writing Club is aligned with these values. To promote students' professional self-care and wellbeing, we developed four strategic programmes: lead and co-author formation, regular sessions, guest lectures, and sharing sessions. These strategic programmes are related to the core values of connection and belonging. The goal was to help students connect to the created academia bubbles, enabling them to develop their manuscripts for publication, meeting the core value of accomplishment. The information about MoRA Academic Writing Club can be accessed on this page: https://magister-tbi.uinsu.ac.id/mora-academic-writing-club/

Lead and Co-Author Formation

We composed the lead and co-author team of a mix of individuals from the three universities. Master's students who had a manuscript draft, named the lead authors, were encouraged to continue refining their manuscript draft with the potential co-authors. However, some students felt anxious about writing up their manuscript drafts. Although some colleagues, including ourselves, confirmed that the students had existing manuscript drafts, we still required them compose a manuscript as an assignment in our courses. We provided encouragement during the class sessions and via direct text messaging for the lead authors that they should feel confident with their writing because we found co-authors to work with them. The co-authors were not only master students – we also invited our colleagues to support our goals by engaging as co-authors. After the lead authors and co-authors confirmed their agreements to refine the draft manuscript, they were encouraged to build communication and a sense of belonging within their writing teams.

Regular Session

We facilitated a regular fortnight session for their communication using a video-conferencing tool. WhatsApp, a social media application, was used to mediate communication among the members. Social media apps such as Twitter (now X) have been studied for their potential to support networking among academics (McPherson et al., 2015). The leads and co-authors were motivated to work on the refinement of the manuscript draft outside the regular meeting by using text messaging, telephoning, or video conferencing. They were expected to distribute jobs evenly within their team and set up a timeline to finalise the draft manuscript in order to submit it to a journal.

Guest Lecture

We held guest lectures on certain themes related to academic writing to help master's students develop their professional writing skills. Our goal was to inspire intrinsic motivation in students to finish writing their manuscripts. We also encouraged research driven by personal curiosity (Grimmer, 2024). Guest lecture activities are designed to provide practical knowledge and professional insights. The purpose of guest lectures is to allow students to learn from the experiences and expertise of professionals, such as educators, researchers, and other scholars. Keynote speakers usually present specialized topics or emerging trends in English education. This activity also can build networking among English education departments on our campus, fostering relationships between students, lecturers, and guest speakers and potentially expanding connections and generating opportunities to enhance students' careers. For example, we invited the managing editor of a national accredited journal to share tips to get accepted into the journal. We also provided topics on academic writing knowledge such as finding high-quality papers in several freely available databases and integrating sources for academic writing. These activities provide students with valuable exposure to real-world insights, practical experiences, and diverse perspectives that enrich their academic and professional self-care.

Sharing Session

We planned sharing sessions for our students to showcase their published manuscripts. They share their published manuscript in the WhatsApp group. They inform their accomplishments through text messaging. Social media has functioedn as a medium for sharing good practices, and it is recommended for continued use in supporting professional development and networking opportunities (Donelan, 2015). By sharing the challenges and solutions encountered during the publication journeys, we are able to motivate other students to stay engaged and committed to publishing their own manuscripts. Using a social media application to showcase achievements can often be useful to establish social presence and show participation in the conversation (O'Keeffe, 2018). Our students may build their profile of expertise and be open to other writing projects with the other members.

Challenges Toward Its Implementation

Although we had carefully thought through the conception of the community support–based SUAW framework, the plan was not smoothly delivered. Several challenges had occurred during the implementation of the community support programme. One obstacle led to other obstacles. Undeniably, we concluded that the community support programme was unsuccessful. We evaluated our plans and strategies to better understand critical causes of this disappointing outcome. We observed and reached out to our students to seek more information regarding their involvement. From this, we concluded the major failure aspects centred on two issues.

Intrinsic Motivation

This section describes several hindrances faced by our students. They reported different barriers to involvement in the online writing community. We gathered student feedback during class sessions in our courses. This feedback was then analysed to categorise barriers related to students' intrinsic motivation.

Some students at each university reported experiencing burnout due to multiple manuscript writing assignments by different lecturers, all intended for journal publication. Having several similar assignments – often three to four – turned out to be overwhelming and burdensome. The students reported frustration at writing manuscripts for multiple different subjects; this excessive workload affected their ability to engage with and participate in the community support programme. This situation led to a lack of motivation to attend regular sessions and guest lectures – a symptom of burnout (Grimmer, 2024). Time management also emerged as an issue for this type of barrier.

Most of our students often skipped the regular session, which made it difficult to integrate them into the academic community we had created. Their absence was largely due to being occupied with daily teaching responsibilities. Low student engagement led to dysfunctional collective support and lack of a shared sense of belonging. As a result, the lead and co-author arrangements that we had prepared become unusable and impractical.

Conflicts within the lead and co-author structure were identified. A few students had withdrawn from the authorship arrangement, reporting that time management issues that limited their ability to engage in the writing process. Other students failed to revise their assignedmanuscripts. Many attributed their withdrawal or delays to the demands of their daily teaching responsibilities.

Extrinsic Motivation

This section reflects our perspectives as the organisers of this online writing community. We openly acknowledge that we struggled withinconsistency in managing this programme. Recognizing the ongoing challenges caused by low students involvement, we decided to lower our expectations to better support our students with professional self-care and wellbeing. As a result, we postponed regular sessions, guest lectures, and sharing sessions for one semester.

Slight Success Towards Its Implementation

Formerly, we completely believed that community support brings no value for students' writing productivity. We reckoned that little achievement can be identified based on our observations and interventions. A small number of dedicated students have managed to complete their manuscripts. Although we had postponed the online activities for a while, we kept supporting our students' writing productivity. We facilitated those who wanted to carry on finalising the manuscript. We figured out that dedicated lead authors and co-authors were the key to the success of the lead and co-author arrangement. Reshuffled lead and co-author formation was also undertaken to support those who wanted to keep going with the writing process.

Dedicated Lead Authors

A female student, who is a fresh undergraduate student and not a teacher, showed her resilience and wellbeing when she was left by one of her co-authors. She continued to finish the manuscript alone. The co-author discontinued her involvement because she got too busy with her role as a teacher. She also was worried about providing misleading information because she did not have sufficient time reading to support writing her part. She experienced "loss of confidence in academic abilities (Grimmer, 2024: p.26)." The dedicated lead author received support from the two of us, a colleague and another master student as the co-authors. We provided feedback to refine the manuscript. We were thrilled with her efforts to take care of her self-care and wellbeing. She admitted that the manuscript is her ticket to complete her master's degree in two years because she is self-financed. This situation motivated her to finalise the manuscript. Finally, this team could submit the manuscript to a journal.

Dedicated Co-authors: Reshuffle Formation

We decided to reshuffle the lead and co-author formation. The previous arrangement of the authorship formation was unsuccessful, but the dedicated co-authors demonstrated their support and collaboration to assist the lead author effectively.

Strategies to Implement Future Concepts of Community Support-Based SUAW Framework

To better support graduate students' professional self-care and wellbeing when receiving community support, organisers should address the following strategies:

1 Lowering organisers' expectations if graduate students frequently demonstrate disengagement. "Lowering expectations does not equate to lowering standard (Grimmer, 2024: p.27)." Understanding graduate students' high pressure in academia is essential to accommodate a healthy writing environment. If graduate students have difficulty to engage in the community support, give them a break. Organisers should trust that graduate students will come back on the main path if they have an unproductive stretch. They are in the transition

process, a time out, from business (Coopmans, 2025). Organisers should provide a positive writing environment; do not push them. Community support is a voluntarily based activity. Reducing the frequency of sessions can give graduate students more flexible time to write their manuscripts.
2 Reshuffling authorship arrangement. Organisers should replan the authorship arrangement. Keep finding "supportive rather than competitive peers" (Grimmer, 2024: p.27); it will create a more enjoyable environment to boost writing productivity.
3 Providing mindfulness training. It can be very useful for graduate students to reduce their stress and anxiety. Organisers may invite colleagues who are able to provide mindfulness training for graduate students. Sharing responsibilities of health promoting actions to support graduate students is pivotal to manage self-care (Barradell et al., 2024).
4 Supporting individual writing growth. Dedicated students who act as lead or co-author should be supported by organisers, although organisers may invest more time to assist them. These students need colleagues and friends, even organisers, who have the willingness to make the same changes in a supportive environment (Grimmer, 2024).
5 Encouraging graduate students to be persistent in refining the feedback that is received from journal editors. Accepting feedback from anonymous reviewers can be challenging. It also can be received as personal attacks that may lead to disconnection to understand the feedback (Little, 2024).

Conclusion

Community support organisers should be prepared for any circumstances that may influence graduate students' involvement in an online writing community. This chapter has indicated that master students could not demonstrate frequent commitments in the online writing community because they were too occupied performing their roles and responsibilities as an employee of an institution. We listened to their feedback. We redesigned the previous community support plan to fit the needs of our students. We understand that an individual's growth may not happen at the same time for every individual. As the organisers of the online writing community, we need to ensure that the MoRA Academic Writing Club is a supportive environment to boost students' writing productivity. We accommodate collective support among three universities to promote professional self-care and wellbeing. We do not force our students to fit our arrangements. We want them to embrace their writing journey so that they may produce good quality papers.

References

Barradell, S., Fortune, T., & Fyffe, J. (2024). Reflecting on university heterotopias and the need for spaces of hope and possibility in higher education (pp. 133–145). In N. Lemon (Ed.). *Prioritising wellbeing and self-care in higher education: How we can do things differently to disrupt silence*. Routledge.

Chin, B. (2024). A cat named Jiji: Belonging, identity, and navigating cultural displacement in academia (pp. 171–182). In N. Lemon (Ed.). *Prioritising wellbeing and self-care in higher education: How we can do things differently to disrupt silence*. Routledge.

Coopmans, C. (2025). Body in the loop: Navigating academic midlife (pp. 15–25). In K. Hammond & N. Lemon. (Eds.). *Navigating tensions and transitions in higher education* Routledge.

Donelan, H. (2015). Social media for professional development and networking opportunities in academia. *Journal of Further and Higher Education*, 40(5), 706–729. https://doi.org/10.1080/0309877X.2015.1014321

Grimmer, L. (2024). Rethinking expectations in academia: How lowering expectations of ourselves and others improves wellbeing (pp. 21–31). In N. Lemon (Ed.). *Prioritising wellbeing and self-care in higher education: How we can do things differently to disrupt silence*. Routledge.

Hammond, K., & Lemon, N. (2024). Lived experiences of transition and wellbeing in higher education: Revealing hidden spaces (pp. 1–12). In K. Hammond & N. Lemon. (Eds.). *Navigating tensions and transitions in higher education* Routledge.

Lemon, N., Bolzle, A., Cruz, M.A., & Saunders, R. (2025). Shut up and write: Fostering wellbeing through collective writing practices. Routledge.

Little, C. (2024). Confronting failure as self-care (pp. 71–81). In N. Lemon (Ed.). *Prioritising wellbeing and self-care in higher education: How we can do things differently to disrupt silence*. Routledge

McPherson, M., Budge, K., & Lemon, N. (2015). New practices in doing academic development: Twitter as an informal learning space. *International Journal for Academic Development*, 20(2), 126–136. https://doi.org/10.1080/1360144X.2015.1029485

O'Keeffe, M. (2018). Academic Twitter and professional learning: Myths and realities. *International Journal for Academic Development*, 24(1), 35–46. https://doi.org/10.1080/1360144X.2018.1520109

Wijetunga, M. (2025). A kitchen of my own: The process of making food as a form of self-care (pp. 195–205). In K. Hammond & N. Lemon. (Eds.). *Navigating tensions and transitions in higher education* Routledge.

World Health Organization (2021). Promoting Wellbeing. https://www.who.int/activities/promoting-well-being

World Health Organization (2023). Self care interventions for health. https://www.who.int/health-topics/self-care#tab=tab_1

Section 3
SUAW across Institutional Boundaries

9 Shut Up & Write! at Varuna, The National Writers' House

Naomi Parry Duncan and Amy Sambrooke

Introduction

> The most sobering month of the year was April, when we closed the doors of Varuna for the first time in almost 30 years. The grounds fell eerily silent and no lights shone from the windows at night. Programs were cancelled one after the other ….
>
> *Veechi Stuart, Executive Director* (Varuna, The National Writers' House, 2021, p. 5).

The foremost institution for literature development in Australia, Varuna, The National Writers' House, initiated a national Shut Up & Write! program during the COVID-19 lockdowns in 2020. This was a pivot from Varuna's long-established program of residencies in Eleanor Dark's former home in Katoomba, on Dharug and Gundungurra Country in the Blue Mountains, west of Sydney. At the outset of the pandemic, the team at Varuna decided to support its community of writers and keep the house lights on with virtual Lamplight Residencies for writers in Australia and a series of international Lamplight Residencies that connected writers in Australia with their peers across the world.

Shut Up & Write! quickly became part of Varuna's regular practice and has continued into 2025. This chapter has been written by Amy Sambrooke, who was Varuna's creative director when COVID-19 struck, and Naomi Parry Duncan, a Varuna alumnus for whom the Shut Up & Write! sessions were a lifeline in a trying year.

This chapter is about a spontaneous program response, which developed iteratively. Varuna acted instinctively to connect and support writers at a time of crisis, and we will discuss what the institution learned from the experience. Co-author Amy Sambrooke explains the genesis of the idea, while Naomi Parry Duncan talks about taking part in the program. We also include insights from Meg Mooney, one of the earliest participants in Shut Up & Write! at Varuna and a mainstay of the weekday writing sessions, and Amanda Niehaus, a science writer who joined an online program Varuna jointly presented with Write On, Door County in the United States.

DOI: 10.4324/9781003633334-12

Image 9.1 Pink flannel flowers (*Actinotus forsythii*) at Narrow Neck, Katoomba in January 2021. These diminutive flowers, pale feathered stars with pink button centres, only bloom the summer after a big fire. They are a sign of regeneration after devastation. (Photo: Naomi Parry Duncan)

Shut Up & Write! at Varuna, The National Writers' House, has forged communities online that have fostered writing and foregrounded the wellbeing of writers, as well as benefitting the institution by enhancing its national and international reach.

Amy, Creative Director of an Emptied Writers Residence

The final weeks of 2019 are memorable in the worst of ways. From one of the highest points in the Blue Mountains, a World Heritage Area of great environmental and cultural significance, we at Varuna watched as each day the fire on the horizon grew closer and closer. A billowing mushroom cloud of smoke from burning ancient trees and the many thousands of mammals, insects and birds that succumbed to the intensity of the fire grew larger and larger. We learned a new word, pyrocumulonimbus, a self-perpetuating dynamic explosion of storm energy that forms above an intense source of heat such as a bushfire, or a nuclear explosion – a storm that can create more lightning, sparking more and more fires below.

At Varuna, a place of quiet and creativity beloved by Australian writers for over 30 years, our staff became responsible for judging ever-changing risk in an unimaginable end-of-days scenario, looking at wind direction and temperature forecasts throughout each day, and helping writers who were sick with asthma from toxic air return to their homes. A colleague came home with me in the afternoons to hold a ladder while I climbed on my roof to clear another day's worth of leaves that had blown in with the smoke. At one point, fire threatened our upper mountains town on three sides. Wide-eyed, we clung to each other in the supermarket and went home to shut ourselves inside while the world turned orange around us. The crisis only passed when torrential rains extinguished the blazes, but this brought disastrous floods that caused road slips and cut train lines in the Blue Mountains and Western Sydney. Nothing felt right, nothing was right.

Weeks later, after the end of the summer of fire and flood, we gathered, still thoroughly exhausted, for a staff meeting. I recall there were just three items on the agenda. The first was pretty run of the mill stuff, not even worth mentioning. The second and third have stayed with me for different reasons. Item two: *Ghosts and what to do about them* (it's an old building and there's always a writer telling us they have had an encounter or heard something in the night). And then there was item three: *Pandemic?*

Within a fortnight our borders were closed, stay-at-home orders were issued, and we were living in the new reality of panic and a very real threat on a global scale. After over 30 years of almost continuous operation, Varuna, a residency-based writers centre, suddenly had no purpose and our small team quickly realised that we had to shut the doors of the house. We were likely to be out of jobs and our consultants and writing mentors would have no income. We needed to identify a way to find purpose – and funding – to exist as a writers' residence, with no writers in residence.

> It seems unbelievable that you are shutting your doors tomorrow for the foreseeable, pandemic-y future … you have been an absolutely essential service for so many writers, and I know that you will be so again soon.
> *Writer Linda Jaivin, on the eve of Varuna's close in March 2020* (Varuna, The National Writers' House, 2021, p. 11)

We work with writers day in and day out. We know how difficult it is to be a writer, juggling work, family and caring responsibilities, the long days and nights of pursuing a solitary artform, as well as the financial unreality of making a living from your creative work. In normal times, Varuna welcomes writers for a much-needed break from everyday life, and steps in to provide recognition of the writer's work, along with the essentials – cooked dinners, a well-stocked fridge, and the time and space to write and commune with the other writers in the house. Each writer first comes to Varuna through a selective and peer-assessed process, either on an awarded fellowship, residency or masterclass-by-application. Over three decades this has fostered a prestigious writing community, a supportive and nurturing culture, and an alumni network of several thousand writers across Australia and internationally. In COVID-19 times, we knew that many of the writers and academics we worked with would be particularly isolated and vulnerable to sudden changes in their already precarious employment.

We knew we wanted to connect with our writing community, to bring people together somehow, to try to provide some routine and normalcy, and perhaps also to lift ourselves out of the sudden isolation – after all, none of us knew how the story ended. We started to work on ideas, to sketch out how we could somehow create writing programs that had the magic of Varuna when writers were unable to be in the place itself. We wondered if we could conjure this from our homes. Our long-standing mentor and book whisperer Dr Carol Major came up with the name that brought together all of our thinking – our online programs were to be called Lamplight Residencies. The idea was that we could be together in our solitude, all writing by lamplight, much like when we at Varuna close the office door of an evening and look up to the second storey of the house to see the writers at their desks, each working separately, but also wonderfully together.

In autumn 2020, Varuna launched these virtual residencies. Six writers met online via Zoom every day for a week, sharing readings with each other, enjoying individual mentoring sessions, and joining eminent authors for intimate workshops about their writing practice. All writers participating in these programs were either from Varuna's extensive alumni network or had a track record as a published writer or academic. In the second Lamplight, the authors inaugurated a daily Shut Up & Write! session and it immediately became a feature of the program.

Buoyed by the participant feedback, and with COVID lockdowns stretching out ahead of us, Varuna offered this concept to our program partners in the United Kingdom, United States of America, and New Zealand, who took it up with enthusiasm. Over the coming months Varuna co-hosted online programs with these partner organisations, with sessions facilitated by literary peers, publishers and authors from around the world. The connections through these programs were brief, but they quickly built depth and trust through the exchange of work and ideas far beyond our expectations. As our Executive Director Veechi Stuart wrote in Varuna's 2020 Annual Report, 'We could never have guessed that it would take the closure of Australian borders to deepen these international relationships so quickly' (Varuna the National Writers' House, 2021, p. 5). Writers were hungry to connect, and were readily putting themselves forward for opportunities to share experiences and learn from each other, even in this online format.

Dr Amanda Niehaus, biologist, academic and novelist, participated in Varuna's 2020 online program jointly presented with Write On, Door County in the United States:

> It's difficult being an emerging writer in the time of pandemic—establishing community, developing skills, and keeping our sensitive writerly brains moving in positive directions. I published my first book in September 2019, a book I never anticipated in my former life as a scientist. There were reviews, and bookstore events, and readers and more

events to come ... and then Covid happened. And we all know how that went. Varuna was an incredible support to writers like me during that time, both via the Lamplight Residency but also via those wonderful daily Zoom writing sessions.

Feedback from writers about their artistic development and the benefits to their sense of connection and wellbeing, alongside the growing expertise of program staff, encouraged Varuna to continue to expand its online offering. In the ever-changing 2020, when whole cities were placed into lockdown, Varuna initiated a weekday Shut Up & Write! session to try and offer a sense of connection, a daily rhythm and to value creativity in challenging times:

> We have been thinking of our Varuna friends who are having a very tough time in Victoria at the moment. Quite a few of you have been in touch to say just how hard the lockdown is this time around, and how difficult it is to focus and find time for your writing. We would love to support you however we can, so starting this Thursday at 11am AEST, we will be hosting daily Zoom writing sessions for alumni every weekday. These sessions are free to join, and no registration is necessary. We plan to run these sessions until Stage 4 restrictions ease in Victoria in mid-September. All Varuna alumni are encouraged to join, wherever you may be! This could help you start a new project, or just find that time to continue developing existing work ... So, why not set yourself a writing goal and join us? *'Free daily writing sessions for Varuna Alumni', email from Varuna to the Alumni network, 4 August 2020.*

This Shut Up & Write! offering, a place of daily connection at a time of immense stress and enforced social isolation, was very well received by Varuna's alumni network:

> How utterly beautiful. What a kind and smart idea. Thank you. I have no idea how tough it must be for Victorians right now, but I will say that as a regionally based writer I often feel like I miss out on being part of a larger community. This opportunity to build that community is lovely – and I'd love to join my interstate peers for a spell. Thanks for the inclusion – and for the initiative.
>
> Thank you from the bottom of my heart. It's such an emotional time at the moment – everyone is struggling in some way or another whether balancing the mental health/anxiety of elderly parents and teenage children, lost income and a general sense of despair – so to receive emails like this is just bloody nice! Thank you and see you online.
>
> Thank you so much for this amazing idea and offer. I found this type of writing session brilliant and so productive during my lamplight residency. I didn't realise I was so emotional about being locked down again, until your email got me all excited and a little teary at the thoughtfulness.

Extending Shut Up & Write! in this way was good for us at Varuna, and it changed how we thought about programming, as I wrote to Jerod Santek, the artistic director of US writing centre Write On, Door County, the following week:

> We were quite alarmed to see Melbourne suddenly go into such a strict lockdown, so we have also started free daily online 'shut up and write' sessions for our alumni wherever they may be, which has been such an interesting thing. Quite a number are joining us each day for an hour and a half of shared writing time. 2020 is certainly making us think differently about our program.

Five years after the first sessions, Shut Up & Write! is integrated into nearly all of the online programs offered by Varuna. Shut Up & Write!, and Varuna's suite of online programs, is seen by the organisation as an essential platform to connect with writers across geographical constraints, and as an inclusive, accessible format for those writers who may otherwise find it difficult to engage with writing communities. Sometimes, Shut Up & Write! sessions are scheduled for those in physical residence at the house, particularly for new writers who are still learning what works for them in structuring their writing day. Program staff learned that Shut Up & Write! provides what so many writers need – dedicated time to write, a sense of camaraderie and connection, and accountability to turn up and do the work, and this now informs programming decisions across the organisation.

Naomi, a Desperate Writer in a Pandemic

> The air in the Blue Mountains was cleared by strafing rains in February but the landscape has not recovered. The forests are blasted sticks and the plateaus are scraped clear of grasses and shrubs. You can see the bones of the country – the layers of sandstone and lava forms glisten with water that was held by hanging swamps that are no more. Regrowth is beginning but it is scar tissue. Some of the eucalypts have shaken off their ashen cloaks but their white marble trunks are stencilled with thin brown lines where the smoke and heat cracked their bark into tiles. Coral-coloured leaf buds are spinning from charcoal trunks and tiny threads of green are beginning to run over the dead grey soil and these are little stitches of hope but really, the damage is too much. The bush will be different than it was before. Walking it right now is an act of reverence, for there is grief for what is gone.
>
> And then ... A virus came from wild creatures who had been stolen from endangered forests and taken to a small market. From there the virus was dispersed by shoppers and tourists and commuters and migrants and spread wide by the climate-choking airplanes and cruise ships and freighters. Small and unseeable, but enough to kill the old and poor, to drive us out of work, to keep us apart and stop us holding each other and burying our dead. We may never return from this either. This is the new normal, people say. How do we live in this time when we cannot even cling together?
>
> *Naomi Parry Duncan, writing produced during Shut Up & Write!,*
> *May 2020 Lamplight Residency*

I had taken 2020 off from paid work, and intended to spend the year living on some funds from grants and my savings while I prepared a long-planned work of creative non-fiction on Musquito, a Gamaragal warrior from Warrane Port Jackson who was executed in Tasmania in 1825. The Blue Mountains had been necklaced by fire during the Black Summer 2019–2020 then flooded, and most Katoomba residents were suffering in the aftermath. It was already extremely difficult to concentrate, but the outbreak of COVID-19 and the subsequent lockdowns were heavy blows for a community that was beyond the limits of resilience. And while most people were complaining about isolation, I had more people in my house than I had ever had before. Beloved friends returned from overseas in a hurry and had nowhere to live so moved into my backyard studio while my partner, a musician and teacher, was completely out of work and was around all the time. As soon as my friends moved out, another whose relationship had not survived lockdown replaced them, and my child returned from university. It was a social time and that was wonderful but the panic of lockdown and the pressure of having so many people in the house meant I could not write a word. I was fortunate to receive a Copyright Agency Cultural Fund COVID-19 Emergency Action Fund Grant that provided me with some funds to keep going, but it was Varuna that shifted me from suspension in the new normal, to animation.

I'm a Varuna alumnus and when the house advertised the Lamplight Residencies I jumped at the chance. I remember the email I got from Amy just as I started, in May 2020:

> Welcome to our third Varuna Lamplight Residency. We hope you are all going okay in these very strange times, and we hope that this coming week can be a special time of connection, reflection and lots of writing!

Along with instructions about uploading our work and the schedule for time with our guest mentors, crime novelist Tara Moss and Aboriginal writer Tony Birch, was the intriguing suggestion that we might try Shut Up & Write!:

> We hope that you are able to commit several hours (we suggest at least 3 hours) of dedicated writing time each day. The second Lamplight group met daily via Zoom for a one hour 'Shut Up and Write' session, which was really productive and a great way of keeping each other accountable!

The Lamplight week did conjure the warmth and stillness that is a week in Varuna, and the sense of solidarity. All of us felt the weight of Black Summer and COVID-19, so it is unsurprising that we placed writing about the environment at front and centre as we wrote – we were on the same page, so to speak. The little video Amy sent us of Varuna's wonderful cook Sheila making her legendary fish pie in her kitchen at home also helped, and we made fish pies in our own kitchens and ate them in front of our computers – my first Zoom dinner party.

And Shut Up & Write! was a revelation. Carving out that precious hour every day, with the camera on and the door closed on everyone in the house, helped me find discipline in a world that was formless. The blue glow and the sense of others sitting there with you, all writing, released the words and they really flowed. With words we all put a shape around what had happened to us and began to adjust to the shock and find a way forward. Varuna's attention to the needs of its writers during this period was a saving grace and Varuna maintained this care throughout that year, introducing Australia-wide Shut Up & Write! sessions so we could all support Victorians when they were plunged back into lockdown in August 2020.

Some of the work I did in this period became the basis of a chapter outline, and then of a book proposal. The book I am preparing for publication now, *Musquito*, was propelled by the feelings of that Lamplight Residency at Varuna and the confidence boost that SUAW provides: you can get down 500 words in an hour. You can even write 1000 words. And they won't be bad. They might even save you.

Meg Mooney, Interviewed by Amy

Meg Mooney is a poet and writer living in Mparntwe/Alice Springs, perhaps the most geographically isolated town in Australia. Meg has been dedicated to her writing practice for many years, publishing several books of poetry while juggling full-time work, and making the trip to the east coast to visit Varuna four or five times for residencies since 2003. In 2020, as COVID hit, Meg had just retired from full-time work and was planning to spend more time writing. It proved to be a serendipitous turning point.

Meg and Naomi met through the same Lamplight Residency, in May 2020. Meg explains what the program meant to her:

> Geographically, Australia is a vast country, and I live in a relatively small town, a long way from others. There are other writers living in Alice, but I don't have regular contact with them.
>
> The local writing group I had been part of for many years had ended some time ago. I hadn't participated in Shut Up and Write but when Varuna initiated the program I was intrigued and I thought I'd give it a go. I've always been reasonably disciplined and haven't needed support or deadlines to write, so I wasn't sure if it was for me.

Meg was one of over 80 writers across Australia who joined Varuna's first national sessions, an incredible number far beyond the organisation's expectations. Initially, it was a bit overwhelming for Meg and others to be in such a large group, but as daily numbers stabilised to approximately 40 for the first six months, connections between writers deepened.

In Varuna's daily Shut Up & Write!, projects get finished, and writers come and go with some of the demands of daily life, but they return and pick up where they left off, in the collegiate support of a group of people with a commitment to writing. Overall, more than 200 writers have participated in Varuna's Shut Up & Write! sessions since their commencement.

It's now five years later, and while the numbers have dwindled to a core committed group, most weekdays Meg logs in for Shut Up & Write!. Her attention is one of the reasons the sessions keep going, but Meg feels the benefits:

> It's had quite an impact on my writing. It's provided a structure, I still go online in the morning at 9:30 and I'll spend the morning writing, usually continuing on beyond the Zoom itself. We occasionally share a little bit of our own writing, though not very much and not often, it's not really about that. It's given me really good contacts around publishing and writing and various courses and types of writing, and it's given me friends and a writing community.

Meg has finished the book she was working on in the earlier years of Shut Up & Write!, and she liaised with one of the others in the group – a highly experienced mentor, academic and writer – who gave paid detailed editorial feedback. Meg has also had a poem published via the networks formed in Shut Up & Write!.

Amy: The Impact of Shut Up & Write! on Varuna and its Community

These programs were central to Varuna remaining relevant and supporting the mental health and well-being of writers during the extended isolation of lockdowns, but they also created unique and ongoing opportunities for writers, including those who may be living with disability, caring responsibilities, geographical isolation or other life circumstances that ordinarily would prevent their participation in the writing and academic community. Importantly, it has provided an opportunity for writers from all over Australia to build connections with each other, to work together, and for Varuna as an organisation to step in and offer support to writers to prioritise their artform and keep up the momentum in their work.

Over the years delivering these initiatives it became clear what writers needed from Varuna as an organisation, and how we could best structure programs to enable meaningful, creatively useful connections and professional development opportunities. With the benefit of hosting daily Shut Up & Write! sessions over many months – now years – we have been able to refine the approach and the clarity of the 'rules' for the sessions we include in our residency programs.

It is essential to create a safe and respectful space where those in the room – whether physical or virtual – are clear on the terms of participation. Writers need to know that they are free to focus their time and efforts exclusively on their own project, without feeling a burden of obligation to give feedback to others or to get drawn into social or professional conversations, unless they choose to do so after the structured sessions. The successful model for Varuna-led sessions has been to join at an agreed time each day, to have roughly five minutes of welcome and brief conversation, followed by 25 minutes of silent writing time. An allocated timekeeper notifies the participants when it is time to break for 5 minutes, giving the option for participants to converse or fix themselves a cup of tea. This invitation to leave the Zoom or room temporarily appears to be successful in reducing social pressure and is a strategy we still use. The second silent writing session recommences sharply after the break. After this, our staff facilitator makes it clear that the session is over and that participants are free to remain if they want to have a social catch up for the next fifteen minutes.

Being clear about the rules of engagement seems to give participants confidence in the level of commitment required. Anecdotally, we know of many small Shut Up & Write! groups that have emerged within Varuna's network. Some have come out of other programs, such as a 2024 masterclass where participants started a 6 am 'wake up and write' session, and some have formed out of social relationships between writers, such as the group that I participate in each week with several Varuna alumni.

Conclusion: Naomi and Amy

Since COVID-19, Varuna's development programs have been informed by the success and outcomes of the Shut Up & Write! sessions. These sessions consciously create accountability for writers and academics and encourage them to 'show up' for the development of their creative and academic work. They provide the opportunity to connect with other writers and discuss challenges and successes and are imbued with the professional understanding of simply working alongside peers in an ordinarily solitary pursuit – for many participants in the weekday sessions this connection is the most important element. These programs have been delivered with the wellbeing and mental health of participants as a key focus and have informed the design of subsequent writer development initiatives.

Without the impetus of COVID-19 forcing the radical reimagining of Varuna's operations, the organisation may not have so intensively explored the possibilities of building writing communities and pursuing writer development through Shut Up & Write! sessions and the many other online programs that have followed. Now, alongside in-person residencies and a writers' festival, Varuna operates an annual program of online writer development masterclasses, online residencies, workshops, mentoring and seminars, which has more than doubled the number of writers the organisation is able to work with each year. Shut Up & Write! remains a part of many online programs, and writers have gone on to create and sustain regular writing practices with peers across Australia. From its beginnings as a tool to bring writers together in a time of great upheaval, Shut Up & Write! has become an integral part of Varuna's care for the wellbeing of writers, a tool used in programs to facilitate intensive and creative productivity, and an initiative that continues to contribute to the successes of a number of its alumni.

Acknowledgement

The authors are grateful to the referees for their advice on this article and thank Amanda Niehaus and Meg Mooney for their contributions. We acknowledge Meg for her important role in making Shut Up & Write! part of Varuna's offerings to alumni and fellows.

References

Varuna the National Writers' House. (2021). *Annual Report 2020.* https://static1.squarespace.com/static/5bb7de23a9ab95700a37b17c/t/6088c296d71d0d5012e9c722/1619575450195/Varuna-AR-2020-web.pdf

10 Shutting Up and Staying Well

Reflections on Community, Belonging, and Mattering from SUAW Exeter

Kelly Louise Preece and Jo Sutherst

Introduction

Over the past 10 years, Shut Up and Write! (SUAW), alongside other models of writing groups and retreats, has emerged as a potential solution to the systemic challenges that researchers face in maintaining productivity. In their work on doctoral writing, Kamler and Thomson (2014, p. 4) establish writing as a situated social practice – and yet it is an activity often undertaken in isolation. We sought to address the experience of writing in isolation through the Supporting Postgraduate Researcher (PGR) Writing project (2017–2021) at the University of Exeter, UK.

The project, initiated by Kelly in her role as Researcher Development Manager, initially drew on Rowena Murray's typing pool model (where time is structured into a series of writing and discussion slots) (Murray & Newton, 2009, p. 541) to create a community of practice where PGRs wrote together in 'Write Clubs'. These Write Clubs slowly began to gain momentum, with feedback demonstrating a positive impact on productivity, community building, and wellbeing. Then came COVID-19, with Write Clubs moving from campus to online and facilitated by PGRs themselves, adopting the format and moniker of Shut Up & Write! (SUAW) Exeter. We went from running two sessions per week to up to four groups per day by the end of 2020, becoming a thriving worldwide peer-led community. Our small, supportive writing community of 50 PGRs grew exponentially in size with engagement increasing by 4484% between 2017/18 and 2019/2020. As the community grew so did its impact, combating the isolation commonly experienced by the PGR community that had been exacerbated by the COVID-19 pandemic. This led to a sense of belonging – of being part of a community – and mattering – adding value to that community, and in tandem an improvement in PGR experiences of wellbeing.

What began as a Write Club for PGRs is now an inclusive, robust SUAW Exeter program that encompasses all research-related work, accessible every single day online on Microsoft Teams from 8 am to 10:30 pm GMT. Some sessions have facilitated Pomodoros, some not – with a timetable that shows when facilitators will be online. Importantly, SUAW Exeter is now run by PGRs for PGRs – overseen by Jo as the 'SUAW student co-ordinator' (a role we created to ensure SUAW Exeter was peer led). The flexible format allows members to participate on their own terms, without any need for commitment. PGRs can enter and exit as they wish, share their projects if they choose to, or simply stay in the background. This setup is especially considerate of those navigating full-time jobs, caring responsibilities, different time zones, and additional needs that resist a 9-to-5 schedule. Facilitators and participants also shape the format and 'feel' of the sessions. For example, each facilitator has their own style and favourite 'race timers' – online timers that can be set to Pomodoro lengths, that visualise the writing time as a race of characters such as cars, ducks, dragons, dinosaurs, and even Santas for Christmas. The format is friendly to people of all backgrounds, neurotypes, and commitments because it acknowledges and accommodates the diverse needs and preferences of individuals. The space offers choices, catering to a wide range of needs and promoting a supportive environment where all individuals can effectively harness their strengths and manage the challenges of being a PGR – and indeed a human being.

In this chapter we borrow from narrative ethnography and feminist research, where there is a 'strong history of use of personal experience and representation of lived experience through autobiographical writing' (Barbour, 2011, p. 17), offering narrative vignettes from SUAW Exeter on how 'shutting up' together has created a vibrant community and had a positive impact on PGR wellbeing. At various junctures we have encouraged members of our community to capture narratives about their experience of SUAW Exeter. These have been part of writing retreats, facilitated by prompts, Lego Serious Play activities, and group discussion as well as an open invitation to write. It was always optional for these to be shared with the group, and the authors of these vignettes have consented to their publication and are included in the acknowledgements of this chapter.

How Shutting Up Leads to Staying Well

Before we dive into discussion, we wanted to acknowledge the bias in the selection of the narratives included in this chapter – both the self-selection of those who wanted to contribute, and in our curation of these to tell a particular story about wellbeing. But whilst we acknowledge this bias, we do not suggest it represents a flaw in our methodology or discussion. We argue that whilst we can capture the impact of SUAW in data – spanning everything from attendances to words written, theses submitted and rating experiences of productivity and wellbeing (Lonka et al., 2019) – the impact of SUAW is most clearly demonstrated in the narratives and the stories of those who participate. It is through those stories that we can capture some of the ephemeral experiences that contribute to staying well, including a sense of community, belonging, and, we would argue most importantly, *mattering*. We propose that

SUAW Exeter has a positive impact on PGR wellbeing – specifically the social, emotional and intellectual dimensions of wellbeing (Stoewen, 2017) – through a combination of combating loneliness and isolation, creating a sense of belonging and providing opportunities for mattering.

SUAW, Loneliness, and Isolation

> In my opinion, SUAW is an easy sell, provided that participants understand the format and concept. It provides you with an online network of PGRs from different disciplines who can offer support and advice. It also reduces the sense of isolation experienced by many PGRs, teaches you tips and tricks to maintain focus and motivation and provides a type of accountability too as we report on our progress during the sessions.
>
> – Dr Anne Blanchflower

In their work on doctoral writing, Kamler and Thomson (2014) argue that writing is not just a set of skills but a situated social practice (p. 4). Writing as a 'situated social practice', therefore, has the potential to be a tool for community building and social wellbeing amongst PGRs. Indeed, Mewburn et al. (2014) argue that "Shut up and Write! is one way of providing the kind of cohort experience" (p. 218) that is so difficult to replicate for PGRs – particularly for our increasingly diverse PGR community whose primary means of connecting with the University, and their fellow PGRs, is online – both during and since the COVID-19 pandemic. We see this sense of community echoed throughout our experiences as developer and co-ordinator, and through Dr. Sam Jones' description of her experience of SUAW Exeter and experiences of friendship and social wellbeing:

> As a part-time, distance learning PhD student living on an island off the west coast of Scotland, I could easily feel isolated and disconnected from the university and the PGR community. However, the SUAW sessions have acted as a bridge across 500 miles to Exeter and I feel connected with the university as well as a full member of the PGR community. I also have an increasing number of friends, the vast majority of whom I have never met in person but I long for the day when I can.
>
> During the first lockdown, my full-time work dried up. I attended most of the SUAW sessions during the day and wrote a chapter of my thesis over the ensuing three months which received very positive feedback from my supervisors. SUAW and the fellowship which it engenders kept me sane at what was a very difficult time for me. I will never forget how my SUAW friends got me through a dark period. I will be forever grateful to them. SUAW was a real beacon.
>
> – Dr Sam Jones

We also see echoes of the findings of Cannell et al. (2023) in our narratives – through poignant descriptions of the SUAW Exeter combating isolation and loneliness, most palpable in Dr Ada Cheong's narrative contribution:

> These are the few coldest truths about doing a PhD: it is a long and lonely road, nobody can write it for you, and sometimes your material just doesn't behave the way you want it to. At my lowest point, I was struggling to write my second (out of four) chapters and would take an entire year to draft it.
>
> I still remember my first SUAW session: it was just past 8 am, before others in the flat were awake, and I was at the living room table. With my first cup of tea beside me, I logged in and typed a hello to Tracey, the only other person online. It brought an immense calm to just have somebody else working in tandem with me, somewhere.
>
> It is a strange thing to be sitting in a studio flat, listening to nothing but the ticking of a clock, as the traffic on Cowley Bridge Road dwindles in the night. At 10 pm, one of us will say that it's the end of the session, and we will trade reflections on our work. Then, I can finally log off, safe in the knowledge that I will continue my work in the company of friends on the next day, and the next, and the next.
>
> – Dr Ada Cheong

We see this theme of shared experience developed further in narratives from Sam Pulman, Rev Dr Nicolle Sturdevant, and Dr Tracey Warren:

> Through SUAW I found 'my people', a group of remote students working on unique and diverse research. I don't think the amazing and sometimes off-beat conversations or connections would have occurred within one faculty or being on-site. It is the co-journey in friendship and with kindness that makes SUAW such a special place and gives it meaning. As a group we share the struggles, and we celebrate the success.
>
> – Sam Pulman

> Being part of the SUAW group helped me to have a community of like/hive minded people. Working on a PhD could be extremely lonely and trying to explain the good and the bad with those who were not doing the same was difficult. In my SUAW group I could share everything, and they understood what I was saying, giving encouragement but most importantly lending an ear and empathetic nod when I most needed it. Even though I have graduated I still look to my SUAW community when I want another opinion or share goals/achievements that only they would understand. They are not just part of my PhD journey but also my lifelong friends.
>
> – Rev Dr Nicolle Sturdevant

> The SUAW groups gave not just a structure to writing but a social opportunity to develop friendships (albeit at a distance) and motivate each other. It has become a great community where we share ideas. The way the SUAW sessions provided an organised way to writing helping to focus to write. By providing an outcome (what I am working on) to the whole group at the beginning of each session also ensured a commitment to achieve the desired outcome by the end of the session.
> – Dr Tracey Warren

Cannell et al. reflect that "[b]y discussing experiences and setbacks [writing groups] members learned that their experiences were shared' (p. 1115). Sam Pulman notes that as a group, SUAW Exeter *"share the struggles, and we celebrate the success[es]"*, and Rev. Dr. Nicolle Sturdevant reflects that *"[i]n my SUAW group I could share everything, and they understood what I was saying, giving encouragement but most importantly lending an ear and empathetic nod when I most needed it."* We see here not just social aspects of wellbeing in the sharing of experiences, but the emotional aspects in the way in which the group support leads to positive emotions. Dr. Pauline McGonagle's narrative gives a deeper understanding of the shared experiences of writing, intellectual wellbeing, and life, that SUAW Exeter gave her:

> SUAW sessions and people were with me through a broken foot, sciatica, disappointing feedback on a chapter, acceptance of a journal article, viva preparations and failed job applications. They were with me when friends died from Covid, when new grandnephews were born and on days of sun, hail and rain. Some days a few lines were written, others resulted in pages of good work or completed admin or marking. The principle however has stayed with me. Time it, get it done, every word is another word, and every line is an achievement.
> – Dr Pauline McGonagle

Indeed, the community building potential of SUAW is well established, but the community building aspect of SUAW isn't just a means to an end – its significance is in how community and shared experiences are "intimately intertwined with well-established theoretical ideas of belonging (Maslow, 1954) and mattering (Schlossberg, 1989)" (White & Nonnamaker, 2008, p. 351).

The concept of belonging stems from Maslow's (1954) hierarchy of needs, where belonging is "the experience of personal belonging in a [...] system or environment so that persons feel themselves to be an integral part of that system or environment" (Anant, 1966, p. 21 as cited in Hagerty et al., 1992, p. 173). Alongside feeling part of SUAW Exeter, our contributors reported a sense of shared identity, which according to McAlpine and Amundsen (2009) can lead to feelings of belonging. We see this shared identity throughout our narrative, in phrases such as "*[t]hrough SUAW I found 'my people'*", a community of "*like/hive minded people*" from Sam Pulman. There is a strong sense throughout of not just being a part of the community but identifying strongly with other members and as a result feeling valued as "an integral part of the [SUAW] system". As reflected by Marlen von Reith:

> From the start, I was embraced as a valued member of an academic writing group and tight-knit research community. SUAW provided structure, both to writing sessions and everyday life as a PhD, but also to research itself, by providing scheduled sessions, a way to exchange stories, or simply silent companionship. Above all, it gave a sense of belonging; even though one was currently miles away from other PhD students and the University itself, it was still easy to feel connected. Fellow students gave practical advice on which social media channels to follow to stay in touch with university events and departments and shared their experiences of academic exams and milestones yet to be reached. In both struggling and succeeding as a PhD student, I felt far from being alone.
>
> One evening, a fellow student asked for my advice on a task, which I myself had struggled to complete weeks before. Yet having struggled and eventually succeeded in writing that particular part, I was suddenly in a position to give advice – without feeling like an impostor. In this particular moment, my experience was valuable to someone else's writing process, and because we were both connected to a wider writing community aimed at supporting each other in SUAW, we were given a platform to exchange these experiences.
>
> –Marlen von Reith

As argued by Cannell et al. (2023) citing Schmidt and Hansson, it is not just the reduction in isolation that has a positive impact on PGR wellbeing through a sense of community, but the ways in which writing groups 'prompt positive wellbeing outcomes such as feelings of "enthusiasm, inspiration, support, meaningfulness, contribution, belonging, worthiness" (Cannell et al., 2023, p. 1108). We see this reflected in the photo collage (Image 10.1) provided by Dr Elsa Urmston, who combines the opportunity for gathering and friendship (and tea) with belonging and meaning in the top right-hand corner:

We argue that in our experience these 'positive wellbeing outcomes' are exemplified by the sense not just of belonging, but of mattering. SUAW is not just about reducing the negative aspects of the PGR experience but developing the positives.

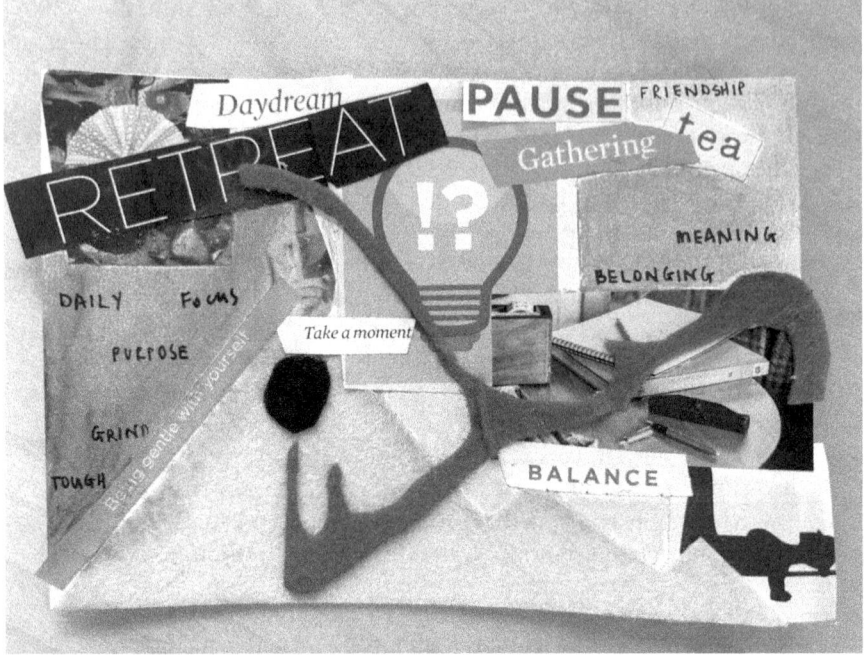

Image 10.1 Mattering. (Photo collage by Dr Elsa Urmston.)

SUAW, Belonging, and Mattering

> This community is not just about writing. It was about empathy. During moments of self-doubt, the group offered validation. When deadlines loomed like insurmountable walls, it provided a ladder of encouragement. And when life outside the academic bubble became too overwhelming, the group listened, shared, and consoled. It bridged the professional and the personal in ways that traditional academic spaces often fail to do.
>
> The pandemic may have upended our lives, but this community adapted, survived, and thrived. It became a symbol of what academia should aspire to: an inclusive, supportive, and nurturing space that prioritises well-being as much as productivity.
>
> – Dr Wafa Rashed Almulaifi

In her work researching the experience of allied health students, Zawada (2024) establishes the important link between a sense of belonging and mattering – with mattering defined by Prilleltensky (2020) as "the experience of feeling valued and adding value (p. 86). We have already discussed some elements of this feeling valued and adding value throughout the narrative – particularly when Marlen offered advice to a peer, developing confidence as a researcher who is *"suddenly in a position to give advice – without feeling like an impostor."*

But it is our assertion that the sense of agency and empowerment experienced by PGRs as they took over the facilitation, running, and ultimately direction of SUAW Exeter that resulted in 'adding value' and 'feelings of mattering'. Co-ordinating and facilitating SUAW Exeter has given Jo and the PGR community agency and independence which allows the sessions to be tailored to fit their unique academic needs and schedules, creating a supportive environment that fosters productivity and creativity.

Although Guerin (2021) argues that "even formal groups run by central university units will inevitably result in more independent doctoral candidates as writing skills develop over time", it is taking control of their experience and journey through running these groups that makes PGRs feel empowered. They are not just recipients of these experiences of community and belonging – they create them through facilitating sessions, coming up with new puns for timers, and deciding on the direction of the group. The initial tentative conversations PGRs had with the 'central university unit' (here, Kelly) about running their own groups and moving formally to the SUAW format, became an important means of 'handing over the reins' of SUAW Exeter to the PGR community. The model of delivery simplified under their leadership, and as argued by Mewburn et al. "[t]he very simplicity of the concept [SUAW] enables complexity to develop" (Mewburn et al., 2014, p. 221). Here, that complexity was a self-sustaining PGR community, a sense of belonging – to SUAW Exeter and to the University – and of mattering and feeling valued for their role in that community. The shift to when the wider community took over co-ordinating and facilitating SUAW Exeter resulted in increased agency for members over the format and structure of the SUAW sessions. This transition has allowed us greater flexibility and the ability to customise the format to meet the specific needs of our community. Having the autonomy to develop the format and frequency of the sessions has also given a sense of ownership and accountability to participants. This has fostered a stronger community spirit, as everyone feels that they matter and have a stake in the development of our group. There are also positive practical implications to the community-led approach – both in terms of sustaining the community and reducing the impetus and workload on institutions. As SUAW Exeter became PGR led, it freed Kelly up to instigate other, new initiatives.

This complexity is also seen in the positive impact on wellbeing. Belonging is easy to describe, but not so easy to create, and "is a fundamental human motivation that links to health and wellbeing" (Zawada, 2024, p. 2). Yet throughout the narratives we see reflections of SUAW Exeter getting PGRs through difficult times and low mental health – for Ada *"At my lowest point, I was struggling to write my second (out of four) chapters and would take an entire year to draft it"* and *"I will never forget how my SUAW friends got me through a dark period"*. We also see evidence of "positive wellbeing outcomes such as feelings of 'enthusiasm, inspiration, support, meaningfulness, contribution, belonging, worthiness" (Schmidt & Hansson, 2018, p. 9 as cited in Cannell et al., 2023, p. 1108). We see these positive wellbeing outcomes embodied throughout experiences of community, belonging and mattering in the narrative of SUAW Exeter:

Outcome	Quotes
Enthusiasm	"*In my SUAW group I could share everything, and they understood what I was saying, giving encouragement but most importantly lending an ear and empathetic nod when I most needed it*" Nicolle
Inspiration	"*It became a symbol of what academia should aspire to: an inclusive, supportive, and nurturing space that prioritises well-being as much as productivity*" Wafa
Support	"*During moments of self-doubt, the group offered validation. When deadlines loomed like insurmountable walls, it provided a ladder of encouragement*" Wafa
Meaningfulness	"*It is the co-journey in friendship and with kindness that makes SUAW such a special place and gives it meaning*" Sam Pulman
Contribution	"*Fellow students gave practical advice on which social media channels to follow to stay in touch with university events and departments and shared their experiences of academic exams and milestones yet to be reached*" Marlen
Belonging	"*Through SUAW I found 'my people'*" Sam Pulman
Worthiness	"*I was suddenly in a position to give advice – without feeling like an impostor*" Marlen

We assert that it is the overlapping of these experiences that leads to a reduction in isolation and a positive impact on wellbeing, and the way in which the simplicity of the SUAW model enables a complexity of experience, having an impact on the social, emotional, and intellectual aspects of wellbeing. In the vein of simplicity, we visualise this in Figure 10.1.:

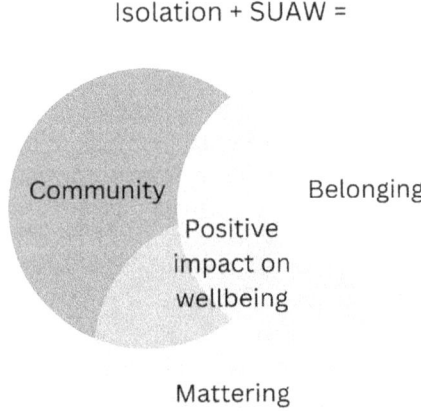

Figure 10.1 Mapping SUAW wellbeing.

As well as theorising the narrative of SUAW Exeter, we have reflected on the way we run our SUAW community, and how this leads to community building, feelings of belonging and mattering, and has a positive impact on wellbeing. To demonstrate this, we have developed our own SUAW manifesto.

The SUAW Exeter Manifesto

To create an inclusive, flexible, and supportive writing environment that fosters productivity, creativity, and community among PGRs, with a particular focus on supporting individuals to develop their own personalised writing rhythms.

The core principles of SUAW Exeter are:

- Inclusivity and Accessibility:
  - We embrace diversity in all its forms, ensuring our writing spaces are welcoming to people of all backgrounds, neurotypes, and commitments.
  - Everyone has the right to a supportive and accommodating environment.
- Flexibility in Participation:
  - Our sessions are designed to be adaptable, allowing members to engage at their own pace and convenience.
  - There are no mandatory sign-ups or rigid schedules; everyone can come and go as they please.
- Autonomy and Empowerment:
  - Members have full control over their participation, choosing when and how to engage, setting their own goals without judgment, and finding their optimal work patterns.
- Community and Support:
  - Our group is a friendly, non-hierarchical community that offers encouragement and reduces feelings of isolation.
  - We foster connections and mutual motivation through shared experiences and support networks.
  - The group is run by PGRs for PGRs, ensuring a peer-led environment that understands and advocates for the needs and challenges faced by members of our community.

Alongside these principles, we employ a range of strategies to promote wellbeing and productivity:

- Embrace Flexibility:
  - Design your writing schedule according to your personal energy levels.
  - Allow yourself to work when you feel most productive, whether that's morning, evening, or alternating.

- Utilise Body Doubling, defined as "using the presence of others to start, stay focused on, or accomplish a task" (Eagle et al., 2024, p. 16:1):
  - Join a writing group session where you can work alongside others. This connection, even virtual, can boost your focus and help overcome procrastination.
- Set Realistic Goals:
  - Set small, achievable writing goals and revise them as necessary.
  - Celebrate all progress, whether you reach the initial target or not. It's the process that counts.
- Customise Your Environment:
  - Choose whether to have your camera or microphone on or off in writing groups, adapt the session length, and find a group that matches your work rhythm.
  - Personalise the space to fit your needs comfortably.
- Engage with the Community:
  - Take advantage of the sense of companionship by participating in discussions, sharing experiences, or simply being present according to your needs.
  - Join sessions that align with your interests and goals.
- Prioritise Self-Care:
  - Remember that your wellbeing is paramount.
  - Take breaks when needed and balance your writing with relaxation.
  - Use the support of the community to discuss challenges and find encouragement.

Through these principles, we aim to create a writing environment that prioritises both productivity and wellbeing and creates an inclusive community in which PGRs both belong and matter.

Conclusion

We have used this chapter to outline the SUAW Exeter model and, using a narrative of contributions from our SUAW community, have argued that SUAW Exeter combats isolation through community, belonging, and mattering, which has a positive impact on wellbeing. We have also argued that the agency and empowerment created through the 'by PGRs for PGRs' aspect of the SUAW Exeter model plays an important role in creating the feeling and experience of mattering, of adding value to the PGR experience.

We have aimed through our small contribution in this chapter to provide contextualisation of the potential social, emotional, and intellectual wellbeing impacts of SUAW *alongside* some principles and strategies for practice so that what we have learned from SUAW Exeter. In that way, through our local context and beyond we hope it can continue to promote positive wellbeing whilst providing structure, support, productivity, belonging, and mattering to PGRs – or indeed, anyone working within a higher education environment. As articulated by Wafa it is, we believe, *"a symbol of what academia should aspire to: an inclusive, supportive, and nurturing space that prioritises well-being as much as productivity."*

If you are considering starting a SUAW community, and we strongly urge you to do so, we want to offer two final nuggets of advice:

1 Keep it simple – simplicity of delivery breeds complexity of impact
2 Let the community lead – even when that means letting go of the institutional hold on initiatives

And equally, if our approach doesn't work for you, and the online environment just isn't a space where you can get folks to engage – ignore all this and find what works for you and your community.

Finally, alongside community, belonging, and mattering, the theme of friendship permeates throughout the narrative. As such, it would be remiss of us to not mention our fellow SUAW-er and friend, Dr Sam Jones, who we lost in October 2024. As Sam said herself *"the SUAW sessions have acted as a bridge across 500 miles to Exeter"* from her home on the Isle of Mull. We dedicate this chapter, and our ongoing SUAW Exeter community, to her.

Acknowledgements

With contributions from Dr Sam Jones, Dr Elsa Urmston, Rev Dr Nicolle Sturdevant, Sam Pulman, Dr Wafa Rashed Almulaifi, Dr Ada Cheong, Dr Anne Blanchflower, Marlen von Reith, and Dr Pauline McGonagle.

References

Anant, S. S. (1966). The need to belong. *Cunoda's Mental Health*, 14, 21–21.
Barbour, K. N. (2011). *Dancing across the page: Narrative and embodied ways of knowing* (1st ed.). Intellect.
Cannell, C., Silvia, A., McLachlan, K., Othman, S., Morphett, A., Maheepala, V., McCosh, C., Simic, N., & Behrend, M. B. (2023). Developing research-writer identity and wellbeing in a doctoral writing group. *Journal of Further and Higher Education*, 47(8), 1106–1123. https://doi.org/10.1080/0309877X.2023.2217411
Eagle, T., Baltaxe-Admony, L. B., & Ringland, K. E. (2024). "It was something i naturally found worked and heard about later": An investigation of body doubling with neurodivergent participants. *ACM Transactions on Accessible Computing*, 17(3), 1–30. https://doi.org/10.1145/3689648
Guerin, C. (2021). *Researcher independence: growing confidence inside a writing group*. Retrieved 22-01-2025 from https://drhiddencurriculum.wordpress.com/2021/09/12/researcher-independence-growing-confidence-inside-a-writing-group/

Hagerty, B. M. K., Lynch-Sauer, J., Patusky, K. L., Bouwsema, M., & Collier, P. (1992). Sense of belonging: A vital mental health concept. *Archives of Psychiatric Nursing*, *6*(3), 172–177. https://doi.org/10.1016/0883-9417(92)90028-H

Kamler, B., & Thomson, P. (2014). *Helping doctoral students write: Pedagogies for supervision* (2nd ed.). Routledge. https://doi.org/10.4324/9781315813639

Lonka, K., Ketonen, E., Vekkaila, J., Lara, M. C., & Pyhältö, K. (2019). Doctoral students' writing profiles and their relations to well-being and perceptions of the academic environment. *Higher Education*, *77*(4), 587–602. https://doi.org/10.1007/s10734-018-0290-x

Maslow, A. H. (1954). The instinctoid nature of basic needs. *Journal of Personality*, *22*(3), 326–347. https://doi.org/10.1111/j.1467-6494.1954.tb01136.x

McAlpine, L., & Amundsen, C. (2009). Identity and agency: Pleasures and collegiality among the challenges of the doctoral journey. *Studies in Continuing Education*, *31*(2), 109–125. https://doi.org/10.1080/01580370902927378

Mewburn, I., Osborne, L., Caldwell, G., Aitchison, C., & Guerin, C. (2014). *Shut up & write: Some surprising uses of cafés and crowds in doctoral writing*. In (1st ed., pp. 218–232). Routledge. https://doi.org/10.4324/9780203498811-18

Murray, R., & Newton, M. (2009). Writing retreat as structured intervention: Margin or mainstream? *Higher Education Research and Development*, *28*(5), 541–553. https://doi.org/10.1080/07294360903154126

Prilleltensky, I. (2020). Mattering at the intersection of psychology, philosophy, and politics. *American Journal of Community Psychology*, *65*(1-2), 16–34. https://doi.org/10.1002/ajcp.12368

Schlossberg, N. K. (1989). Marginality and mattering: Key issues in building community. *New Directions for Student Services*, *1989*(48), 5–15. https://doi.org/10.1002/ss.37119894803

Stoewen, D. L. (2017). Dimensions of wellness: Change your habits, change your life. *Canadian Veterinary Journal*, *58*(8), 861–862.

White, J., & Nonnamaker, J. (2008). Belonging and mattering: How doctoral students experience community. *NASPA Journal*, *45*(3). https://doi.org/10.2202/0027-6014.1860

Zawada, C. (2024). Student drop out and feelings of belonging and mattering in UK undergraduate allied health students. *Journal of Learning Development in Higher Education* (31). https://doi.org/10.47408/jldhe.vi31.1172

11 SUAW and Creating Inclusive Student Learning Communities

Sian Robinson

Introduction

This chapter explores the experiences of using focus/writing retreats as a version of SUAW for students on our large programme at the University of Exeter Business School. This chapter explores the SUAW initiative from two sides, firstly, from my own perspective, that of a neurodivergent lecturer who has ADHD and has found the use of focus/writing retreats to be revolutionary for my productivity and work, which has positively impacted my wellbeing. Secondly, a focus on how this translated into the creation of programme-level focus/writing retreats for a large undergraduate programme, supporting the students to develop an inclusive learning community through my role as programme director. These retreats have supported the wellbeing of the students through the creation of an inclusive community of learning that supports both productivity and developing relationships. This chapter focuses on wellbeing aligned with self-determination theory, aligning the challenges and benefits of the retreats with the three elements of autonomy, competence and relatedness. Focus/writing retreats have helped to develop relatedness through increased and direct mechanisms of support for students and being part of a community and allowed for increased autonomy and competence in line with being more productive and developing further time management and goal-setting skills. As a programme director, this also supports my own wellbeing as I am creating meaningful and supportive relationships with my students, whilst also making progress with my own work. I have ADHD, so productivity and executive function can be a challenge; therefore, for me, the use of SUAW retreats works as a fantastic method of body doubling.

Body Doubling for an ADHD Brain

I have ADHD. This means although I am creative, enthusiastic, curious, empathetic and good at problem-solving, I also have challenges with executive function. Executive function is the actions that we take to change our behaviour that will positively influence our future, including major functions such as self-directed attention, self-restraint and self-motivation (Barkley, 2022). For me, this includes difficulty with starting and continuing tasks, especially if they are onerous or boring. I also have trouble with regulating focus, prioritisation and time management. I can either have no capacity for focus, even though I want to, or I hyperfocus and forget everything else exists. Unfortunately, managing these contradictions constantly can be very stressful, which negatively impacts my psychological wellbeing.

Last summer I was cajoled into joining an in-person writing retreat. I initially resisted attending, as I felt that it wasn't a space for me and to my mind, I didn't have anything to write. Luckily, my friend persuading me to attend asked, 'Aren't you writing a textbook?'. This was very true, and therefore I resigned myself to going, but with little enthusiasm for it being useful to me. Little did I know that it would completely revolutionise how I work, and in turn have incredibly positive impacts on my wellbeing. What I found during this session was that a community setting was perfect for providing positive peer pressure for my ADHD brain as a form of body doubling, supporting me to be able to focus. For neurodivergent individuals, body doubling is the use of others being present to support in accomplishing tasks, supporting their ability to be productive, accountable and to get tasks done (Eagle et al., 2023). The image that I have created (Image 11.1) provides a visual representation of how chaotic my thoughts and processes are, and how the use of body doubling helps to streamline and focus my thoughts and focus.

I initially found the populated space distracting, but I developed strategies for creating a focused environment by using noise-cancelling headphones and specific goal setting. Meeting short-term goals and feeling like I was progressing on a larger task helped me to stay positive and keep going. I continue to use writing retreats and regularly co-work online with colleagues, which gives me the space to break down my work into manageable tasks and provides further accountability. This has positively impacted my psychological and social wellbeing more than I could ever have imagined. Being able to be productive and having support from a community has allowed me to be kinder to myself and to feel I am more competent at my work.

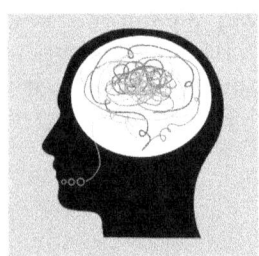 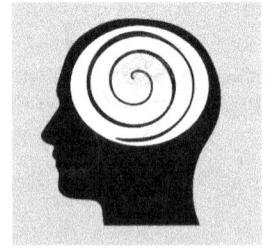

Image 11.1 Body doubling for an ADHD brain.

Having realised that writing retreats were revolutionary for my own productivity and wellbeing, this led me to consider how this might impact my students. I lead a large undergraduate programme in my role as programme director with over 1200 students enrolled, which brings unique challenges. The main challenges can be aligned into three key areas: community, outcomes and support. It is difficult to build a cohort identity when there are so many students and to create a learning community that gives a sense of belonging as well as develops relationships with peers. It can be difficult to create and maintain student engagement, both with their learning but also with programme events and the programme team. There are challenges with providing effective communication whilst also giving support that is personalised and inclusive, giving students a sense that they matter as individuals. Having experienced the positive impacts of writing retreats for myself, I decided to implement this as a programme-level event. I reframed them as 'focus/writing retreats' (hereafter FWRs) so that they could be used for any form of focused work, not just writing. The retreats aimed to create an inclusive community within the programme, enhance student outcomes and provide inclusive support at scale.

Impacts of Writing Retreats

When developing the rationale for adding these FWRs as a programme-level intervention, I recognised the need to go back to the literature and explore what potential impacts it could have backed by research. This highlighted that the use of writing retreats with students had a dearth of research. There was exploration of their usage and impacts for academics, PhD students and some studies on undergraduate researchers, but the focus here was always on writing for research. The neurodiversity literature explores body doubling more widely as a concept and how this supports the creation of inclusive learning environments, but there seems to be limited crossover.

Wellbeing

Firstly, it is important to explain how the concept of wellbeing is viewed in alignment with writing retreats and the student experience. It has been recognised that education innovations show signs of enhancing the wellbeing of students through embedding the principles of self-determination theory (Baik & Larcombe, 2023); as such, this links to the fulfilment of the three basic psychological needs of autonomy, competence and relatedness (Ryan & Deci, 2001). These three elements align with the challenges which the FWRs aim to help solve. The FWRs aim to increase student autonomy, as the students set their own goals and help to develop the skills of self-regulation. The FWRs align with increased competence as students are being effective and productive during sessions, supporting better outcomes. The FWRs also support relatedness by creating a community where students have the opportunity for both connection and support from their peers and staff.

Writing Retreats for Academics

Most of the research on the impacts of writing retreats aligns with their use for academics, particularly writing for research. Murray and Newton (2009) found that writing retreats can support academics in many ways, that they create dedicated writing time and increase learning through participation and support to build collegiality, which in turn leads towards creating a community of practice. Aligning with this, Kornhaber et al. (2016) found similar outcomes, that writing retreats developed a community of practice, which included increased collegial support and interaction as well as shared vision and mentorship. Kornhaber and colleagues also found that writing retreats developed their competences in academic writing and goal setting, and increased outputs, providing a dedicated and protected time and safe and supportive space for writing. The writing retreats also give intrapersonal benefits, including increased self-awareness, motivation and confidence, and help to reduce writing-related anxiety. Eardley et al. (2021) explore wellbeing, finding that writing retreats can positively impact both hedonic wellbeing, the affective quality of a person's life, and eudaimonic wellbeing, linking to the actualisation of potential and flourishing through personal growth, as well as supporting to mediate threats to wellbeing.

Writing Retreats for Researcher Students

There is some research on PhD students and on undergraduate researchers regarding the impacts of writing retreats. Writing retreats can support PhD students in developing writing self-efficacy and self-regulation through the use of goal setting and time-management practices (Vincent et al., 2023). Retreats also support providing positive results for their academic writing abilities through the impact of a community of practice (Tremblay-Wragg et al., 2021). For undergraduate researcher students, research by Cunningham (2022) indicates the biggest challenge is to find the space and time to write their research, and the use of writing retreats helped to create this, especially with the lecturer also working during the retreats. Cunningham (2022) also found that writing retreats increased the sense of support for the students, increased their productivity, gave them the ability to protect time and space for writing both during and after the writing retreats and gave them an increased capacity to effectively set goals.

Body Doubling

As mentioned at the start of this chapter, for neurodivergent people, particularly those with ADHD, body doubling is the use of others being present to support to accomplish tasks supporting their ability to be productive, accountable and to get tasks done (Eagle et al., 2023). Writing retreats and other forms of coworking meet the criteria of body doubling to support creating a conducive and inclusive environment for neurodivergent individuals to work and learn.

Student Wellbeing

Research by Baik and Larcombe (2023) has found that it is possible to improve the wellbeing of students through their learning environments and the teaching practices utilised, and that their experiences on their course accounts for more variance in wellbeing outcomes than other factors that are more commonly investigated such as finances, job prospects and care commitments. Some of the key experiences that were strongly associated with positive wellbeing were a sense of belonging, teacher support, motivation/intrinsic interest and peer support for learning, and in reverse, some key elements that impacted psychological distress included social disconnection, assessment stress and work overload (Baik and Larcombe, 2023). The benefits of writing retreats align well with increasing the experiences related to positive wellbeing by providing a place for them to belong, direct access to teacher support and peer support for learning. The retreats can also mitigate impacts on psychological distress of social disconnection, assessment stress and work overload by providing a community setting to actively progress on work that will reduce academic overload and stress.

Students with ADHD

When considering students with ADHD, there are challenges for those with severe symptoms that can result in lower academic achievement as a result of impacting academic enablers such as study skills, motivation and engagement (Dou et al., 2022). Promoting the development of these enablers can support increased educational outcomes for students (Dou et al., 2022). Similarly, Kwon et al. (2018) found four key challenges associated with ADHD: issues with daily routine due to poor time management, academic struggles linked to procrastination and difficulty prioritising tasks, struggles with building and maintaining relationships, and ongoing worries that impact self-esteem. Kwon et al. (2018) also argue that part of the university experience should involve educating students on how to manage time effectively, along with strategies to express emotions and reduce worrying. The benefits of body doubling, but more specifically through structured retreats, can be seen to align with supporting these difficulties, including providing a strategy to develop study skills, especially time management, prioritisation and goal setting.

Research exploring neurodivergent students and wellbeing has found that performing arts students who are neurodivergent are especially vulnerable to lower wellbeing, with ADHD students having lower levels of educational self-efficacy and reporting a desire for more education-based support (Buckley et al., 2024). Again, this highlights that the use of writing retreats can help to develop levels of self-efficacy through goal setting and providing direct educational support.

Summary

Overall, the literature serves to justify the potential benefits of FWRs for students, particularly for those who are neurodivergent. The potential impacts of using writing retreats also aligns well with the challenges of leading a large programme that were explored at the start of this chapter, of creating a community, supporting increased outcomes and providing a sense of support for students, aligning with supporting the wellbeing of the students through the three areas of autonomy, competence and relatedness. The use of writing retreats also links to the student-specific wellbeing impacts, including developing a sense of belonging, providing teacher support, providing peer support for learning and developing motivation and intrinsic interest in studying, as well as mitigating social disconnection, work overload and assessment stress.

Focus/Writing Retreats

Following an exploration of the literature and based upon my lived experience, when I moved to implement the FWRs into the programme, I believed the retreats would build an inclusive learning community that would support students' sense of belonging to their cohort and more widely at the University. That they, as an individual, matter to staff and peers and that the retreats would give direct access to support, both from the programme team and peers. This would lead to improved wellbeing, as aligned with developing autonomy, competence and relatedness, as well as improved educational outcomes and increased satisfaction for those students involved.

Facilitation and Structure of Our FWRs

The FWRs are facilitated in person, on campus. In the first iteration, FWRs were run as a hybrid format, but students wanted to meet in person, so we moved to a solely on-campus format. Retreats are run for two hours, and I lead the retreat as the programme director. Students and staff set their own goals for the two-hour retreats, which could be starting an assignment plan or other academic work. I emphasise that students can use the space for anything they need to do, but we invite them to share their goal with the group at the beginning of the session. Students then work individually on their goal in two slots of focused time, each of 45 minutes. There is a ten-minute break in the middle of this where students are encouraged to take a break and get up and move around, but if they want to carry on through the break they can. This is also a good point to check in on how things are going for the student and remind them they can readjust their goals or make efforts to refocus for the second focus period if needed. At the end of the session, everyone is invited to feed back on the progress they have made towards their goal. There is a focus on encouragement for any successes, and a reminder that any progress, no matter how small, is still progress.

This structure works well for all participants but is particularly beneficial for neurodivergent students as it manages the time for the students, with the external pressure of others working at the same time. The time periods are enough for in-depth work, but not so long that students feel overwhelmed. The check-in and readjustment of goals also supports the participants to get back to their work if they have become unfocused.

There is also free lunch provided for the group, before or after the retreat, depending on the time of the day. The intention of this is for everyone to gather together to talk generally, socialise and enjoy some free food. This meal, and the time and space to socialise, is a key element of cohort building and developing meaningful relationships with peers and staff and provides further space to develop relatedness.

Key Considerations for Running Our FWRs

There are some ground rules that we implement in the retreats, and alongside this some key considerations for ensuring the retreats are inclusive and effective. Firstly, retreats are open to all students in the cohort; although we know they are particularly helpful for neurodivergent students, this doesn't mean they aren't also useful for neurotypical students. Having retreats open to all helps to create an inclusive environment, and as everyone is using the tool of the session, it can help neurodivergent people feel part of that community.

Secondly, the retreats aim to create a positive and productive atmosphere, and therefore I ask for quiet working during the focus periods to minimise distractions. If students want to discuss something, I suggest that they move out of the room into the corridor to discuss. Students tend to work quietly in the focus period and then use the break to have a short discussion. An important part of creating this atmosphere is to have staff working alongside students, modelling what is expected in the session and working on their own project during that time. The lunch element of the retreat is important, as it gives participants time to socialise and develop relationships.

Thirdly, the retreats need optionality to ensure that they are inclusive. I don't force the sharing of goals for the session but instead highlight that this supports accountability. However, if people prefer not to share, this is respected. I recommend the use of headphones or earplugs if participants have noise sensitivities. Individuals can take extra breaks if they need them. No one is heavily monitoring participation, so students can leave when they need to. This is particularly important to support their wellbeing through autonomy during the retreats.

Finally, the setting is also important. When these retreats started, they were both in-person and online, but the online attendance was very low, so the focus moved to in-person only. This was specific to our cohort of students, but this could be different for students from other demographics, for example, online-only students. The retreat format still works well online but having it either online or in-person seems to work better than a blended approach. For in-person retreats, it is important to consider the space itself, having a classroom format with larger tables for students to be able to set up and be comfortable has worked well.

Our Student Feedback

The implementation of these retreats is now partway through its second academic year. The feedback from students attending the retreats has been positive. To illustrate this, some of this feedback has been included here from the students who gave informed consent for this to be shared. The outcomes also align well with supporting to solve three areas of specific challenges faced with leading this cohort that were explored at the start of this chapter: creating a community, supporting increased outcomes through better productivity and providing a sense of support for students, which in turn align with supporting wellbeing through increased competence, autonomy and relatedness.

Creating a Learning Community

The students found that the retreats helped them to feel part of a learning community, with the time to socialise at lunch positively contributing to that experience as reflected in this statement from a participant, *'The lunch at the end was a great incentive, it gave me something to look forward to but also was nice to speak with people and actually get to know some people on my course a bit better!'*

Students also found the space itself to be enjoyable, motivating and encouraging, with time and space for both goal setting and reflection. Students felt the community provided positive peer pressure to support focus on their work, for example, *'Being surrounded by others working created a productive atmosphere, which made me match the focus of those around me and concentrate better.'*

Increasing Productivity

Students have specifically highlighted that in terms of productivity, they felt the FWRs supported them to make significant progress in their work or assignments, and they were more productive during the retreat compared to regular studying, supporting them to achieve their competence needs. One student said:

> The focus retreats have been revolutionary to maximising my productivity (...) Having a set schedule where we meet with likeminded people similarly determined to reach their work goals created a unique environment that is far superior to the usual study sessions I would have in the library or other on-campus study spaces (...) I usually got more done during those 90 minutes than I would if I had spent 3–4 hours independently in the library, or even 5–6 hrs of trying to study with friends.

Feedback such as this highlights the focused and conducive environment the FWRs are creating. There was not only a positive impact on productivity within the retreats, but the environment also supported participants in developing their skills in this area for autonomy outside of the retreats. Students shared the retreats '...*contributed to shaping my view of what it means to be productive*' and '*The focus retreats have been revolutionary to maximising my productivity.*'

The retreats are also particularly helpful for neurodivergent students, as a student with ADHD highlighted:

> With my ADHD I have trouble focusing on tasks, the retreat helped me focus on tasks by providing a new setting made for focus (…) the halfway 5–10 minute break to reevaluate goals helped me not to get too stuck on small details and look at the bigger picture, I tend to get distracted by small details when starting a project but being reminded to focus on overall progress and that readjusting goals is okay [and] helped keep attention to a more helpful place of overall goals.

Feeling Supported

The retreats also helped to make the students feel more supported by creating a community and knowing that other students were in the same position as them which helps to develop relatedness, with one sharing; '*it feels very supportive, especially when the same people tend to show up (…) It was nice (…) to feel less alone with any deadlines approaching.*' Another key element of support was that they matter to staff as individuals, with students highlighting that:

> …checking in with us individually and making sure we felt motivated and empowered to do our very best (…) Knowing that someone within your department is looking out for you and cares for you does a lot for students' academic performance.

This is particularly important, and also difficult in such a large programme, which was also acknowledged by one student:

> At such a big university, and considering the size of the business cohorts, it is easy to feel lost in the crowd. However, (…) events this year have helped improve my motivation, mental health and have made me feel more connected to the university. (…) creating a safe, inclusive atmosphere.

Students felt that this not only supported a sense of mattering but also improved their academic performance, for example, '*Knowing that someone within your department is looking out for you and cares for you does a lot for students' academic performance. You're no longer a number or a face in a packed lecture hall, you're an individual.*'

These outcomes help to demonstrate the impact and difference that events like FWRs can make for a student and their journey through university.

Overall Feedback

Overall, the outcomes of the FWRs align with supporting the wellbeing of the students, from giving them a supportive community to be a part of and directly providing them with further support from peers and staff linking to increased relatedness and increasing their outcomes positively, including developing skills aligned with productivity, supporting both autonomy and competence. These FWRs seemed to have a large positive impact and students showed this through the following feedback, *'I really needed the focus retreat more than I knew'* and *'I honestly cannot rave about this initiative enough, and I can only imagine how much other students would also benefit from it'*. One student also highlighted that they could be used more widely, saying, *'I would love to see more of these writing retreats in universities.'*

The Main Challenges and Our Solutions

Although the FWRs have been a success for the students who attend, there are some challenges with their implementation. The first and most challenging is attendance levels; up to 20 students attend a regular session, despite the whole cohort being invited via email. This brings questions about the best way to get the word out about the initiative and to highlight its value. Students who have never attended a retreat might think, like I previously did, that it wasn't for them. FWRs are not a solution for everyone, as some prefer to work in a solo environment, but without trying it I would argue it is difficult to know whether it is right for you. However, if many more students attend, this would be difficult to manage, requiring a larger room size and the need to introduce a booking system.

The range of students that attend also varies, with mostly final years, some second years, and a few first years. This aligns with the increasing importance of their grades across these years. However, first years could gain from the development of time management skills at an early stage in their degree. It can also be difficult to ensure that timings work for students, especially across such a large programme that covers both compulsory and a variety of optional modules across three years. Similarly, the timetabling of rooms can be difficult in a busy University. There is also the element of cost; currently timetabling of rooms doesn't directly cost for the retreats, but the free lunch can add up to a larger expense and students have highlighted this is a key benefit to them attending. This means there needs to be buy-in from those with the budgets and as part of that, this requires the ability to present the positive impact of the retreats.

Although there are a range of challenges, there are some ways in which these can be addressed. Firstly, getting more students to attend can be supported by inviting students personally, in lectures or other events when you see them, and snowballing through word of mouth. I suggest that if students find it helpful that they share this with their friends in the cohort. I also remind the students via email regularly that the retreats are on, as they aren't timetabled currently the students need to add this to their own schedules. Some form of event booking platform is something that could help with this. Although there are many struggles with timetabling, I try to timetable the retreats for when most of the cohort are available or at least not when the compulsory modules are timetabled. Finally, we highlight the benefits of the retreats, from the social element to increased productivity, using student testimonials in our advertising and highlighting the free lunch, as this is a key draw for many students.

Conclusion

The use of FWRs for a wider range of students than just those who are undertaking and writing research has value in many areas of improving the students' experience and also their wellbeing. The retreats align well to support neurodivergent students, as a form of body doubling, but the space needs to be inclusive and considerate of different needs. Within a large undergraduate programme, the outcomes of FWRs help to align with solving some of the key challenges as well as supporting wellbeing. FWRs support the development of a learning community for students, which gives space to develop relatedness and build relationships with peers and staff. FWRs also increase productivity, both during the retreats but also outside of retreats, helping to make students feel they are meeting their academic outcomes and increasing their competence, but also supporting development of skills for further autonomy. Although the format we use is rather specific, these types of retreats can be tailored to different student and course needs.

References

Baik, C., & Larcombe, W. (2023). Student wellbeing and students' experiences in higher education. In C. Baik, & E. R. Kahu. *Research handbook on the student experience in higher education* (Online ed.). Edward Elgar Publishing. https://doi.org/10.4337/9781802204193.00013

Barkley, R. A. (2022). Improving clinical diagnosis using the executive functioning—Self-regulation theory of ADHD. *The ADHD Report, 30*(1), 1–9. https://doi.org/10.1521/adhd.2022.30.1.1

Buckley, E., Sideropoulos, V., Pellicano, E., & Remington, A. (2024). Higher levels of neurodivergent traits associated with lower levels of self-efficacy and wellbeing for performing arts students. *Neurodiversity, 2*. https://doi.org/10.1177/27546330241245354

Cunningham, C. (2022). "It's exciting and rewarding!": Structured mini writing retreats as a tool for undergraduate researchers. *Journal of Further and Higher Education, 46*(10), 1421–1433. https://doi.org/10.1080/0309877X.2022.2085031

Dou, A., Oram, R., Rogers, M., & DuPaul, G. (2022). The effects of ADHD symptomatology and academic enabling behaviours on undergraduate academic achievement. *Psychology in the Schools, 59*, 574–588. https://doi.org/10.1002/pits.22632

Eagle, T., Baltaxe-Admony, L. B., & Ringland, K. E. (2023). Proposing body doubling as a continuum of space/time and mutuality: An investigation with neurodivergent participants. *Proceedings of the 25th international ACM SIGACCESS conference on computers and accessibility.* https://doi.org/10.1145/3597638.3614486

Eardley, A. F., Banister, E., & Fletcher, M. (2021). Can academic writing retreats function as wellbeing interventions? *Journal of Further and Higher Education*, *45*(2), 183–196. https://doi.org/10.1080/0309877X.2020.1744542

Kornhaber, R., Cross, M., Betihavas, V., & Bridgman, H. (2016). The benefits and challenges of academic writing retreats: An integrative review. *Higher Education Research & Development*, *35*(6), 1210–1227. https://doi.org/10.1080/07294360.2016.1144572

Kwon, S. J., Kim, Y., & Kwak, Y. (2018). Difficulties faced by university students with self-reported symptoms of attention-deficit hyperactivity disorder: A qualitative study. *Child and Adolescent Psychiatry and Mental Health*, *12*(12). https://doi.org/10.1186/s13034-018-0218-3

Murray, R., & Newton, M. (2009). Writing retreat as structured intervention: Margin or mainstream? *Higher Education Research & Development*, *28*(5), 541–553. https://doi.org/10.1080/07294360903154126

Ryan, R., & Deci, E. (2001). On happiness and human potentials: A review of research on hedonic and eudaimonic well-being. *Annual Review of Psychology*, *52*, 141–166.

Tremblay-Wragg, E., Mathieu Chartier, S., Labonté-Lemoyne, E., Déri, C., & Gadbois, M. E. (2021). Writing more, better, together: How writing retreats support graduate students through their journey. *Journal of Further and Higher Education*, *45*(1), 95–106. https://doi.org/10.1080/0309877X.2020.1736272

Vincent, C., Tremblay-Wragg, É., Déri, C., Plante, I., & Mathieu Chartier, S. (2023). How writing retreats represent an ideal opportunity to enhance PhD candidates' writing self-efficacy and self-regulation. *Teaching in Higher Education*, *28*(7), 1600–1619. https://doi.org/10.1080/13562517.2021.1918661

Section 4

Innovative Approaches to SUAW for Wellbeing

12 Writing Together Online
A History of Online SUAW in the Southern Hemisphere

Katherine Firth

Image 12.1 My hand, my laptop, my cat.

Visual Narrative

Since 2012, I have taken dozens of similar photographs of my laptop, plus sometimes a pile of books and papers, sometimes my cat Jelly, often a cup of coffee or tea. Multiple campuses, houses, desks, and libraries turn up in the background of these photos. I used this picture to illustrate the second of my blog posts about how to run Shut Up & Write! online (Firth, 2017). It is unusual because a part of my body appears in the picture, and I wanted to place my body into this history alongside my technology and environment.

Introduction

Many online Shut Up & Write! (SUAW) programs arose as a response to the COVID pandemic lockdowns of the early 2020s, but this chapter tells a story that starts significantly earlier than that and continues to the present day. I was part of some of those stories, and in this chapter I collate eyewitness accounts, blog posts, and published articles to piece together some of the stories of Shut Up & Write! online in the southern hemisphere, from mine and others' experiences.

I live in Naarm (Melbourne) in Australia, which has been a southern SUAW epicentre. I have set up, led, and participated in SUAWs as an Academic Skills professional staff member, a freelance researcher, a researcher developer in an academic role, and a manager of academic programs. It's been strange and joyful to reconnect with people I haven't talked to in a decade, and to reach out to new people, to piece together this chapter, telling a story spanning the southern half of the globe.

This chapter firmly locates itself in the southern hemisphere and draws connections laterally (sideways) rather than longitudinally (linking to the north) (see further Connell, 2007). To date, Shut Up & Write!, along with similar peer writing groups, has been a site of academic activity in the southern hemisphere for a decade and a half. Researchers in Australia, Aotearoa (New Zealand), southern Africa, and South America identify their groups as a wellbeing response to isolation and stress in the writing process (e.g. Jeyaraj, 2018 writing from Malaysia); to provide transformative spaces for researchers to develop their writing identity (e.g. Chihota and Thesen, 2014; Oluwole et al., 2018; Wilmot & McKenna, 2018 writing from South Africa); or to create positive perceptions among writers (e.g. Manzano-Nunez et al., 2020 writing from Colombia).

Shut Up & Write! originated in North America, and the experience of creating and belonging to similar writing groups has been well documented across the northern hemisphere (Driscoll et al., 2023). Where southern hemisphere researchers have published about their writing groups, it has typically focused on a single country or university, or in collaboration with northern hemisphere colleagues (e.g. Aitchison & Guerin, 2014). By focusing solely on southern Shut Up & Write! programs, we can see trends emerging of how they show evidence of community, word-of-mouth, pragmatism, and contingency. Online SUAW programs in the south are typically a response to a problem or unmet need and show how digital tools are used creatively to build and sustain communities of writing.

A History of Online SUAW in the South

In Anglophone settler colonies like Australia, New Zealand, and South Africa, metropolitan cities are often spread out and many hours distant from each other. It is common for staff and students at all levels to continue to live in their family home and commute to campus. In 'regional' (often remote and sparsely populated) areas, small towns are surrounded by a vast penumbra of bush, small hamlets, and farms, requiring many hours of driving to get into the office. Capital cities are over an hour's flight from each other, added to the already many hours of flying required to visit Anglophone colleagues in Asia, let alone in Europe and North America. For this reason, almost as soon as Australians learned about Shut Up & Write!, we were working out ways to put it online.

In 2011, nearly 4 years after the first SUAW started in the northern hemisphere, a group of researchers at RMIT University in Melbourne Australia started meeting face-to-face (Mewburn et al., 2014, Mewburn et al., 2018). They talked about their experiences at the QPR conference in Adelaide (700 km away) in early 2012, which is how it found its way back to us at the University of Melbourne, even though we were only 1 km up the road. In mid-2012, Peta Freestone, Liam Connell, and I launched our first face-to-face SUAW directly after the first ever Thesis Boot Camp (Firth et al., 2020).

Very quickly, participants asked if there could be an online version, and so, a few months later, I created a Twitter SUAW that ran twice a week on Wednesdays. Because Peta and I were both professional staff, our managers were only comfortable for us to regularly have an hour for our writing, which is why the #shutupandwrite @AcadSkillsMelb on Twitter was only ever two Pomodoros, as opposed to the usual four (Firth, 2013).

Synchronous online options were already just becoming possible, with regional and multi-campus universities using 'web conferencing tools' to come together to write (Kozar & Lum, 2013). For example, Cassily Charles was using Adobe Connect in 'later 2012 or 2013' to run Shut Up & Write! online four times a week across a widely spread-out New South Wales university covering about 400,000 square kilometres (personal communication, 21 January 2025). As she explained on the Doctoral Writing blog in 2015:

> Metropolitan/single campus universities may have less need, but regional and multi-campus universities in Australia tend to find working together online a pretty normal way of doing business – because we have no alternative. At Charles Sturt University more than half our research candidates are off-campus, compared to less than 10% at most metropolitan universities. We also have more than a dozen campuses (depending on how you count them). Some of these are relatively small, so even if research candidates are officially 'on-campus', they may still be far away from peers and people like me whose job it is to help them develop their academic writing.

In October 2013, Siobhan O'Dwyer was an academic in Brisbane (1,800 km up the coast). She tells her story of setting up Shut Up & Write! Tuesdays (SUWT, O'Dwyer, n.d.) this way:

> Siobhan O'Dwyer was part of a Shut Up & Write group that met monthly in Brisbane, Australia. On the way to one of these monthly writing sessions, Siobhan was chatting, via text message, with Sharon McDonough, an academic based in another state of Australia. Sharon was also keen to write, so they agreed that Siobhan would send an SMS at the start and end of each writing block. In this way, Sharon became a 'virtual' participant in the 'real world' Shut Up & Write.
> (O'Dwyer et al., 2017, p. 252)

Soon, this SMS became a public text message via Twitter. 'Spontaneous' sessions were also being run occasionally by Jason Downs (then at RMIT) under the hashtag #suaw on Twitter by 2013 (Firth, 2013).

In 2016, Tseen Khoo (then at La Trobe in Victoria) set up their first All Campus SUAW, using video conferencing technology to link rooms from each regional campus, with local SUAW groups meeting both face to face and online.

In 2017, on the other side of the continent, Katrina McChesney was getting to the end of her PhD at Curtin University (in Perth, 4,300 km from Brisbane). As a parent, she wrote about her experience of the *Virtual Shut Up and Write – Parents' Edition Facebook Group* (McChesney, 2017) as a completely asynchronous support network.

And then in 2020, the pandemic hit. Immediately, cities all over the globe entered various kinds of 'lockdowns' and work-from-home orders. It was inadvisable, or often illegal, to gather on campuses or in cafés and write together.

The uptake of video software over the previous 8 years had been highly differentiated. Regional universities like La Trobe and Charles Sturt had been using Skype, Zoom, and Adobe Connect to provide synchronous online teaching for years. And yet, for many researchers in metropolitan universities, the idea of video SUAW was so new we had to explain how to set up a video meeting (e.g. Firth et al., 2020).

By the end of March 2020, a group of us Twitter old hands had gathered a global survey of how people were doing 'Virtual Shut Up and Write, Now with Added Video' (Firth et al., 2020). This brain trust, which included Tseen Khoo, Debbie Kinsey, Hannah James, Inger Mewburn, Siobhan O'Dwyer, Victoria Firth-Smith, Justin Canty, and Elizabeth Morgan, showed that early in the pandemic, online SUAW showed a lot of creative experimentation. We heard about people trying to meet together on multi-directional platforms like Zoom, Skype, MSTeams, WhatsApp, and Instagram Live, as well as uni-directional platforms like YouTube and Twitch.

However, the most common version used online meeting software, as Tseen Khoo (then at La Trobe) explained:

> We all meet on Zoom. We have a nominated host for the session, and they are the timekeeper for the 25-min pomodoros. When a pomodoro is on, everyone's muted but video on. The host comes back when time's up. Everyone can unmute and chat.
>
> We have short intros from everyone at the beginning – name, dept, what they're working on. We also use the chat screen for other side conversations and any issues that people might be having with the session.
>
> (Firth et al., 2020)

This was the model used across the southern hemisphere. For example, in Ecuador, Elisabeth Rodas (2022) worked with a research team coordinator at her university to transition the long-standing in-person writing groups online in response to the COVID-19 pandemic; she wrote: "the main change consisted of incorporating Zoom-based synchronous virtual conferences to replace the in-person meetings previously held at the university's writing center" (p.169).

Meanwhile, in South Africa, SUAW had been running since 2014 at the University of Cape Town, when Associate Professor Carolyn McKinney set up a Shut Up & Write!/Thula Ubhale (McKinney, n.d.) in the School of Education, influenced by the *Thesis Whisperer*, Inger Mewburn's blog (Mewburn, n.d.). In 2020, in response to the repeated lockdowns, the central Office for Postgraduate Studies and Researcher Development set up online Shut Up & Write! sessions, initially on Zoom and later on Teams (as the university shifted its standard remote platform) (P. Meissner, personal communication, 28 January 2025). Dumisa Dlodlo and later Amanda Bessick as senior officer in the department set the sessions up, when the office was managed by Professor Peter Meissner.

Lockdown mandates were lifted unevenly across the southern hemisphere, and back-to-campus moves are still showing significant variation across the sector in 2025. Part-time researchers, disabled researchers, regional and remote researchers, and carers continue to have differential access to safe or easy face-to-face contexts. Researching 'at a distance' is experienced by choice as well as imposed by external factors (Burford & Hook, 2019; McChesney et al., 2024).

As I write this chapter, there continues to be a mixture of online-only, hybrid, and face-to-face SUAW across universities in the south. For example, the Graduate Student Association at Melbourne (who inherited the Shut Up & Write! I helped to found) meets both online and face to face. At the University of Cape Town, Just Write/Thula Ubhale meets face to face (and with a new English name as not everyone likes being told to 'Shut Up', although the isiXhosa name remains 'be silent, write'), but online options remain from the central office for researchers living outside Cape Town. In one city in Aotearoa/New Zealand, The University of Aukland SUAW is hybrid, while at Aukland University of Technology, it is online. La Trobe university currently only meets online.

How to Shut Up and Write Online

Shut Up & Write! works online, and it works for a diverse group of people. For people who live and work in places that make it inconvenient to get to campus, people who have caring responsibilities for themselves and others, as well as the many people whose writing days happen at home, SUAW online gives them the best of both worlds.

I found lots of different ways people use 'online' to run SUAW.

Many early versions of online SUAW used scheduled text-based social media prompts. For example, I wrote in 2013,

> I run a virtual Shut Up and Write session twice a week (both on Wednesdays) on Twitter. As I say in under 140 characters: "#shutupandwrite is 2 times 25min writing sprints with a 10min break between them. We do it in a group, for motivation and accountability".
>
> (Firth, 2013)

This reflected a moment in time when Twitter was the academic town square, and when messages were limited to 140 characters. (The timeline was real-time not algorithmic until 2016, character limits were expanded in 2017, the platform was renamed X in 2023, and the online academic town square is still in flux as I write this in 2025). I used a scheduling program to pre-prepare the prompts and send them out at the correct times, including information about what we were doing, prompts for getting set up, starting to write, stopping writing, a fun thing to do in the break, and encouragement. Each session was slightly different, so the words, tone, and energy were fresh, topical, and human each time.

Just as important is what to do in the breaks. I spent a lot of time thinking about the 5-minute break activity—perhaps linking an upbeat song to listen to, a soothing video to watch, or a fun quick offline activity to promote like going outside and looking at a tree. Sometimes people engaged in real time, and at other times they merely appreciated the sense other people were also out there on the web trying to write.

#SUAWTues took a similar approach:

> SUWT began with one Twitter account (@SUWTues), a hashtag (#suwtues) and a basic Wordpress website. Sessions were held on the first and third Tuesday of each month, at 10am Australian Eastern Standard Time, with the Pomodoro method used to guide the session (2 x 25-minute blocks of writing, with a 5 minute break in between; Cirillo, 2015). Participants were encouraged to tweet their writing task (e.g. journal article, thesis chapter) at the start of the session and tweet their progress at the end, with Siobhan and other participants providing personalised feedback and encouragement. Sharon and Michelle Redman-MacLaren participated in the sessions and also served as guest hosts when Siobhan was unavailable.
>
> (O'Dwyer et al., 2017, p. 252)

Connectedness without necessarily strict synchronicity was an important element across these early online SUAW platforms. For example, Kristina McChensney writes about her experience of the *Virtual Shut Up and Write – Parents' Edition Facebook group* (2017) about the benefits of impromptu Facebook group solidarity,

> There are no fixed schedules, start times, obligations or expectations here. Instead, it's a place where someone is always online no matter where you are in the world. Even if it's the middle of the night (not an

uncommon time for members of *Virtual SUAW – Parents' Edition* to be writing), you'll find company, encouragement and moral support almost immediately.

Usually we end up with one or two threads each day where those who are working share informal updates. People pop in and out throughout the day and there is no need to apologise for the realities of PhD parenting.

If the Twitter online Shut Up & Write! programs took the real-time Pomodoro/breaks elements from 'classic f2f SUAW', then Facebook groups took the accountability elements—stating your writing intentions and reporting back (and celebrating) your writing goals (McChesney, 2017). As McChesney (2017) quotes from the group:

"I'm here! I want to write 1000 words today."
"Five graphs done; now doing another five with the same dataset"
"Happy to have company".

The switch to video SUAW, using multi-directional meeting platforms (like Zoom) and uni-directional platforms like Twitch, brought about a new phase in the way online SUAW functioned. Online meetings are synchronous, and they do not exist beyond their allotted time. Unlike the extreme flexibility of parents in the SUAW Facebook group—logging on at 5 am, 1 am, and public holidays—online meetings require attendance at the same time as each other. This does not mean that they are tied to business hours however, as Michael Healey explains in his blog post about the regular meetings he attended since 2018, both on Saturdays with Melbourne Write Up and in the evenings with a group of colleagues on Tuesday Night Write (7–9.30 pm) (Healey, 2024). Like Cassily Charles' sessions across regional campuses, Healey was based in Toowoomba (almost two hours' drive from the closest major city) and collaborating with regional Australian colleagues.

At the University of Cape Town, synchronous online meetings were used to try to bring cohorts together during the pandemic. Peter Meissner told me, 'students were encouraged to choose which weekly sessions suited them and attend regularly' (personal communication, 27 January 2025), and some did, while others dropped in and out. Peter Meissner explained how they did it:

Facilitators were senior Postgrad students whose role it was to:
- Prepare the rules for engagement to be posted in the chat before the session starts;
- Open the platform used 10 minutes before the session starts;
- Ensure that the session is recorded;
- Be in possession of the register and check that those registering sign in at the beginning and end of the session – on the chat;

- Divide students up as they request – by faculty, department or theme, – into breakaway rooms;
- Encourage videos and sound on for introductions, to keep the space human and engaged at the start; advise microphones off for silence to facilitate writing, but check cameras left on (unless bandwidth is an issue);
- Set a personal timer of 30 minutes (or an agreed time limit) and facilitate students setting goals for either/or/and the entire session or segments of time;
- Check at 30 minutes in each breakaway room, for microphones to be switched on, to hear the progress on the goals and to encourage students who are struggling to write (training is given for this);
- Ensure that each student signs off in the chat, and elicit some comments on how helpful the session was;
- Debrief the OPGS (my office at the time) on challenges and improvement suggestions. (Personal communication, 27 January 2025)

More recently, the online MoRA Academic Writing Club was set up to support students from three different universities across disparate Indonesian provinces to support master's students who need to publish as part of their degree by Dewi Wahyu Mustikasari, Maslathif Dwi Purnomo, and Anugrah Imani (see Chapter 8).

By contrast, at La Trobe it was decided to leave the online SUAW writing room open 24/7 once the security on Zoom had improved enough that it would be safe to do so. That meant that La Trobe's online SUAW functioned for the next 5 years more like the earlier versions, where strict synchronicity is less important than a general sense of there being other people writing out there. Researchers reflected that this constituted both one of the best things about online SUAW, as Corina Modderman reflected in 2020 "Why I love SUAW online: 1. Because it is so flexible, you can come and go when you want"; and a major challenge, as Lauren Lawson reflected in the same blog post, "I find myself more easily distracted because there is less accountability" (Fyffe and SUAW Participants, 2020).

Writing together, and making our writing process public, has been demonstrated to have multiple wellbeing effects (for example Cannell et al., 2023; Firth, 2023; Le Goix et al., 2022; McPherson & Lemon, 2021; Vincent et al., 2023). Shut Up & Write! in particular has the benefit of requiring breaks every 25 minutes, combating loneliness and isolation by bringing people together to write, and making other people's writing processes visible (Firth, 2013). Not all forms of SUAW in the southern hemisphere included explicit accountability on writing progress. For example, when we set up our chapter at Melbourne, we didn't have time to go around the table and state our writing goal for the day, but we often talked about it in the breaks anyway. Writing publicly online has similar benefits to writing together in person, but the capacity to include more dispersed physical spaces enables more diverse forms of individual embodiment in place for researchers. As Bayne et al. have argued, "online can be the privileged mode. Distance is a positive principle, not a deficit" (2020, p.139).

Writing together online offers multiple affordances for comfort and ease. At La Trobe, my colleague Meagan Tyler told me, a recent experiment to run a special face-to-face SUAW for Academic Writing Month ended early because researchers realized that typing on a laptop in a generic classroom is less comfortable than working in an ergonomic chair and with the big screens in their campus office. A new online Shut Up & Write! is being proposed by Gabra Biik Indigenous Post-graduate Engagement Project Officer Samantha Gilmour, specifically for First Nations researchers, also at La Trobe. She reflected to me that out of the dozen or so researchers in her target cohort, most lived in regional and remote areas, or out of the state, so online was the only way to bring them together. At the same time, she wanted to build a SUAW specifically for First Nations researchers to enable peer connections across fields, in a community space of 'familiarity, safety, ease' instead of 'sitting in isolation' (personal communication, 28 January, 2025). This sense of cultural safety is as important as the ease of connection across distance or physical comfort.

Still, online writing productivity is not without its problematics. Online writing, making writing visible, can fold our communities of writing into structures of surveillance (Bayne et al., 2020); and supporting writers to write regardless of external factors can feed into cultures of toxic productivity in a university system where writing is metricised. In their advice to get away from the computer and do things other than research and writing, Siobhan and Sharon, the founders of #SUAWTues, wrote together in a later article with Sarah Pinto:

Wind wool around needles
Survive a spin class
Go to the movies in the middle of the day
Exist.

Write a list of self-care activities
Publish it in a good journal
Encourage your colleagues to reflect on their own self-care
Resist.

(O'Dwyer et al., 2018, p. 248)

Online SUAW is not a silver bullet for SUAW inclusion. In places with limited, expensive or unreliable internet bandwidth (including regional Africa and Australia), synchronous writing groups are not accessible. Online SUAW often struggles to provide the multisensory experience of being surrounded by others writing, such as the clatter of keys in a face-to-face group—typically the sound and often also the video is turned off during online writing sprints, removing the visual, auditory, and proprioceptive cues that other people are writing, that writing is now the norm. There are no snacks or cups of coffee to reward you in the breaks, unless you provide your own!

Like all online learning, online SUAW requires greater self-regulated learning capacity (Wong et al., 2018). It is easy to not write when no one is watching. Research writers often find that a significant challenge is to force themselves to make time to write, not undertake other tasks in that time, and make progress on their writing projects. Online writing spaces can only partially mitigate such writing challenges.

Conclusion

Online SUAW has been a persistent part of the writing-together ecosystem in the southern hemisphere since the early 2010s. While almost every face-to-face SUAW drew its influence from the northern hemisphere (most often via the RMIT group), the online SUAW models typically responded to pragmatic challenges like geographic distance, caring responsibilities, and time constraints and drew inspiration from each other. With the global emergency response to the COVID pandemic, even more SUAW went online, and it has stayed that way in many parts of the southern hemisphere.

As I write this in 2025, 'online Shut Up and Write' firmly means synchronous, video meetings; however, this short history demonstrates that this was not always the case. As the kinds of social connections made possible via technology develop and transform, what it means to write together online will also continue to change and grow. Regional and remote communities in the southern hemisphere will continue to be engines of innovation, reaching out to one another and to our northern hemisphere colleagues. This chapter also traces outlines of friendship, co-authorship, and diaspora, as researchers move between institutions and countries and migrate across software systems and social media platforms. It also traces new collegialities, for example the University of Cape Town colleagues who replied to me cold-emailing them and contribute so fully to the story of SUAW in the south.

Making writing public and communal and visible is embodied, it's messy, it's contingent on external factors, it has feelings involved, and still, it gets done. SUAW is here to stay, online and offline, viral, partial, hybrid. The academic networks of the southern hemisphere are widely separated by less-populated oceans and interiors from one another, and from our northern hemisphere colleagues. Again and again, we demonstrate that pragmatic, inclusive, and social interaction makes space for the experience of writing, and of writing together in communities of support, online across the world wide web.

References

Aitchison, C. & Guerin, C. (Eds). (2014). *Writing groups for doctoral education and beyond: Innovations in practice and theory*. Routledge.

Bayne, S., Evans, P., Ewins, R., Knox, J., & Lamb, J. (2020). *The manifesto for teaching online*. MIT Press.

Burford, J., & Hook, G. (2019). Curating care-full spaces: Doctoral students negotiating study from home. *Higher Education Research & Development*, *38*(7), 1343–1355. https://doi.org/10.1080/07294360.2019.1657805

Cannell, C., Silvia, A., McLachlan, K., Othman, S., Morphett, A., Maheepala, V., McCosh, C., Simic, N., & Behrend, M. B. (2023). Developing research-writer identity and wellbeing in a doctoral writing group. *Journal of Further and Higher Education*, *47*(8), 1106–1123. https://doi.org/10.1080/0309877X.2023.2217411

Charles, C. (2015). All in the room together: Doing things with writing in real-time, online with web conferencing. *Doctoral Writing*. https://doctoralwriting.wordpress.com/2015/09/10/all-in-the-room-together-doing-things-with-writing-in-real-time-online-with-web-conferencing/

Chihota, C., & Thesen, L. (2014). Rehearsing 'the postgraduate condition' in writers' circles. In L. Thesen & L. Cooper (Eds.), *Risk in academic writing: Postgraduate students, their teachers and the making of knowledge* (pp. 131–147). Taylor & Francis.

Connell, R. (2007). *Southern theory: The global dynamics of knowledge in social science*. Allen & Unwin.

Driscoll, D. L., McDevitt, T., & Kerry-Moran, K. J. (2023). Writing Groups: Three Models of Practice to Support Academic Authors. In M. R. Jalongo, O. N. Saracho (Eds.), *Scholarly Writing: Publishing Manuscripts That Are Read, Downloaded, and Cited* (pp. 189–212). Springer.

Firth, K. (2013, May 7). Generative Writing and Shut Up and Write. *Research Degree Insiders*. https://researchinsiders.blog/2013/05/07/generative_writing/

Firth, K. (2017, June 14). Generative Writing and Shut Up and Write: Second Edition. *Research Degree Insiders*. https://researchinsiders.blog/2017/06/14/generative-writing-and-shutupandwrite-second-edition/

Firth, K. (2023). *Writing Well and Being Well for Your PhD and Beyond: How to Cultivate a Strong and Sustainable Writing Practice for Life*. Routledge.

Firth, K., Connell, L., & Freestone, P. (2020). *Your PhD survival guide: Planning, writing, and succeeding in your final year*. Routledge.

Firth, K., Khoo, T., Kinsey, D., & James, H. (2020, March 29). 'Virtual shut up and write: Now with added video. *Research Degree Insiders*. https://researchinsiders.blog/2020/03/29/virtual-shut-up-and-write-now-with-added-video/

Fyffe, J., & SUAW Participants. (2020). Virtual Shut Up and Write: Zooming in with the cheer squad. *RED Alert Blog*. http://redalert.blogs.latrobe.edu.au/2020/05/virtual-shut-up-and-write-zooming-in.html

Healey, M. (2024). *Tuesday Night Write*. https://mojohealy.com/post/tuesday_night_write/

Jeyaraj, J. J. (2018). It's a jungle out there: Challenges postgraduate research writing. *GEMA Online Journal of Language Studies*, *18*(1), 22–37.

Kozar, O., & Lum, J. (2013). Factors likely to impact the effectiveness of research writing groups for off-campus doctoral students. *Journal of Academic Language and Learning*, *7*(2), A132–A149.

Le Goix, R., Houssay-Holzschuch, M., & Noûs, C. (2022). Multiple binds and forbidden pleasures: Writing as poaching at French universities. *Environment and Planning A: Economy and Space*, *54*(7), 1475–1485.

Manzano-Nunez, R., Ariza, F., & Rengifo, J.E. (2020). A scoping review of peer support writing groups in academic medicine as a valuable tool for physician-scientists in the publish or perish era. *Medical Science Education*, *30*, 1313–1319.

McChesney, K. (2017, November 13). Survival and solidarity: Virtual shut up and write, parents' edition' *Doctoral Writing*. https://doctoralwriting.wordpress.com/2017/11/13/survival-and-solidarity-virtual-shut-up-and-write-parents-edition/

McChesney, K., Burford, J., Frick, L., & Khoo, T. (2024). *Doing doctoral research at a distance: Flourishing in off-campus, hybrid, and remote pathways*. Taylor & Francis.

McKinney, C. (n.d.). *ThulaUbhala*. https://thulawrite.wordpress.com/about/

McPherson, M., & Lemon, N. (2021). Table chats: Research relations and the impact on our wellbeing as academics. In N. Lemon (Ed.), *Healthy Relationships in Higher Education* (pp. 132–142). Routledge

Mewburn, I. (n.d.). *The Thesis Whisperer*. https://thesiswhisperer.com/

Mewburn, I., Firth, K., & Lehmann, S. (2018). *How to fix your academic writing trouble: A practical guide*. McGraw-Hill Education.

Mewburn, I., Osborne, L., & Caldwell, G. (2014). Shut up & write!: Some surprising uses of cafés and crowds in doctoral writing. In C. Aitchison & C. Guerin (Eds.), *Writing groups for doctoral education and beyond* (pp. 218–232). Routledge.

O'Dwyer, S. (n.d.). *Shut Up and Write Tuesdays*. https://suwtuesdays.wordpress.com/about-2/

O'Dwyer, S., Pinto, S., & McDonough, S. (2018). Self-care for academics: A poetic invitation to reflect and resist. *Reflective Practice, 19*(2), 243–249.

O'Dwyer, S. T., McDonough, S. L., Jefferson, R., Goff, J. A., & Redman-MacLaren, M. (2017). Writing groups in the digital age: A case study analysis of shut up & write Tuesdays. In A. Esposito (Ed.), *Research 2.0 and the impact of digital technologies on scholarly inquiry* (pp. 249–269). IGI Global Scientific Publishing.

Oluwole, D. O., Achadu, O., Asfour, F., Chakona, G., Mason, P., Mataruse, P., & McKenna, S. (2018). Postgraduate writing groups as spaces of agency development. *South African Journal of Higher Education, 32*(6), 370–381.

Rodas, E. L. (2022). Sustaining writing-for-publication practices during Covid-19: Online writing groups at an Ecuadorian university. In J. Fenton, J. Gimenez, K. Mansfield, M. Percy, & M. Spinillo (Eds.), *International perspectives on teaching and learning academic English in turbulent times* (pp. 167–177). Routledge.

Vincent, C., Tremblay-Wragg, É., Déri, C. E., & Mathieu-Chartier, S. (2023). A multi-phase mixed-method study defining dissertation writing enjoyment and comparing PhD students writing in the company of others to those writing alone. *Higher Education Research & Development, 42*(4), 1016–1031.

Wilmot, K., & McKenna, S. (2018). Writing groups as transformative spaces. *Higher Education Research & Development, 37*(4), 868–882.

Wong, J., Baars, M., Davis, D., Van Der Zee, T., Houben, G. J., & Paas, F. (2018). Supporting self-regulated learning in online learning environments and MOOCs: A systematic review. *International Journal of Human Computer Interaction, 35*(4–5), 356–373. https://doi.org/10.1080/10447318.2018.1543084

13 Writing 'Alone Together' in a Nourishing and Supportive Online Environment

Andi Salamon, Natalie Thompson, and Belinda Downey

Prologue

Visual Narrative

This visual narrative (Image 13.1) illuminates the actual and abstract Story of this chapter. In it you can see Belinda and Andi writing alone together online. In two different geographic locations, they share a timer and safe psychological space. In the background are mixed traces of elements that make up teaching and research-focused academic jobs. At left is a partial view of Andi's teaching-related documents with file names such "… education 2023 workshop" and "… Student feedback – mid semester". Peeking out from the desktop is a partial view into Andi's research about infant communication, and, if you look closely, traces of a personal life (her son's Minecraft Education program) and past professional life (a snip of a COVID travel meme from a visiting scholar visit at the end of the pandemic). These are individual and shared stories of teachers and researchers with personal and professional lives, coming together and "learning how to go on" (Kemmis et al., 2017) in academic practices.

Introduction

> The one thing all Australians, or people living in Australia, have in common is that they walk in Aboriginal Countrys every day. Countrys that, when respected, seen and read appropriately, when listened to and heard, when felt, teach us about our interconnectedness to everything around us.
>
> Blair & Collins-Gearing (2017, p. 63)

Indigenous ways of being and knowing are often at odds with Western, neoliberal academia. The frenzy to move through its hierarchical stages of positional leadership and associated power enables some and constrains others. Habibis et al. (2019) discuss this concept as "dollar dreaming", linking it to a hegemonic Western drive for competitiveness and individualism. Finding others who share qualities of professional respect, responsiveness, and reciprocity, outlined in Blair and Collins-Gearing's (2017) reflection of relationships with

DOI: 10.4324/9781003633334-17

160 *Cultivating Wellbeing and Community through Writing in Academia*

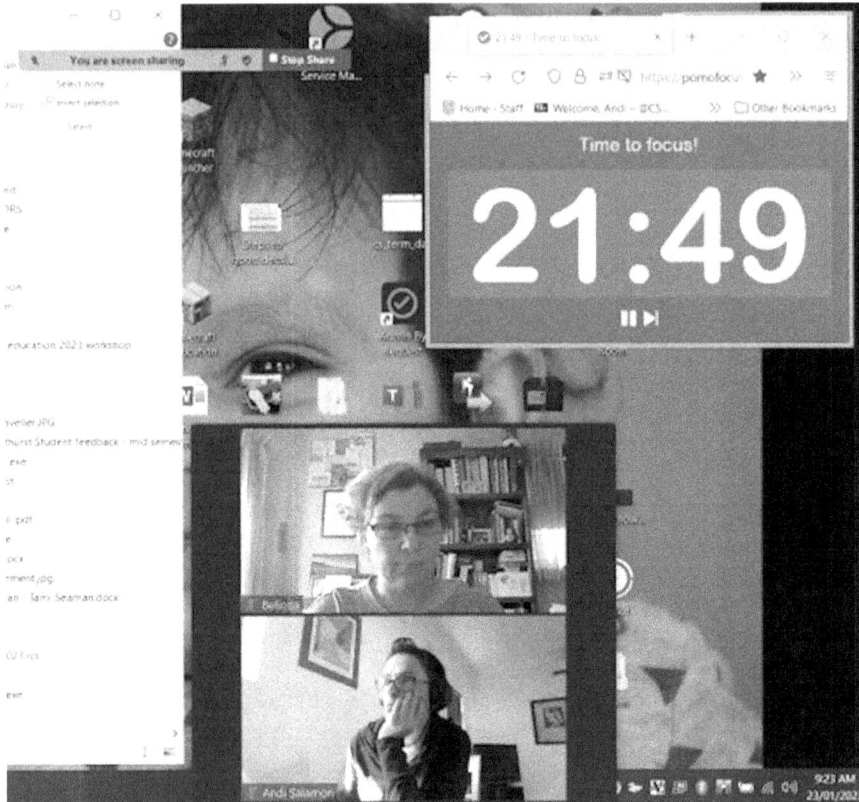

Image 13.1 Foreground (writing "alone together" online) and background (teaching, research, life).

Countrys, can be a saving grace for those constrained by Western academic norms. The practical 'doing' of academia adds its own unique challenges, especially when what needs to be done is to think, read, and write. For many teachers entering academia as professionally active and conceptually interactive practitioners, finding ways to maintain respectful and authentic interconnections with others helps create the collaborative environments in which they thrive. This chapter tells the story of such a nourishing and supportive online environment where three academics at various stages of their careers were able to write 'alone together' during Academic Writing Fortnight (AcWriFo).

We must start by acknowledging that none of us have Aboriginal or Torres Strait Islander heritage. We respectfully draw on personal and professional connections with the notion and practice of 'Storying', which is different to Blair and Collins-Gearing's (2017) definition of Storying as embodying "Indigenous Story telling from an Indigenous context and centre" (p.64). Andi (living on Gundungurra and Darug Country) first learned about Storying as a young academic during early morning yarning with Indigenous elder (and first author of the chapter on which we draw) and mentor, Professor Nerida Blair. With permission, Andi shared her own learning about 'Acknowledgement of Country as Storying' on the first slide of every presentation since listening to and hearing Professor Blair do the same eight years ago. In doing so, Andi helped Nat (living on Wiradjuri Country) learn about Acknowledgement of Country as Storying, through listening to and hearing Andi and seeing her slides. The slides had developed to include a screenshot of Blair and Collins-Gearing's (2017) abstract and the intention of their chapter to "Story the power of reflective practice" (p.63). Reflection was framed as an ancient wisdom enhancing connectedness and relatedness to "*new old knowledge*" (Blair & Collins-Gearing, 2017, p. 64), piquing Nat's interest as a deeply reflective practitioner and pedagogue. Belinda (also living on Wiradjuri Country) learned about Storying in the co-creation of this chapter.

In the spirit of Storying as acknowledging the stories of the people whose lands you are on, sharing your own story, and moving forward together in a new shared story (Blair, 2017), Storying connected our past, brought it into the present, and is taking us into a shared future. Like Blair and Collins-Gearing (2017), in this chapter we Story our individual and collective experience as both a framework and methodological approach to answer the question of how AcWriFo shaped our wellbeing. To do so we outline the context of our shared Story, each at different stages of our academic careers, with different roles, and on different campuses, but connected by a deep and committed relationship with pedagogy within a School of Education. We then share our individual Storys, with a sense of a "slowly emerging awareness" (Blair & Collins-Gearing, 2017, p.64) of how AcWriFo mattered in important ways. We outline AcWriFo's main goal as an inclusive and collective experience of achieving alone together, instead of a competitive, individualistic neoliberal endeavour, and reflect on the unexpected outcomes of fostering wellbeing through our collective practices. We conclude with implications for practice of applying the same sensibility of maintaining humanity in the 'mess' of a neoliberal academy, and the constraints of our academic lives as they become entangled with our pedagogical and scholarly integrity, and personal wellness.

The (Bigger) Story of AcWriFo

The job of an academic requires skills in teaching, conducting research, and writing at a high standard to publish and secure grants, which are necessary for academic career advancement. Individual writing attitudes (self-efficacy) and strategies (self-regulation) are essential for strengthening and refining these skills. In a recent review on academic wellbeing in teacher education (2023), Turner and Garvis highlight the intensifying stressors, identifying workload intensification and policy-driven reforms as eroding autonomy and wellbeing that, in turn, erase opportunities for developing positive dispositions and strategies for writing. One evidenced-based way these skills and dispositions can be developed is through low-intensity writing interventions such as Shut Up &

Write! (SUAW) and, in our case, AcWriFo. AcWriFo was one of several online writing initiatives that built on existing weekly four-hour SUAW sessions in our school. AcWriFo added alternate Bootcamp Days, that is, 9 am to 5 pm writing days, to SUAW days over a fortnight. 'Doing' AcWriFo was thus more intensive than SUAW alone, however the inclusive, collaborative, and nourishing space for writing remained the same. SUAW is, and AcWriFo was, a time to write quietly with others, a sharing of individual goals and the commitment to prioritise the writing process. It has been shown that writing intervention models can assist with self-efficacy and self-regulation, by way of goal setting, planning, and self-reflection (Proulx, et al., 2023). What is more, Hintz (2024) argues, online writing groups can become spaces of healing, solidarity, and co-regulation, particularly in times of personal or institutional change or hardship. While AcWriFo was not born from a crisis, like the writing group referred to in Hintz (2024), its structure similarly prioritised connection, care, solidarity, and collective motivation as the core conditions for writing. Nevertheless, how a writing intervention model is created, nurtured, and evolves will influence what individuals (and groups) gain from the experience. This can depend on whether the intervention does, or does not, provide opportunities to foster communities of practice (CoP) around the process of academic writing (Mewburn et al, 2014 cited in Proulx et al., 2023).

Costello et al. (2024) identify "Care in the academy" as an essential element that can determine the development of quality CoP around academic writing. This aligns with the community-building aspect of Storying. Neoliberal ideologies that have swept through higher education echo earlier reflections of how academic individualism leads to competition and increased workloads for already complex jobs. Costello et al. (2024) add teaching to this complexity, which is now considered as a time-intensive demand that involves increasing amounts of student support and welfare. As a result, some academics prioritise research and career advancement over teaching, pedagogy, and student engagement. For others, taking on positional leadership roles may be a strategic way to reduce teaching responsibilities, creating more time for other academic pursuits. These shifts draw them away from the care-full, creative, and often all-consuming work of teaching and learning. With that time comes more conceptual, physical, and relational space to prepare and publish journal articles, book chapters, research grants, and books. In doing so academics with lower teaching loads are less likely to feel the intensity associated with juggling a full academic life and are more likely able to fulfil expectations for performance reviews and career advancement (Vicars & Aronson, 2023).

In this AcWriFo Story, an important thing we all shared was our own professional careers as care-full, critical pedagogues. As critical pedagogues, we understood that "Learning and teaching should not stand on opposite banks and just watch the river flow by; instead, they should embark together on a journey down the water. Through an active, reciprocal exchange, teaching can strengthen learning and how to learn" (Malaguzzi, 1998, p. 83). Similarly, our academic work did not place teaching and research as separate or binary entities that stood on opposite banks of a fast-flowing academic river. Rather, through an active, reciprocal exchange, our teaching strengthened our research, and vice versa. Our shared narrative, constructed from decades of meshing together teaching and research in our care-full professional practice with children, colleagues, families, and communities, was the glue that held us together in our corner of the academy. As a result, a collectivist approach to caring for ourselves and others already existed within our AcWriFo community. The benefits of this ethic of care in our collective academic community, "where groups of people act together to achieve something" (Costello et al., 2024, p.2), was evident in AcWriFo. But how did we get there?

Andi's Story

AcWriFo was one of a few creative residuals from a long and successful history with SUAW. SUAW is where (this part of) my Story begins, a most positive and lasting influence from the beginning of my doctorate. As a neurodiverse preservice teacher and then practitioner, coming into academia was never in the cards. The SUAW initiatives I participated in early in my PhD study were the first most sensible way to overcome my culture shock. After a rewarding decade-and-a-half-long physical, tangible, and usually busy people-oriented career as an early childhood teacher and leader, sitting at a desk at 9 am on day one of my return to fulltime study with only a computer and my busy brain before me was challenging. Iyengar et al. (2023) outline the usefulness of the Pomodoro technique (on which SUAW is based) for breaking research projects and associated tasks into manageable chunks, which helped me write well and be well during my PhD and into my career (Firth, 2023). As a quick convert, I organised SUAW wherever else I worked, for myself and others.

The AcWriFo initiative took place in early 2023, before the intensity of Semester 1 preparation had begun, a kooky play on words borne from (and rhyming with) AcWriMo, the acronym for Academic Writing Month. At the time, I was chair of the School of Education (SoE) Research Committee, and regular SUAW sessions had already been established to create a rich research environment. The personal benefits of nourishing online writing spaces where you can work alone together are outlined in other sections of this chapter (and book). However, such spaces are also beneficial from a zoomed-out organisational perspective. The writing initiatives were a strategic choice developed through my own understanding that rich research environments support academic grant applications whereby researchers applying for funding must demonstrate their "activities, outputs and achievements in the context of career and life opportunities and experiences" (Australian Research Council (ARC), 2023). Additionally, the writing initiatives were designed to help build research capacity and work towards meeting the school's goals and the university's research strategy. Given the challenging academic landscape and prospects of the university's ongoing viability in a challenging higher education environment, space and time to prepare, produce, and publish research seemed a winner.

Time is important in my Story, and our AcWriFo Story. One of the clear benefits of SUAW for me has always been the structure of timed writing sessions, shared on-screen and gently curated during my PhD with, in the olden days, a real little 'ding-a-ling-a-ling' bell (I can't go into shops with a little bell on the door and not stop my brain or lift my hands in a conditioned response). Sometimes it was hard to stop writing, especially when in flow, but as a participant who benefitted greatly from such a concrete frame in which to focus and (co) regulate, the timer was my friend. As 'driver' of the Pomodoros in AcWriFo, the timer became an interesting (a) ethical, (b) physiological, and (c) strategy-based phenomena:

a The five-minute breaks were clearly beneficial for participants and conversations often ran well over time. Some people came for the social connection and to feel less isolated in their work – AND the point of the sessions was to keep us focused on chunks of work that, in theory, matched people's capacity to focus in optimal ways.
b Because of my tendency for task orientation, personal and professional respect for the timer, and deeply embedded visceral readiness to get back to work after 5 minutes (perhaps another conditioned response), stopping the conversation after breaks took some nuanced inner and outer relational work.
c Strategies to manage included (1) gauging the right amount of time to end the break, (2) lightening how I ended it, (3) finding a break in the conversation, (4) balancing everybody being able to share and contribute, and (5) gently yet clearly declaring "Should we keep going?".

From the beginning, AcWriFo was a space that invited inclusion and belonging, with my initial email invitation to 'opt in' sent to everyone in the Faculty. Daily morning emails were then sent with targeted subject headers to show what kind of day it would be, for example, "AcWriFo (Bootcamp Day)" or "AcWriFo (SUAW 9-1)". It also included the link to the online SoE Writing Room, a group goals google document to support accountability and track progress towards set goals, and a reminder of the day's schedule. For example, if the day started at 9 am, the timer started at 9:15 and the first 15 minutes were slated as "Good morning, talk about/set your goals, make your cuppa, get settled". Costello et al. (citing Bergmann et al., 2023) consider the sociality this transition into the shared space affords as crucial in building supportive and productive online groups. It seems I organised and led AcWriFo with the same spirit of collegiality, scholarship, and focus I had experienced myself, a wonderful return on investment to the place I became an 'academic'.

Nat's Story

AcWriFo materialised in the form of an email from Andi, the chair of our school's research committee, that arrived in January 2023, just a few months after I had submitted my PhD. The acronym sounded like fun, as did the 'luxury' of a fortnight of writing. I had been working full-time as a lecturer throughout my PhD and had developed, already, a sense of unease about the ways my work was affected by a neoliberal discourse that included, among other things, the responsibilisation of individuals. As described by Morrissey (2015), this means that individual academics are seen as solely responsible for the quality of their teaching and the quantity of their writing outputs with little responsibility assigned to the institutional processes and demands that shape their work (Morrissey, 2015). At the university I work at, our workload is split across three teaching sessions. Two are for teaching and research, and one for research-focused activity. We have a sole solitary session (usually from December–February) to concentrate on research and writing. This is an already short window of time that is being aggressively eroded by the demands of accountability and neoliberal governance. And so, in January 2023, while emails about a new learning management system, initiatives for improving student experiences, business development opportunities, reminders for mandatory training, and demands from accrediting bodies streamed in, I signed up for AcrWriFo as an excuse to prioritise the real other work of being an academic.

Each morning, for a fortnight, I shut down Outlook, turned on my webcam and thought only about my teaching and writing. Faced with the constant fear of an over-flowing inbox, AcrWriFo become an act of resistance – a way of speaking back to oppressive forms of power by blocking out time and becoming-unavailable (while becoming-academic). It was a calendared disruption to the hierarchies of my day-to-day university work, which went something like this:

1 meetings,
2 student emails,
3 administration,
4 marking and moderation,
5 teaching,
6 writing.

Motivated by my commitment to a collective, I showed up to AcWriFo, even when the reminders about missed emails escalated. I continued to show up, nourished by the connections I had made, even when my writing goals became teaching goals and then writing goals again. Guided by Malaguzzi's (1998) invitation to bring teaching and learning closer together, this became a way to allow pedagogy and writing to flow in the same stream, rather than on opposing banks. Some members of this collective became regular allies: Andi, in charge and juggling the role of mentor, organiser, facilitator, and busy academic with individual writing goals; and Belinda, finding a way to finish her PhD, wearing a layer of exhaustion that was all too familiar. Other members popped in and out offering new faces, new names, and strange stories from other research worlds. At times, my own writing was shaped and enhanced by the conversations we had as a group. In one session, I was supported by the collective to perform the daunting task of reopening my thesis post-submission. Although it was apparent that each of us were deeply embedded within the complexities of our own projects and lives, the conversations we had, in breaks between writing, highlighted our shared Story of trouble within the academy and a sustained commitment to writing, scholarship, and each other. Our time together reminded me that although each of us are not the same, we are in this together (Braidotti, 2014). I have come to understand that it was this element of AcWriFo, not just the blocked-out time or the Pomodoro technique, that made this practice effective for me. AcWriFo opened opportunities to become academic through new relations with others – other people, other spaces, other times, other discourses. This kooky-named figuration conjured possibilities for writing and scholarship that were otherwise unimaginable for me.

Belinda's Story

As a tired part-time higher degree research student and full-time academic pushing towards the penultimate draft of my doctoral thesis, the idea of AcWriFo was exciting and daunting. My youngest child would soon start school and I was trying to juggle my family, PhD, and teaching, feeling like I was failing them all. Spending two weeks solely focused on my PhD seemed selfish, but with a looming deadline and depleted wellbeing I thought AcWriFo could be a life jacket that might keep me afloat a little longer. At the same time, my inner critic was terrifying me – Would others think my PhD progress was to slow? Would my daily goals be enough? However, the SUAW community established by Andi prior to this fortnight emboldened me to ignore the self-doubt and grab hold of the lifeline. My overarching goal was simple; finish the PhD and by the end of AcWriFo the penultimate copy of my doctoral thesis was complete. More importantly, what I found in the AcWriFo sessions was not just accountability, space, and time to work on my research; what I found was a supportive and inspiring community of practice.

CoP can vary in size and structure but typically include a core group of people whose passion about a topic unites them (Wenger and Snyder, 2000). The AcWriFo CoP was a passionate group of pedagogy-focused academics who were intent on creating ethical and transparent educational research that made a difference. Andi modelled the expectation of a group that was honest, inclusive, and supportive, creating a psychologically safe space for all. This safe, shared space, seemed to enable individuals to take interpersonal risks, such as asking for help and voicing opinions (Foster, 2022). After 12 years as a research higher degree student, my physical, social, emotional, intellectual, and financial wellbeing was at capacity (Robbins et al., 2017). Having a supportive and safe space to write in re-ignited my passion and motivation to finish.

At the end of each session the group would debrief and note what had been achieved against their set goals (e.g. completed four out of five sections, made good progress though all feels very slow). I was surprised to discover that this process of goal setting supported my wellbeing. My intellectual wellbeing was improving as the goal-setting process assisted improving my self-direction and motivation by providing purpose, and removing other lists of menial mental tasks for the day (Weintraub, et al. 2021). While my intellectual wellbeing was supported through the goal setting process my emotional wellbeing was supported by the end of day debrief. Others in the AcWriFo CoP were at different stages in their careers, some were mid PhD, others were just starting out or in the final push like me, and others had finished long ago. The varied experience within the CoP helped shift any negative feelings I had by clarifying and refocusing me on the achievements made. As the fortnight progressed, what was being achieved become more visible to me because (whether the progress was large or small) I could now visually see the forward movement.

During AcWriFo the Pomodoro technique was applied daily, where the task for the day was broken into manageable focused intervals followed by breaks (Iyengar et al., 2024). Another gift of the AcWriFo CoP were the conversations and reflective practice that occurred within these breaks, not just around my research but around my pedagogy. The Pomodoro breaks often provided more wellbeing support than the task achieved through the goal -setting process and focused intervals. The safe space Andi established within the AcWriFo was a CoP where participants felt free from the fear of social rejection or reprisal (Agarwal & Farndale, 2017). This environment fostered creative discussions and debates around pedagogy, academic teaching, and research leading to a sharing of Storys, resources, and ideas. Ultimately, what I gained from the collaborative and supportive atmosphere of the AcWriFo CoP was much more than my penultimate PhD draft. I found a community whose shared Story created lasting impacts on my teaching and research.

So What? Implications for Theory and/or Practice

The threads of Andi's, Nat's and Belinda's individual Storys weave together to form a shared narrative about AcWriFo's unexpected outcomes. By the end, we collectively wrote thousands of words, achieved research goals, and improved our wellbeing by allowing us to meet deadlines, get published, finish projects, and write meaningful things. In this sense, our shared Story demonstrates that innovative online approaches to SUAW are worth pursuing. However, our collective Storys suggest that it was not just the notions of performance and productivity, understood in economic terms of outputs and competition, that were enhanced. The benefits were much more complex and relational, and stretched beyond the framework of capitalism and profit that contribute to academic stress. While dominant discourses locate burnout and academic stress in the personal failure to cope, Turner and Garvis (2023) highlight that the systemic sources of exhaustion are audit-driven reform, increasing accountability, and a shift towards performativity. AcWriFo responded not by offering "resilience" training, but by cultivating conditions of care, autonomy, and mutual recognition as preconditions for sustainable scholarship. In fact, AcWriFo shifted our relationship with these neoliberal terms. In ways that echo Malaguzzi's (1998) vision of the productivity of reciprocal and reflexive exchanges between teaching and learning, performance was reimagined as contribution to a collective academic wellbeing and productivity reconfigured to be about daily participation with a focus on sustainable and regenerative work in our learning, through our writing, and our teaching. These more empowering relations align with Barnett's (2010) idea of "decentralised coordination" where decisions and responsibilities are distributed across multiple actors and competition between individuals removed. Our Story demonstrates how AcWriFo shaped, and was shaped by, the practices of individuals coming together as a collective.

The daily connection over the fortnight developed trusted professional relationships and a genuine collaborative CoP that was focused on more than individual research. Rather than a by-product of collegiality, care was a deliberate structuring principle of AcWriFo, echoing Costello et al.'s (2024) finding that writing communities thrive when care is materially enacted and mutually recognised as part of the scholarly process. The safe space allowed individuals to be vulnerable and share stories about their workloads, pedagogy, research queries, and themselves. The relationships forged during AcWriFo continue to support our individual academic careers but more importantly continue to nourish our collective wellbeing. The smallest kindnesses were often the pivotal points of difference during AcWriFo. For example:

- the inclusive invitation to all,
- group goal articulation,
- regular debriefs,
- reminders that we did not need to be present 100% of the time and that missing a Pomodoro or a session was okay and even encouraged if this supported our wellbeing,
- changes to Pomodoro timing to suit the group movements,
- changes in the Pomodoro alarm to birds chirping to suit the group sensibilities.

Drawing on Hintz's (2024) conceptualisation of online writing groups as blueprints for new academic possibilities, AcWriFo's focus on care and flexibility led to a sustained form of distributed co-presence that allowed participants to self-determine their involvement while remaining connected to a shared scholarly rhythm.

As a reflexive and relational practice, this shared Storying enabled a better understanding of our own subjectivities as academics in the context of the neoliberal university. In this sense, AcWriFo is an example of what Braidotti (2014) calls affirmative action, and the insights that flow enable us to continue to act in productive and nourishing ways amidst increasingly restrictive conditions. Pedagogical hand-me-downs of inclusion and caring were key to cultivating CoP for AcWriFo and this began in the creation stage. For example, Andi's knowledge of the SUAW process and the intentionality in her leadership fostered respectful, responsive, and reciprocal relationships with individuals and groups that centred the CoP communication, intentions, and interactions around the shared writing process. This foundation then permeated through the CoP evolution via effective interpersonal communication and interpersonal risk taking that further engendered inclusive practices within the CoP (Moloney & McCarthy, 2018). These inclusive practices fostered the sense of community within the group and nurtured our combined wellbeing, as the inclusive practices were also practices of care (Costello et al., 2024).

Haraway's 1987 warning that "our machines are disturbingly lively, and we ourselves frighteningly inert" (p. 5) seems an accurate description of our current moment. We experience inertia from competition, individualism, administrative fatigue, and from the difficulty of working slowly through complex and oppressive conditions of the present. In this context we need more of the academic nourishment, increase in wellbeing, and the healing effect of better understanding our positionalities that were made possible through AcWriFo. In response to Turner and Garvis (2023) call for more qualitative accounts and context-sensitive interventions to respond, this chapter contributes a Storying-based account of collective care and writing. In fitting with the multiplicities of our working, thinking, and being, AcWriFo attempted to reconcile the position/s of the smaller group of a School with the whole group of a University, in addition to reconciling the position/s of individual academics with small groups within the School. From an even more zoomed-in perspective, Andi reconciled a personal and professional love for writing to time with (and without) others, Nat reconciled finding time for **all** parts of being an academic, and Belinda reconciled completing and submitting a PhD not believing she could. This AcWriFo Story was a transformational one.

Conclusion

> Storytelling was and will always be a cultural conduit utilised by Aboriginal people as a pedagogical approach for imparting and sharing of knowledge as well as understanding and formulating new knowledges.
> (Holt & Perry, 2023, p. 29)

Respectfully following Aboriginal approaches to Storytelling, and Storying (Blair & Collins-Gearing, 2017) as both a framework and methodological approach, this chapter outlined the Story of AcWriFo, an intensive fortnight of academic thinking, reading, and writing, told through the individual and shared Storys of three academics working at a regional university in Australia. Though we were at different stages in our academic careers, we shared commitment and care as pedagogues, who are always already both teachers and researchers, connecting us in a respectful, responsive, and reciprocal academic relationship.

The process of "doing" AcWriFo developed professional relationships and the personal conversations that connected us, motivated us, and encouraged us to show up both for the writing process and each other. The fortnight moved AcWriFo beyond a productivity intervention into an intentionally fostered CoP built on a foundation of caring, inclusion, and collaboration. Andi's intentional leadership encouraged a sharing of knowledge, Storys, teaching praxis, and care practices transforming us from individuals working alone into a community working alone together. The creation of this flexibly structured writing environment transformed our individual efforts into a collective experience that successfully supported our productivity and, importantly, enhanced our wellbeing.

AcWriFo was only made possible, however, by the participation and courage of attendees, to be open, honest, and true to their own and others' processes, pains, and successes. In this sense, AcWriFo was a political act of resistance within the neoliberal academy, echoing Flo Kennedy, prominent civil rights activist and feminist who implored us not to agonise but organise, both alone and together.

References

Agarwal, P., & Farndale, E. (2017). High-performance work systems and creativity implementation: The role of psychological capital and psychological safety. *Human Resource Management Journal, 27*(3), 440–458. http://www.doi.org/10.1111/1748-8583.12148

Australian Research Council (ARC). (2023). Research Opportunity and Performance Evidence (ROPE). Australian Government. https://www.arc.gov.au/sites/default/files/2023-12/ROPE%20Statement%20updated%20template%202023_0.pdf

Barnett, C. (2010). Publics and markets. What's wrong with neoliberalism? In S. J. Smith, R. Pain, S. A. Marston and J. P. Jones (Eds.). *The Sage Handbook of Social Geographies*, (pp. 269–296). Sage.

Blair, N. (2017). *Personal communication.* Sydney.

Blair, N., & Collins-Gearing, B. (2017). Reflective practice: Ancient wisdom and practice—Australian indigenous reflections in teacher education through shared storying. *Reflective Theory and Practice in Teacher Education*, 63–83.

Braidotti, R. (2014). Writing as a nomadic subject. *Comparative Critical Studies 11*(2), 163–184. http://doi.org/10.3366/ccs.2014.0122

Costello, M., Nyanjom, J., Bailey, S., & Ireson, D. (2024). Care in the academy: How our online writing group transformed into a caring community. *International Journal of Educational Research, 127,* 102441.

Firth, K. (2023). *Writing well and being well for your PhD and beyond: How to cultivate a strong and sustainable writing practice for life* (1st ed.). Routledge. https://doi.org/10.4324/9781003307945

Foster, R. (2022). Creating a psychologically safe space. *Nursing Management, 53*(11), 48–48. http://www.doi.org/10.1097/01.NUMA.0000891452.18867.b2

Habibis, D., Taylor, P. S., & Ragaini, B. S. (2019). White people have no face: Aboriginal perspectives on white culture and the costs of neoliberalism. *Ethnic and Racial Studies, 43*(7), 1149–1168. https://doi.org/10.1080/01419870.2019.1642504

Haraway, D. (1987). A manifesto for cyborgs: Science, technology, and socialist feminism in the 1980s. *Australian Feminist Studies, 2*(4), 1–42.

Hintz, L. (2024). Academic solidarity in the wake of disaster: Blueprint for an online writing support group. *Political Science & Politics, 57*(3), 370–377.

Holt, L., & Perry, J. (2023). Shaping the narratives—Indigenous knowledges through storying. In M. Vicars & L. Pelosi (Eds.) *Storying pedagogy as critical praxis in the neoliberal university: Encounters and disruptions* (pp. 29–47). Springer Nature Singapore.

Iyengar, K. P., Vaishya, R. & Botchu, R. (2024). Can we apply pomodoro technique in academic publishing? *Apollo Medicine, 21*(2): 176–177. http://www.doi.org/10.4103/am.am_193_23

Kemmis, S., Edwards-Groves, C., Lloyd, A., Grootenboer, P., Hardy, I., & Wilkinson, J. (2017). Learning as being 'stirred in' to practices. *Practice theory perspectives on pedagogy and education: Praxis, diversity and contestation,* 45–65.

Malaguzzi, L. (1998). History, ideas and philosophy, In C. Edwards, L. Gandini, and G. Forman. (Eds.). *The hundred languages of children: The Reggio Emilia approach.* Ablex Publishing, Greenwich.

Moloney, M. & McCarthy, E. (2018). *Intentional leadership for effective inclusion in early childhood education and care: Exploring core themes and strategies.* Taylor & Francis Group.

Morrissey, J. (2015). Regimes of performance: Practices of the normalised self in the neoliberal university. *British Journal of Sociology of Education, 36*(4), 641–644. http://dx.doi.org/10.1080/01425692.2013.838515

Proulx, C. N., Rubio, D. M., Norman, M. K., & Mayowski, C. A. (2023). Shut up & write!® builds writing self-efficacy and self-regulation in early-career researchers. *Journal of Clinical and Translational Science, 7*: e141, 1–7. https://doi.org/10.1017/cts.2023.568

Robbins, G., Powers, D., & Burgess, S. (2017). *A wellness way of life* (11th ed.). McGraw-Hill Higher Education.

Turner, K., & Garvis, S. (2023). Teacher educator wellbeing, stress and burnout: A scoping review. *Education Sciences, 13*(4), 351.

Vicars, M., & Aronson, G. (2023). Doing it on your own terms: Narrating time and place in the neoliberal university. In M. Vicars & L. Pelosi (Eds.) *Storying pedagogy as critical praxis in the neoliberal university: Encounters and disruptions* (pp. 1–13). Springer Nature Singapore.

Weintraub, J., Cassell, D., & DePatie, T. P. (2021). Nudging flow through 'SMART' goal setting to decrease stress, increase engagement, and increase performance at work. *Journal of Occupational and Organizational Psychology, 94*(2), 230–258. https://doi.org/10.1111/joop.12347

Wenger, E., & Snyder, W. (2000). Communities of practice: The organizational frontier. *Harvard Business Review, 78*(1), 139.

14 The Time of Our Lives

SUAW as a Space for Academic Writing Wellbeing

Abigail Winter, Jenna Gillett-Swan, Naomi Barnes, Catherine Challen, Keri Freeman, Danielle Gordon, Tessa Rixon, Tom Long, Zoe Mellick, Jane Turner, Alethea Blackler, Julie Arnold, Cassandra Cross, Nicole Vickery, Stine Johansen, David Pyle, Emily Woodman-Pieterse, and Dannielle Tarlinton

Introduction

We all have different needs for and definitions of wellbeing, at different points in our lives. Using a framework of academic writing wellbeing based on the models of Narelle Lemon (2021b, 2024) and Joan Tronto (1993, 2013), this chapter analyses reflections from 18 academic writers at a large metropolitan Australian university about the ways that leading and participating in regularly scheduled Show/Shut Up & Write! (SUAW) sessions meet their wellbeing needs. Responding to the question "What does SUAW give you?", the reflections come from SUAW facilitators and participants, staff and students, and academics at all levels from casual tutors to tenured full professors. Some have used SUAW for over a decade (Blackler, 2021), while others have joined for the first time this year.

As the number of co-authors shows, our SUAW is a community, a collective, a collaboration. Using Sarah Haas' (2014) typology of writing groups, our SUAW can be characterised as an expert-led, interdisciplinary writers' group that supports individual academics' writing through regular meetings in hybrid format. Our meetings are scheduled at the start of each year by the lead author in her Outlook Calendar from 10 am–12 pm. We meet in the mornings, because that is most attendees' peak writing time, for two hours. A Zoom link as well as a physical meeting room is included as the hybrid location. We set goals for ourselves during each SUAW session (sometimes for each "Pomodoro" – the shorter writing sessions within the SUAW). New goals are often set at the end of the session to "finish this by…", if a piece of writing is close to completion or a deadline is looming.

Our SUAW sessions always begin with checking in. Sometimes it takes only a few minutes, but other days take longer – and not always associated with the ebbs and flows of the academic calendar. We don't work in strict 25-minute writing Pomodoros – we usually work to the half or full hour, so if we have chatted more, then we have less time available to write. During the stretch-and-check-in break, the facilitator (Abbe) makes sure to ask "How are you, and what are you working on today?" because our SUAW is a place of collegiality and care, not just neoliberal production. Our membership is large – all of the academics in the faculty are invited, plus others who find out and ask to be included, from research students to professional staff. Our attendance is usually around 10–12 at each session, with a rotating regular attendee list of about 30.

SUAW gives us a place to practice our academic writing wellbeing, which demonstrates Lemon's (2021a) four critical areas of work-life harmony. First, SUAW provides a place of *emotional* support, where issues ranging from the personal (a car literally falling apart on the way to work) to the common-to-many in the neoliberal academy (marking, student grade reviews, curriculum development …) can be shared and empathised with, and sometimes even helped towards a solution. Second, SUAW provides *instrumental* support by being a place where work can be done – whether that work is lecture preparation, clearing emails, or actual academic writing. Third, SUAW provides a place of *role modelling*, not only as a place for people to touch their own writing (Belcher, 2019), but also as somewhere to draw on the wisdom of the community. Finally, SUAW provides *creative management* by making us all feel part of an academic writing community in the broadest sense of the word. SUAW is not just a community of practice (Wenger, 1998) but is a genuinely caring, care-full community, where we are emotionally engaged in each other's achievements. Achievements are celebrated, regardless of size – from meeting goals in SUAW to submitting an article or publishing something.

It is in the light of this that we come to SUAW as a collaborative. Our sessions offer a grassroots dismantling of the myth of the writer flying solo in the abstract and refined upper atmosphere of academia. Something very subversive happens in the safety of a SUAW session. The act of sharing 'session writing goals' is similar to the format of a yarning circle (Barlo et al., 2020) where the outcome is the sharing process itself, building relational connections and understandings. This tends to create what Huizinga (1949) calls 'a magic circle', usually used to describe a place for ritual play, a playground where everyone within the circle agrees to a set of rules or protocols. However, as a place for play created through an accord, a magic circle can also be framed as a safe place (Taboada et al., 2024) because of the manner in which consensus and agreement affords imaginative creativity.

There is considerable depth in this rich nexus of the magic circle, the safe imagination space, and the multiple community space. Huizinga's concern in his analysis of the role of play in creativity and his notion of the magic circle is the way that ritual scaffolds culture. His magic circle is the space in which the normal rules and reality of the world are suspended and replaced by a liminal temporary reality. There is a fluid, relational aspect to this that combines with the ebbs and flows of our SUAW community to create something called 'communitas' (Turner, 2012; Turner, 1969). Communitas is subversive and radical, describing an unstructured community where individuals are equal and share a deep sense of intimacy that arises from collective experiences of liminality. It is a feature of groups engaged in pivotal moments, be they celebration, crisis, or support.

Communitas reflects a group's joy in shared experiences (Turner, 2012), yet it remains fleeting, contextually dependent, and difficult to commodify (Agamben, 1993). What this means is that fostering communitas is a very different activity from fostering or mobilising a community into some kind of activism. Our own SUAW community provides us with a safe place to deal with some of the tensions involved in writing, in being an academic writer, in a small way. More importantly, our SUAW space allows us the collective opportunity for connection and to tell stories that disassemble some of the paradoxes of writing, to make even the driest piece of thesis writing or research data reporting a more storied experience through the sharing of our writing process in SUAW.

Academic Writing

The act of scholarly writing in particular is anti-relational, formalist, containing, restrictive and "the death mask of its conception" (Benjamin, 1979/2016, p. 47). The expectation of 'the written word' as a respectable source of information and knowledge that will bring the reader to wisdom is very much part of the same legacy of the Enlightenment that prioritises product over process and depends on the world of consumable things for its values. In this system, non-conformity, the experiences and ways of others, as Haraway (1991) searingly observes, are the subject matter of the written word, even when they attempt to claim these tools for themselves.

Sharing the challenges of writing is one of the more extraordinary subversive things we can do. Finding ways to share and collaborate in a system focused on 'authorial' production and extraction of the idea into the coldness of the page is often at odds with our understandings of ourselves as academics.

As Alison Eardley et al. (2021, p. 193) argue, "providing academics with a structured institutionally-validated space to write enhances wellbeing in a stressed and overworked environment". It provides "institutional endorsement" (p. 190) for spending time writing. This aligns with what Rowena Murray (2014) terms "organisational support" – SUAW is a sanctioned activity available to all staff and students in the faculty (and selected invitees from beyond it). In other ways, it reflects what Nancy Stevenson (2021) notes – that community among writers grows naturally, particularly when conversations are allowed to move beyond the work of writing and into the realm of caring.

Ethics of Care

Joan Tronto's Ethics of Care was first detailed in her 1993 book *Moral Boundaries* and included four elements: Attentiveness, Responsibility, Competence, and

Responsiveness. By 2013, she had expanded the model to include Reciprocity. Each element of her model describes a different step in the care process. *Attentiveness*, or *caring about*, focuses on identifying needs and things that deserve attention in another. *Responsibility*, or *caring for*, is about the things we could do on the basis of our attentiveness. *Competence*, or *care giving*, is about the actions we take on the basis of our care for another. *Responsiveness*, or *care receiving*, is about the actions of the person we gave care to in response to our actions. *Reciprocity*, or *caring with*, is about our collective caring for one another, in this case as part of our SUAW community. Reciprocity, therefore, also describes the care we receive for ourselves. Tronto's model (1993, 2013) has also been extended to include an additional element of *Maintenance*, or *self-care* (Grant-Smith & Payne, 2021).

Maintenance of Self-Care

Narelle Lemon proposed her Dimensions of Self-Care model in 2021. Arising from research during the COVID-19 pandemic, she used poetry to represent the thematic analysis of her findings, as well as presenting the themes in her model of self-care. Like Tronto, Lemon's model (2021b, 2024) has five dimensions. *Mindfulness* is about being non-judgemental about what is needed in the present moment. *Self-compassion* is about realising and accepting what is actually needed with kindness and humanity. *Time* is about recognising the amount of time necessary to look after ourselves – whether moments or months. *Habits* are about building small, frequent actions into impactful consequences. *Empowerment* is the agency and ability to be able to make the choices that we need to.

Method

In mid-2024, following the call for this book, Abbe sent out an invitation to all of the regular SUAW attendees, asking if they would like to be involved in co-authoring a chapter about our Faculty SUAW. Those who responded as interested were asked to provide a response to the reflective prompt: **What does SUAW give you?** Those who provided a response are listed as authors, in order of their acceptance of the invitation. Responses varied from a couple of sentences to three pages with references. All were analysed deductively by Abbe, firstly using the theoretical frame of Tronto's (1993, 2013) Ethics of Care, and then secondly using Lemon's (2021b) Maintenance of Self-Care.

Image 14.1 shows our model of academic writing wellbeing, expanding Tronto's Ethics of Care on the left into Lemon's Maintenance of Self-Care on the right via the connection point described by Grant-Smith and Payne (2021) as Maintenance (self-care). We use an infinity symbol to indicate that all these elements are interconnected and necessary, building on each other to enable and enhance our academic writing wellbeing in our SUAW community of care.

Image 14.1 A framework for academic writing wellbeing.

Discussion

In this section, we provide example reflections from the author/participants, deductively themed to the elements of each theoretical framework. Following that, we draw together commonalities and differences across the reflections with other writing in the academic writing and wellbeing space.

Attentiveness

> The establishment of this group came at a time when I was in a new role, as part of a new faculty, with new colleagues I had never met before, in disciplines I knew nothing (or very little) about.
>
> – Cassandra

> Writing can be difficult to do and to find time for in exceedingly busy schedules.
>
> – Cate

> SUAW helps me to connect with others, share wins and achievements (no matter how big or small), vent to others who can relate and understand my frustrations … get ideas and tips … learn about interesting work and projects that other colleagues are doing … and get to know others in the Faculty across all career stages, many of whom I would be unlikely to meet or know about.
>
> – Jenna

Responsibility

> The very nature of this community is the push for mutual development in that everyone wants everyone to succeed.
>
> – Tom

> The physical space of our SUAW sessions is a calm and quiet space. It is warm (not just metaphorically), and it is a bright space.
>
> – Stine

It costs very little as the leader running the sessions can continue with their own work during each Pomodoro, so the only time requirement is setting up the meetings and then the few minutes of chat at the start and end. I believe it has been enormously valuable to individual attendees and has contributed to addressing some of the faculty goals in my role as Associate Dean (Research).

– Alethea

Competence

I believe that SUAW can create a culture of writing and research in a school or faculty just as most have a culture of teaching because it is a shared endeavour of all academic staff. The regular commitment works just like any other regular habit, and people have shared that having something in their diary that looks just like any other meeting helps to carve out protected writing time that is less likely to get booked over.

– Alethea

In listening to my colleagues share their progress – as well as their feelings about research – I found myself being very open and accepting of however someone else chose to approach the task of writing. I never judged them for 'failing' to write a certain quantity of words during a 25mins session – so therefore, maybe I should stop judging myself. Maybe I could apply some of that perspective, that understanding, that kindness, to myself when I approach research writing.

– Tessa

Responsiveness

Knowing others were navigating similar challenges was comforting, and the shared encouragement helped me stay motivated during difficult periods.

– Dannielle

As this community hosts different schools, fields of research and levels of experienced academics, I have always had novel and valuable feedback provided that has been instrumental in developing my own research approach.

– Tom

One aspect I particularly enjoy is the debriefs during breaks. It's a privilege to hear snippets of what my colleagues are working on, especially since we often only see the final results of academic work, not the process behind it. Hearing about their work in progress can be both inspiring and motivating, even when they are in a completely different field.

– Zoe

Reciprocity

Through SUAW, people who would never have met each other otherwise saw each other regularly, built relationships and collaborations, shared tips and tricks and encouragement, and started to understand and appreciate a wider variety of research approaches.

– Alethea

What I draw from the community who also practise in that space, in whatever way makes sense to them, is calendar space (I'll bet everyone says this) and a rhythm of commit-write-pause-relate. Community, and the visibility and empathy that brings, is accessible, non-judgemental, and appreciated. The option of practical support is accessible and helpful.

– Julie

Our SUAW space allows us the collective opportunity for connection and to tell stories that disassemble some of the paradoxes of writing.

– Jane

Maintenance

SUAW provides an excuse to shut the mental door to all and sundry, knuckle down and get stuck into it for a couple of hours.

– David

The quietness and companionship that shuts up my overactive brain for a couple of precious hours.

– Naomi

The session happens to fall within my golden hours of productivity, meaning that I can really get the most out of each session. I am naturally inclined to prefer numbers over words, and I find writing tasks much more mentally draining than 8 hours of data analysis and interpretation. I try to adapt by making sure I save these 'big brain' writing tasks for the weekly SUAW session to maximise my output.

– Emily

Habits

When I was a PhD student, the Pomodoro helped me keep focus on my thesis while raising two babies, sustaining a marriage and paying a mortgage. Today, as a newly minted Associate Professor I still have those responsibilities (though the babies more closely resemble teenagers). But now I also look for time amongst teaching, learning, meetings, research and leadership. The Pomodoro has always been there whether I put it in a calendar myself, join a research group who also recognises the importance of the humble tomato timer, or accept calendar invitations from the Faculty. The Pomodoro technique is integral to my academic practice and what I have managed to achieve.

– Naomi

No matter what I am working on, regardless of how much I have procrastinated, I can almost always work on something for at least 20 minutes. And, usually, once I get started, inertia keeps me going.

– Cate

Having the sessions scheduled into my calendar by someone else helps me view the sessions as a commitment to others, meaning I'm less likely to prioritise other work.

– Emily

SUAW sessions provide a haven for focused, uninterrupted productivity – something I struggle to maintain on my own. In a career that often feels fragmented and chaotic, SUAW offers me structure: a dedicated time block reserved exclusively for writing, free from the usual distractions … When writing becomes overwhelming, progress feels slow, or other competing priorities arise, just being in the company of others engaged in the same process helps me persevere. It's a reminder that even on difficult days, progress is possible.

– Zoe

Agency

SUAW provided a dedicated space for focused writing amidst the many demands of research. Having a structured time designated each week allowed me to make consistent progress on my work, especially during moments when balancing competing priorities felt overwhelming. It became a dependable part of my routine, where I could fully immerse myself in writing.

– Dannielle

It put me on the path to discovering that my writing wasn't fixed; I could adapt and learn. I learned that I wasn't just stuck submitting to the same series of conferences and journals considered king in my PhD research lab where my work was perceived as uninteresting - that there were other venues. It taught me as a supervisor, that I shouldn't just celebrate my publication successes with my students, that I should also commiserate my defeats.

– Nicole

Our SUAW community … provides us with a safe place to deal with some of the tensions involved in writing, in being an academic writer.

– Jane

Mindfulness

SUAW has slowly but surely helped me address this tendency towards perfection. Through constant, regular exposure to how other people tackle writing tasks, I have learnt there is no 'right' way to write.

– Tessa

By committing to SUAW, I'm finding a better balance between my teaching role and my research goals and I'm getting better at prioritising my weekly research writing. This creates healthier boundaries around my time and helps me remember that my research goals are just as important as answering emails.

– Keri

These SUAW sessions allow me to engage in this metacognitive process (Archer, 2003, 2007, 2012) – a reflective practice where I evaluate my goals, align them with my daily realities, and determine the best use of my energy within a supportive community.

– Danielle

Self-Compassion

SUAW gives me a productive and positive writing community that brings joy to my work.

– Jenna

In SUAW, I find the discernment to prioritise, the deliberation to plan, and the dedication to carry through – each essential for balancing both work and wellbeing.

– Danielle

The camaraderie is second to none, as is the access to a superb 'brains-trust' of advice and help from a diverse skillset that the participants generously provide each week.

– David

SUAW gives me social space. The sessions create connections between other researchers that I would not otherwise have met. We are scattered across campus areas and buildings but with SUAW, we come together (physically or virtually) and support each other. The social space is key to what SUAW gives me.

– Stine

Time

It gives me space in terms of time to deepen my engagement with a task. As my time is usually very chaotic, with multiple tasks that seem immediately urgent to be done, participating in SUAW allows me to use 2 hours for one, single task.

– Stine

SUAW removes one of the barriers to writing – finding time for it. In much the same way that writing things on a to-do list removes some of the cognitive load associated with tasks, having dedicated writing time in my calendar removes the need for me to stress about when my writing will get done.

– Cate

By setting clear intentions, I can tune out distractions and fully commit to the work that best serves my goals for that day. SUAW facilitates the necessary deliberation that follows, weighing the importance of different tasks alongside discussion with colleagues who face similar challenges. This community insight allows me to reflect on how I am investing my time, helping me find a balance while juggling many roles.

– Danielle

Reflections on the Analysis

Our reflections show the importance to us of having a community. SUAW offers a regular moment of ritual (Bickel, 2009; Turner, 1969), creating a space for what Marni Binder (2022, p. 33) calls "detoxifying the academic environment". Unlike the writing groups and activities described by Nancy Stevenson (2021), SUAW is a place of support, community, and trust. As Tseen Khoo and Jonathan O'Donnell (2024, p. 114) note about SUAW, "they came for the writing time and stayed for the community". Like Stevenson's (2021, p. 727) writing retreat participants, our SUAW "draws attention to the significance of non-writing aspects, the importance of conversation with others, the sense of satisfaction arising from sharing and supporting one another". It is a place of professional empowerment, agency, and efficacy.

SUAW is a regular place of productivity within the working week, rather than a special writing retreat "from the responsibilities associated with daily life" (Stevenson, 2021, p. 723). SUAW provides group flow (Eardley et al., 2021), where being with others all immersed in their own writing makes it easier (or perhaps provides peer pressure) to immerse in your own writing. As Abbe reflects, *I try to make my SUAW a place that people want to come to – an antidote to the university's usual "monotonous work of computers and meetings"(Yngvesson et al., 2023, p. 117). I make its hybrid mode into a place of invitation and possibility, enabling those in other places to still join the community and get some useful work done in good company, because the focus is on the people and our writing, not the technology that brings us together.*

Strategies Unpacked as Tips

Aware of Sarah Haas' (2014) assessment that there are no courses on actually getting writing done (despite Wendy Belcher's subsequent course and book), we use SUAW to affirm that writing is a long-form, usually slow process, with multiple phases. Abbe builds in common writing advice terminology – chunking

(Murray, 2021), rhythm (Le Guin, 1998), touching the writing (Belcher, 2019) – to normalise the terms for those who are not reading in that academic writing development space, because it is the professional language of the academic writer.

In SUAW, it's important to reiterate frequently that "any progress is great progress", and "that's how the work gets done – one (small) chunk at a time". Academic writing is hard, and it needs places of support.

SUAW is a place of role modelling, not only as a place for people to work on their writing, but also as a place where we can all contribute. In a recent conversation, Alethea shared her tab management tool (https://www.gettoby.com/) with a research student who was overwhelmed by all of the things they had found and in fear of turning off their computer in case they lost all of their open tabs. SUAW is a place of collective efficacy (Bandura, 2000). We use the wisdom of the group. We lean on each other for support and celebration.

Conclusion

SUAW is a place of care for academics in the neoliberal academy – a place of living "well within the academy" (Garbett & Thomas, 2020, p. 296). It is not just a place of writing. Sometimes the most important thing to do is to prepare for the next lecture (whether that's next week or tomorrow), or deal with the never-empty email inbox (which, like the Celtic myth of the Cauldron of Cerridwen, magically regenerates its contents without overt action by its user). SUAW is an accepting, supportive community of like-minded enablers of getting the work done – whatever "the work" is or what "done" looks like for each of us.

At the same time, for many of us, SUAW is a time of writing, and our SUAW community enables this. As Katherine Firth (2024, p. 175) concludes, "When we have a writing community based on acceptance, generosity and authenticity, then the writing we produce will be ethical, productive, readable and useful – in other words, 'good writing'". Our research poem uses key words from our reflections to summarise our wellbeing gains from SUAW.

    Our SUAW is
      Care
      Capability
      Celebration
      Choice
      Collaboration
      Collective
      Communication
      Community
      Compassion
      Empathy

Engagement
Flourishing
Hybrid
Inclusive
Offered
Opportunity
Participation
Reflective
Regular
Relationships
Supportive
Time.
Academic
Wellbeing
Writing
Self-care.

SUAW is just one piece of our toolkit of academic writing wellbeing. But its value is in being consistently there – a group that meets (currently) twice a week for two hours of dedicated writing community. Through SUAW we find our play, join our magic circle, and emerge with a feeling of communitas as we have the time of our lives.

References

Agamben, G. (1993). *The coming community* (Vol. 1) (M. Hardt, Trans.). University of Minnesota Press.
Archer, M. (2003). *Structure, agency and the internal conversation*. Cambridge University Press.
Archer, M. (2007). *Making our way through the world: Human reflexivity and social mobility*. Cambridge University Press.
Archer, M. (2012). *The reflexive imperative in late modernity*. Cambridge University Press.
Bandura, A. (2000). Exercise of human agency through collective efficacy. *Current Directions in Psychological Science, 9*(3), 75–78.
Barlo, S., Boyd, W. E., Pelizzon, A., & Wilson, S. (2020). Yarning as protected space: Principles and protocols. *AlterNative: An International Journal of Indigenous Peoples, 16*(2), 90–98.
Belcher, W. L. (2019). *Writing your journal article in 12 weeks: A guide to academic publishing success* (2nd ed.). University of Chicago Press.
Benjamin, W. (1979/2016). *One-way street and other writings*. Verso.
Bickel, B. (2009). Unveiling a sacred aesthetic: A/r/tography as ritual. In S. Spriggay, R. Irwin, C. Leggo, & P. Gouzouasis (Eds.), *Being with a/r/tography* (pp. 81–94). Sense.
Binder, M. J. (2022). Finding the spaces in-between. In N. Lemon (Ed.), *Reflections on valuing wellbeing in higher education: Reforming our acts of self-care* (pp. 28–40). Routledge.
Blackler, A. (2021). Research leadership. In A. Blackler & E. Miller (Eds.), *How to be a design academic: From learning to leading*. CRC Press.

Eardley, A. F., Banister, E., & Fletcher, M. (2021). Can academic writing retreats function as wellbeing interventions? *Journal of Further and Higher Education*, 45(2), 183–196. https://doi.org/10.1080/0309877X.2020.1744542

Firth, K. (2024). *Writing well and being well for your PhD and beyond: How to cultivate a strong and sustainable writing practice for life*. Routledge.

Garbett, D., & Thomas, L. (2020). Developing inter-collegial friendships to sustain professional wellbeing in the academy. *Teachers and Teaching, Theory and Practice*, 26(3-4), 295–306. https://doi.org/10.1080/13540602.2020.1832062

Grant-Smith, D., & Payne, R. (2021). Enacting careful engagement in the (post)pandemic care-less university. In A. Bozkurt (Ed.), *Handbook of research on emerging pedagogies for the future of education: Trauma-informed, care, and pandemic pedagogy* (pp. 169–190). IGI Global.

Haas, S. (2014). Pick-n-mix: A typology of writer's groups in use. In C. Aitchison & C. Guerin (Eds.), *Writing groups for doctoral education and beyond* (pp. 30–47). Routledge.

Haraway, D. (1991). *Simians, cyborgs, and women*. Routledge.

Huizinga, J. (1949). *Homo ludens: A study of the play-element in culture*. Routledge.

Khoo, T., & O'Donnell, J. (2024). Tensions of aspirational activism: Developing the research whisperer community. In M. Aarnikoivu & A. T. Le (Eds.), *Building communities in academia* (pp. 107–123). Emerald.

Le Guin, U. K. (1998). *Steering the craft: A 21st-century guide to sailing the sea of story*. Harper Perennial.

Lemon, N. (2021a). Vulnerability, self-care, and the relationship with us and other in higher education. In N. Lemon (Ed.), *Healthy relationships in higher education: Promoting wellbeing across academia* (pp. 1–9). Routledge.

Lemon, N. (2021b). Illuminating five possible dimensions of self-care during the COVID-19 pandemic. *International Health Trends and Perspectives*, 1(2), 161–175.

Lemon, N. (2024). *The 'how' of self-care for teachers: Building your wellbeing toolbox*. Routledge.

Murray, R. (2014). Practical strategies for writing for publication: It's not just about time. *International Journal of Therapy and Rehabilitation*, 21(2), 58–59.

Murray, R. (2021). *How to write a thesis* (3rd ed.). Open University Press.

Stevenson, N. (2021). Developing academic wellbeing through writing retreats. *Journal of Further and Higher Education*, 45(6), 717–729. https://doi.org/10.1080/0309877X.2020.1812549

Taboada, M., Turner, J., Seevinck, J., & Foth, M. (2024). A worldbuilding approach for pluriversality in codesign. *CoDesign*, 20(1), 218–241.

Tronto, J. (1993). *Moral boundaries: A political argument for an ethic of care*. Routledge.

Tronto, J. (2013). Joan Tronto: Interview. *Ethics of Care: Sharing Views on Good Care*. https://ethicsofcare.org/joan-tronto

Turner, E. (2012). *Communitas: The anthropology of collective joy*. Palgrave Macmillan. https://doi.org/10.1057/9781137016423

Turner, V. (1969). *The ritual process: Structure and anti-structure*. Aldine de Gruyter.

Wenger, E. (1998). *Communities of practice: Learning, meaning, and identity*. Cambridge University Press.

Yngvesson, T., Wank, A.-C., & Garvis, S. (2023). The personal and professional blur: Work-life family balance with COVID-19. In N. Lemon, H. Harju-Luukkainen, & S. Garvis (Eds.), *Practising compassion in higher education: Caring for self and others through challenging times* (pp. 103–119). Routledge.

15 Sprinting Towards Academic Writing Wellbeing

Reflections from a Care-Full and Compassionate Friday Writing Community

Abigail Winter, Jenna Gillett-Swan, Deanna Grant-Smith, Francis Bobongie-Harris, Michelle Jeffries, and Sophia Mavropoulou

Introduction

The language of agile management (Gillies, 2011) has infused higher education – we create deliverables and work in sprints. This chapter provides reflections from a group of women academic writers who participated in organised weekly full-day Friday sessions, rather than traditional 25-minute Pomodoros of writing (Duke, 2024), to manage our writing marathons (Tarabochia et al., 2022; Yngvesson et al., 2023) in small, manageable sprints. In particular, we reflect on how these Friday Shut Up & Write! (SUAW) sprints supported our productivity, wellbeing, and connection during COVID-19 and beyond.

Understanding SUAW as Care-full Practice

The sprints began as a way to maintain some structure in a largely turbulent, uncertain period in the world and in work. As classes were cancelled, postponed, or switched to online delivery at a moment's notice with the onset of the COVID-19 pandemic, our academic work was disrupted. Friday was a day that seemed immune from the chaos (at least initially) and we wanted to end the unpredictable work week with a sense of calm, control, and connection. Early in 2020, Jenna set a goal to complete a writing marathon of 42 sprints (as 42 km is the length of a running marathon). To do this, she scheduled blocks of time (sprints) in the calendar. Generally, three blocks were scheduled each Friday – the first, 1.5 hours followed by a 30-minute break, the second and third for two hours each, with a one-hour break between them. Jenna initially invited co-authors and encouraged them to invite others, leading to multidisciplinary participation through targeted invitations and professional network snowballing. The sessions were also advertised in the member mailing list of a university research centre of 40 participants, male and female, from early career academics to professors.

Given other commitments, there were 14 female attendees overall, with five regulars across the year. Each session contained writing blocks, debriefing, and 'brains trust' discussions based on attendees' needs for the week; Table 15.1 shows a typical pattern.

Table 15.1 Typical sequence of activities occurring in SUAW sessions

Sprint/session	Duration (in min)	Activities
Writing Block 1a	25	Participants usually used this time to orient themselves, plan what they were doing for the other blocks, and complete some easy writing tasks.
Debrief	5	Participants did a check-in with one another and briefly shared what they would be working on in the next block.
Writing Block 1b	50	Participants tended to prefer long blocks to make significant headway with whatever they were working on.
Debrief + Brains Trust	10	This debrief often extended into the break. It was also a time that participants would ask the 'brains trust' for advice, problem-solving, devil's advocate, etc. Over time, these debriefs and brains trust discussions turned into valuable mentoring, learning, and growth opportunities for participants including learning about new techniques, theories, or data representations; fostering new multidisciplinary collaborations; and seeing synergies across disciplines that participants may have otherwise been less aware of, as well as learning more about one another and their personal and professional interests.
Break	30	Participants tended to use this time to get a drink/snack and stretch.
Writing Block 2a	50	Independent Writing.
Debrief + Brains Trust	20	(As above in Debrief + Brains Trust)
Writing Block 2b	50	Independent Writing.
Lunch Break	60	Participants often used this time to catch up on emails or quick tasks unrelated to their writing. Some took a brief walk outside or did some stretching.
Writing Block 3a	50	Independent Writing.
Debrief + Brains Trust	20	(As above in Debrief + Brains Trust)
Writing Block 3b	30	Independent Writing.
Debrief	20	Debrief/progress check from morning goal.
Writing Block 3c	20+	Typically, participants stayed on and continued working until they had finished what they wanted to, or until they felt they were done for the day. This third block would often end up being extended for another hour or more past the scheduled finish time. The remaining participants would decide among themselves the blocks of time between working and check-ins.

Methodological Approach

To develop this chapter, each of the five regular Friday writing sprint participants was invited to respond via email to six prompts:

1. Why did you attend the Friday writing sprints?
2. How did the Friday writing sprints support your wellbeing (especially during COVID-19)?
3. Did the Friday writing sprints have any impact on your productivity?
4. Have you stayed in touch with other Friday sprinters? If so, how?
5. Since the Friday writing sprint, have you found an alternative place/space/community for connection and collegiality?
6. If the Friday writing sprints started again, would you join?

Replies to each prompt varied from a sentence to a half-page, with most authors providing paragraph-length short responses. Then, using Joan Tronto's (1993, 2013) Ethics of Care as a framework, we deductively analysed these self-reflections on the SUAW sprint community as a vehicle to enable mindfulness, self-compassion, habits, time, and agency as academic writers seeking wellbeing in a time of global crisis.

Joan Tronto's Ethics of Care model (1993, 2013) has five elements: (a) *Attentiveness* (caring about) – the things we pay attention to; (b) *Responsibility* (caring for) – the people we care for; (c) *Competence* (care giving) – the ways in which we show that care; (d) *Responsiveness* (care receiving) – the ways in which we permit others to care for us; and (e) *Reciprocity* (caring with) – the ways in which we, as a group, care together. We used those five elements of care as a lens to analyse our reflections on the Friday writing sprints.

To preserve the unique voice of each contributor, where possible we have used their direct quotes within our prose in italicised script.

Participation in SUAW as a Place of Caring

COVID-19 was a time of professional and personal isolation for many in higher education (Gao & Sai, 2020). Unsurprisingly, most responses to the first prompt (*Why did you attend?*) included elements of Reciprocity, such as Michelle's desire for "*company, building connections/relationships*" and Jenna's hope for "*strengthening [her] connection and relationships with existing colleagues as well as being the start of new relationships and connections with new colleagues*".

While some in the group had prior relationships, for many this was their first experience of working together. Despite this, the desire to create supportive relationships was evident, with Deanna noting that "*the other members were so welcoming ... We were just a group of women struggling to find [time] to write and in desperate need of an affirming cheer squad*". This notion that writing together would have benefits beyond the words produced was clear in Sofia's reflection where she wrote about "*the advantage of receiving collegial support*", and how she

> wanted to connect with colleagues while they were working on their creative writing adventures… [because] when you share these Friday writing sprints with colleagues you are connecting with them at a deeper level — I believe you get to know them better as people — you know their habits, their passions, their sentiments and their aspirations as writers.

Francis's reflection, by contrast, was presented primarily in terms of Responsiveness: "*The invitation came at a time when I wasn't consciously taking time just to write, and this was always in the back of my mind*". Michelle's reasons also included the need to receive of care: "*Writing support (as someone who is anxious about writing)*".

Not surprisingly, as the initiator of the Friday writing sprints, Jenna wrote a lot about giving care (Competence):

> Knowing that other colleagues were grappling with challenges… I blocked out the chunks of time in my calendar and invited colleagues… who I liked to work with to come along, while making it open to others, who I may not know, that might also like to come.

Receiving Care Supports Wellbeing in SUAW

Connection and care matter in academia (Bosanquet et al., 2014). The most common response to the second question (*Support for wellbeing?*) related to Responsiveness (receiving care). Michelle noted that "*it helped me with doing writing with a baby! … it was definitely an important connection point*". Sofia described it as "*a positive and supportive online community*". For Deanna, it felt like "*a necessary act of self-care rather than a selfish act*", as well as an act of Responsibility:

> The fact that the time in my calendar was blocked for a meeting where others would be present made me feel I should go, and quarantined that time from others trying to create meetings with me, and in a sense gave me permission to go.

For Francis, participation was grounded in Reciprocity:

> It was nice to know that once a week, you'd have a group of colleagues to talk to and get advice from about your writing. There was a definite social aspect too which was a welcome relief, after not seeing people physically at work.

For Jenna, it was a mixture of Competence, Responsiveness, Attentiveness, and Reciprocity:

> To begin with, it was so nice to be able to see people and know they were going okay [Competence]. I genuinely enjoyed my Friday sessions as a space to connect and develop collegial relationships (many of which also turned into friendships) … even when most other aspects of work life may have been causing a lot of burnout, fatigue, and stress [Responsiveness]. It was basically the only part of my work life that I could control, and any writing work that was achieved and completed during these sessions felt like a huge achievement [Attentiveness]… Every session the group also celebrated each other's achievements in the session no matter how big or small … even small wins [are] wins worth celebrating [Reciprocity].

Promoting Productivity Through What We Care About

In the neoliberal academy, productivity matters (O'Dwyer et al., 2017). Responses to the third question (*Impact on productivity?*) broadly map to the Care Ethics element of Attentiveness (caring about). Francis notes:

> I wasn't consciously finding time to write at this point. Joining the Friday writing sprints forced me to block out time in my calendar. I haven't written much since I began working at QUT, so this was a conscious effort to plan a publication trajectory and begin writing.

For Jenna,

> the Friday writing sprints helped me progress several publications as well as initiate many more, especially with those in the group also attending the sprints… I genuinely believe that if I hadn't blocked the time in my calendar each week AND if others hadn't joined the writing sprint community (i.e., it had just been time that I had blocked out without anyone else attending) that I probably wouldn't have stuck with it as long and/or would have found it easier to progress other work-related things that weren't writing, and would have ended up being nowhere near as productive.

Deanna suggested that she "*certainly took advantage of this quarantined time in a time of quarantine*".

For Michelle, the Friday writing sprints were about Reciprocity:

> In this group, I connected with colleagues in an intimate environment which encouraged us to be real, honest, ask questions, connect, share

our challenges, share our worries, share our successes, celebrate with each other. We built relationships… we did a lot of writing, and the format was really helpful in getting writing done in a way that helped to combat my panic about writing (PhD PTSD?) – because of the format of Pomodoro and coming back together to chat afterward. Setting writing goals and then coming back after a period of writing to check in with each other, share how it's going, get support/feedback/advice, and then write again, it was incredibly helpful.

Participation also helped Michelle to develop her professional identity as an early career academic:

Sometimes, we didn't do much writing, and instead did a lot of talking – but that was also incredibly helpful to me because I learned an enormous amount about the institution and academia in general—this knowledge helped me so much.

Creating Community Beyond Friday Writing Sprints

Maintenance of writing habits through being part of a community have been shown to be necessary for many academics (Macoun & Miller, 2014; Silvia, 2018). As Ai Tam Le and Melina Aarnikoivu (2024, p. 159) note, there are challenges to building writing communities – the work is often "voluntary … [and the] benefits are not always clear-cut, measurable, or predictable", however the rewards can include "a sense of belonging and solidarity … concrete outcomes including publications … and feeling part of a group". Responses to the fifth question (*Replacement community?*) also broadly map to Reciprocity. Sofia reflects:

As a result of being a regular member of the Friday writing sprints, I have become more open to being part of sessions with the intent to write, together with colleagues, sections of a journal paper or a grant proposal. In retrospect, I think the Friday writing sprints prepared me well for these opportunities to think and write with colleagues for a common purpose.

For Jenna,

Since the Friday writing sprints, I don't think I have found an alternative place/space/community for connection and collegiality in quite the same way as the conditions for the Friday writing sprints seemed to create, but the regular Faculty SUAW [see Chapter 14] has been a good alternative for some connection when I have been able to attend.

Michelle reflects that *"there was something very intimate about the Friday sprints. Perhaps it was the same faces each week. So, we were really able to be open with everyone about any frustrations, goings-ons, etc."* Francis works *"in a niche area. There aren't a lot of opportunities to have professional conversations unless there are intentional meetings, which are rare."* But she is *"hopeful that there will be more opportunities in the future, now that I am about to take on a more research-intensive role"*. Deanna is *"now part of a quiet writing circle at [her] new university* [Grant-Smith et al., 2025]. *Rather than writing online we are trying face-to-face, and I think I might actually prefer that, as I am less likely to 'just' check an email, or to not turn off my phone."*

Staying in Touch After SUAW Enhances Self-care

Connection to others, including maintenance of existing productive working relationships, is a well-established way of supporting wellbeing in the neoliberal academy (Bosanquet et al., 2014; Winter, 2023). As a place of community, the Friday writing sprints prevented us from becoming, as Herrmann (2014, p. 336) describes, "the walking dead in the workplace". The fourth question (*Stayed in touch?*) generally maps to Reciprocity for most. Deanna has *"long-standing personal relationships with some of the members, and it was because of those connections and their care that I accepted their invitation to attend, even though none of the members were from my discipline."* For Jenna,

> I still talk and see many of the 'core sprinters' fairly regularly, particularly those with whom I subsequently have collaborations or other shared activities with … Some of the group now regularly also attend the weekly Faculty-run Shut Up and Write sessions [see the previous chapter] that now run. While different to our Friday sprints, these have also served a similar purpose of connection, productivity, and celebration of writing achievements of those in the group no matter how large or small … The community created is positive, productive, and professional.

Francis has *"stayed in touch with other Friday sprinters. Fortunately for me, there have been opportunities to join some on other research and teaching projects, and the supervision of research students."*

Reflections on the Value of SUAW

Responses to the final question (*Join again?*) were mixed in terms of mapping to Tronto's (1993, 2013) Ethics of Care. Sandra Tarabochia and her colleagues (2022) describe academic writing as a marathon, rather than a sprint, noting, "support for faculty writers too often emphasises strategies for increasing productivity rather than building a healthy, sustainable writing life" (p. 88).

The Friday writing sprints were a place where participants could join and achieve both goals – productivity and a sustainable writing practice. It was by doing the Friday writing sprints that we were able to maintain the marathon that is the working life of an academic. As Jenna reflects,

> I found it much more productive to be able to make substantial headway with writing in the dedicated chunks over a full day, rather than 1.5–2 hours on random days, usually while also running between meetings, teaching, emails, and other work commitments,

indicating that she clearly is what Katherine Firth (2024) calls a 'stacker' rather than a 'spreader' of her writing time. She also notes, in her reasons for initiating the Friday writing sprints, that *"I thought that turning my Fridays into a series of writing 'sprints' could help to keep me motivated and give me a goal to aim for (42 sessions = writing marathon)"*.

Deanna's reflection on not joining again has elements of Competence, Reciprocity, and Attentiveness:

> I do take forward from it a range of learnings that I am applying to my new writing circle [Competence]… [including that] it is important to allocate time to enthusiastically celebrate each other's small writing wins and progress [Reciprocity]… [and] it helps when the writing time looks like a meeting with others in the calendar, as it will be less likely to be cancelled in favour of other work, by others and me, as it is a true commitment to writing alongside others [Attentiveness].

Francis' response is also about Attentiveness: *"Absolutely. I would like to put together a writing plan and carve out time specifically for writing."* However, Michelle also has family Responsibility to harmonise: *"I would, but I will have almost full-time care of my toddler [this] year, so likely am not able to fit it in. However, if the timing works with naps, perhaps that would be a possibility!"* Sofia simply gave an enthusiastic *"Yes, certainly!"*

SUAW as a Strategy of Self-care and Productivity

Maintenance, or self-care, although not part of Tronto's (1993, 2013) original Ethics of Care (Grant-Smith & Payne, 2021), is crucial because we cannot be productive in an ongoing, career-long way unless we look after our own needs for restoration. For Sofia,

> The Friday writing sprints strengthened my determination to write on Friday despite several pending tasks piling up at the end of the week. I was looking forward to it! My mind had been habituated, and it felt like escaping from the administrative load for a worthy reason!

While she has *"not stayed in touch with other Friday sprinters…that experience laid the seeds for my own search for writing coach sessions, useful books and podcasts about stylish and pleasurable academic writing"*.

Similarly, Jenna speaks to self-care when she notes:

> In a time of such uncertainty and change, always having to be on high alert and responsive with minimal notice, made this one day, this one pocket of time that was perhaps the only thing that I could potentially control, quite reassuring and calming.

For Deanna, *"hearing that others were experiencing similar challenges balancing all of their expectations but taking time out together to concentrate on our writing was really great for my wellbeing"*. She adds, *"I think its greatest impact was on my state of mind, which will have helped my productivity"*.

Friday SUAW Sprints as a Mosaic of Care

As shown in Image 15.1, our Friday writing sprints can be understood as a mosaic of care. The SUAW sprints offered a place for coming together and sharing, where the whole was greater than each individual's contribution, each offering and accepting support and encouragement. This practice resulted in a mosaic writing community, with each member contributing their own unique

Image 15.1 Mosaic of care.

pieces – fragments of ideas, perspectives, and experiences – that came together to form a cohesive whole. In a mosaic some pieces are bold and striking, others subtle and intricate, but every piece adds depth and texture to the shared vision. Together we were able to create a space to be academic writers working together, revealing patterns of support, inspiration, and mutual growth that make the final picture richer than any single piece/participant alone. For many of us, the writing sprints not only gave us a space to write, but also nourished our intentional collaborative interdisciplinarity.

The mosaic metaphor can also be extended to each of our individual writing experiences. We are all made up of "the little bits", as Jenna reflected about doing academic writing – *"even a seemingly small amount of progress on something adds up, which makes it worth doing, even if it is chipping away at something little bit by little bit"*. Our time is shattered among multiple tasks, but by coming together for the Friday writing sprints each writing chunk can be combined to create a coherent whole.

Strategies Unpacked as Tips

- SUAW as Attentiveness (caring about): Dedicate time to your writing – block it out in your calendar as an appointment. Aim for small weekly writing goals that add together to achieve big outcomes.
- SUAW as Responsibility (caring for): You don't have to be in a formal leadership position to start a writing group. If you need it, others probably do as well.
- SUAW as Competence (giving care): Invite others, so that you're less likely to cancel or allow 'more important' things into your dedicated writing time.
- SUAW as Responsiveness (receiving care): Make the most of opportunities to receive advice and support (like the brains trust) no matter your career stage or discipline.
- SUAW as Reciprocity (caring with): Spend time getting to know your co-writers as people. Celebrate lives as well as writing achievements.
- SUAW as Maintenance (self-care): SUAW communities can offer a sense of connection, which can be comforting, particularly during otherwise stressful, uncertain, and busy times.

Conclusion

In terms of Tronto's Ethics of Care (1993, 2013), this research shows that Reciprocity was the most common element in discussions of the Friday writing sprints, followed by Attentiveness, Competence, and Responsiveness. Responsibility was not a common theme in the responses, although it was certainly present in people's thoughts about their writing. Much like Donna Pendergast et al.'s (2023) option of invisibility yet belonging for camera-shy members of a COVID-19 online work group, the Friday SUAW sprints built a space of comfort and empowerment, where we could be ourselves and not feel forced to perform as neoliberal workers, let alone as researchers. Sometimes people would only turn up for five minutes simply to say "hi" and check in. In other weeks, the check-ins would run long, finding us still chatting half an hour later. We also found, similar to Sharon McDonough and Narelle Lemon (2021, p. 70), that spending this time together helped us to build "authentic relationships that are supportive, both with connection but also accountability that assists with discovery, growth, and maintenance of self".

The Friday writing sprints were a stable island among the ever-increasing chaos, overwhelm, and uncertainty of the modern neoliberal university (Poulos, 2014). To use Asilia Franklin-Phipps' (2024, p. 250) words, "some of the ways we cope with being overwhelmed [are] solidarity, community, and connection" – the sprints gave us a place to get writing work done each week. The sprints were a compassionate interruption (Lemon, 2024) to the neo-liberalised workday in Australian higher education, where teaching, administration, and meetings conspire to expand like a gas and take up all of the time and space we have, and more if we let them. Our SUAW sprints provided a place of shared accountability, where we could each focus on our micro-level engagement with academic writing, within a broader connected practice of care, compassion, and understanding.

For the early career academics in the group, the sprints provided a place of collegiality, support, and scaffolding, as well as being a place both modelling and enabling good academic writing practice, which is at the heart of their professional identity – academics teach, research, and serve, and write about their teaching, research, and service. For the more experienced academics, it provided a space to model good writing practice and to engage in mentoring, as well as to get their own writing done. Responding to Andrew Gibson and Taina Saarinen's (2024, p. 152) call to action, this chapter has shown that SUAW is a way for "senior academics to model 'vulnerable academics' and to dare to learn together with early career colleagues". We may be academic workers in the neoliberal academy, but, in our Friday SUAW sprints, we found ways to fill our writing spaces with care and compassion for ourselves and each other.

References

Bosanquet, A., Cahir, J., Huber, E., Jacenyik-Trawöger, C., & McNeill, M. (2014). An intimate circle: Reflections on writing as women in higher education. In C. Aitchison & C. Guerin (Eds.), *Writing groups for doctoral education and beyond* (pp. 204–217). Routledge.

Duke, D. C. (2024). When the words just won't come. In K. Townsend & M. N.K. Saunders (Eds) *How to keep your research project on track: Insights from when things go wrong* (pp. 126–134). Edward Elgar Publishing.

Firth, K. (2024). *Writing well and being well for your PhD and beyond: How to cultivate a strong and sustainable writing practice for life*. Routledge.

Franklin-Phipps, A. (2024). Being overwhelmed. In J. B. Ulmer, C. Hughes, M. Salazar Pérez, & C. A. Taylor (Eds.), *The Routledge international handbook of transdisciplinary feminist research and methodological praxis* (pp. 249–258). Routledge.

Gao, G., & Sai, L. (2020). Towards a 'virtual' world: Social isolation and struggles during the COVID-19 pandemic as single women living alone. *Gender, Work & Organization*, *27*(5), 754–762. https://doi.org/10.1111/gwao.12468

Gibson, A. G., & Saarinen, T. (2024). What if academia was not a gladiator fight? Reflections on trying to change the discourse from competition to community building. In A. T. Le & M. Aarnikoivu (Eds.), *Building communities in academia* (pp. 141–154). Emerald.

Gillies, D. (2011). Agile bodies: A new imperative in neoliberal governance. *Journal of Education Policy*, *26*(2), 207–223. https://doi.org/10.1080/02680939.2010.508177

Grant-Smith, D., Hands, K., McIntyre, K., Schmidtke, D., Mulcahy, R., & Scheepers, R. (2025). Moreton Bay Fridays: Creating community in a regional university campus through convivial co-located quiet writing. In N. Lemon, A. Bozle, M. Santa Cruz & R. Saunders (Eds.), *Fostering wellbeing through collective writing practices: Shut up and write! in higher education settings*. (pp. 33–40). Routledge.

Grant-Smith, D., & Payne, R. (2021). Enacting care-ful engagement in the (post)pandemic care-less university. In A. Bozkurt (Ed.), *Handbook of research on emerging pedagogies for the future of education: Trauma-informed, care, and pandemic pedagogy* (pp. 169–190). IGI Global.

Herrmann, A. F. (2014). Ghosts, vampires, zombies, and us: The undead as autoethnographic bridges. *International Review of Qualitative Research*, *7*(3), 327–341. https://doi.org/10.1525/irqr.2014.7.3.327

Le, A. T., & Aarnikoivu, M. (2024). Conclusion: Cam communities be cornerstones of future academia? In A. T. Le & M. Aarnikoivu (Eds.), *Building communities in academia* (pp. 155–162). Emerald.

Lemon, N. (2024). Unmasking wellbeing: Voices redefining self-care and wellbeing in higher education. In N. Lemon (Ed.), *Prioritising wellbeing and self-care in higher education: How we can do things differently to disrupt silence* (pp. 1–18). Routledge.

Macoun, A., & Miller, D. (2014). Surviving (thriving) in academia: Feminist support networks and women ECRs. *Journal of Gender Studies*, *23*(3), 287–301. https://dx.doi.org/10.1080/09589236.2014.909718

McDonough, S., & Lemon, N. (2021). Stepping into a shared vulnerability: Creating and promoting a space for self-care and wellbeing in higher education. In N. Lemon (Ed.), *Creating a place for self-care and wellbeing in higher education: Finding meaning across academia* (pp. 187–196). Routledge.

O'Dwyer, S. T., McDonough, S. L., Jefferson, R., Goff, J. A., & Redman-MacLaren, M. (2017). Writing groups in the digital age: A case study analysis of shut up & write Tuesdays. In A. Esposito (Ed.), *Research 2.0 and the impact of digital technologies on scholarly inquiry* (pp. 249–269). IGI Global.

Pendergast, D., Sammel, A., Rowan, L., O'Brien, M., McCann, T., Kanasa, H., Geelan, D., Exley, B., Dennett, C., & Alhadad, S. (2023). Spaces to care and places to share: Fostering a sense of belonging during the global pandemic through digitally mediated activity. In N. Lemon, H. Harju-Luukkainen, & S. Garvis (Eds.), *Practising compassion in higher education: Caring for self and others through challenging times* (pp. 120–147). Routledge.

Poulos, C. N. (2014). Under pressure. *Cultural Studies – Critical Methodologies*, *17*(4), 308–315. https://doi.org/10.1177/1532708617706122

Silvia, P. (2018). *How to write a lot: A practical guide to productive academic writing*. American Psychological Association.

Tarabochia, S. L., Brugar, K. A., & Ward, J. A. (2022). Running, writing, resilience: A self-study of collaborative self-care among women faculty. In N. Lemon (Ed.), *Creative expression and wellbeing in higher education: Making and movement in mindful moments* (pp. 87–104). Routledge.

Tronto, J. (1993). *Moral boundaries: A political argument for an ethic of care*. Routledge.

Tronto, J. (2013). Joan Tronto: Interview. *Ethics of care: Sharing views on good care*. https://ethicsofcare.org/joan-tronto

Winter, A. (2023). Taking a text and tweaking it: Using Wendy Belcher's 12-week journal writing program to support writing wellbeing for busy educators. *Student Success*, *14*(3), 120–127. https://doi.org/10.5204/ssj.2764

Yngvesson, T., Wank, A.-C., & Garvis, S. (2023). The personal and professional blur: Work-life family balance with COVID-19. In N. Lemon, H. Harju-Luukkainen, & S. Garvis (Eds.), *Practising compassion in higher education: Caring for self and others through challenging times* (pp. 103–119). Routledge.

16 Fear of a Blank Page

Discovering My Writing Superpowers in a Two-Day Pomodoro Writing Workshop

Nadezhda Chubko

Image 16.1 Imaginary chain of self-doubt.

Introduction

Once upon a time, there was a brilliant writer. She could naturally produce a perfect academic article from a first attempt at literally any time. She sincerely enjoyed filling the pages with words and never had to force herself to start writing….

Unfortunately, it is a fairy tale, and in real life, even the best writers from time to time face resistance to writing (Bane, 2012). It is safe to argue that an author is extremely vulnerable at the very starting point of the writing process when our subconscious mind tries to protect us from exposing our vulnerabilities. Our own mind stalls us from openly communicating our ideas, trying its best to protect us from the possibility of being painfully rejected by our prospective readers. This is the time when we are confronted by our self-doubt and eagerly put our knowledge and system of values under question. Under the pressure of high-stakes and little-guidance academic writing requires a huge amount of mental effort and courage which undoubtedly impact our wellbeing.

I was trapped in this mental cage of self-doubt for months, confident that my knowledge of the topic was insufficient. The frustration was growing as time was ticking away, but I did not feel ready to write. The thoughts about the volume of the expected output and the approaching deadline for proposal defence were making things even worse. It seemed like there was no way out. The piles of literature were occupying a significant part of my living space and each and every piece looked important for the bigger picture, but not enough to commit to writing. Despite all the literature consumed, I could not think of anything worthy of writing.

By the end of the first month as a PhD candidate, I started questioning my research proposal. Procrastination to write was disguised as a belief that more background reading was needed to cover the blind spots in my knowledge. I became exceptionally good at identifying additional concepts to explore. Five months into my candidature I was physically drowning in the mounds of books and papers piled up in my study room. I was reading article after article, reading aloud to stay focused. The tension was growing. Every additional piece of reading carried me further away from my initial topic of interest. Eventually, I lost my precious 'Why?' Why was I reading all those papers in the first place? It felt impossible to bring it all together. I could not squeeze even a word out of my pen. All I could feel back then was an overwhelming guilt for not writing.

My experience is a typical example of a 'writer's block', a phenomenon commonly known as 'fear of a blank page' or a 'white page terror' (Ahmed & Güss, 2022; Bane, 2012; Huston, 1998; Rose, 1984). Although it tends to happen at the initial stage of the writing process, it can happen at any other stage as well. Ironically, despite being an absolute torture, writer's block is a mechanism devised by our brain to protect us from potential failure (Bane, 2012; Cirillo, 2018). The good news – it is all in our heads. Meaning we can remove writer's block at will (Huston, 1998). Easier said than done though.

Being a teacher of academic writing, I had a range of strategies up my sleeve to steer my students away from writer's block. When it happened to me, I was not quite ready for this big-stake writing challenge. My teaching role mainly involved reading, analysing, and giving feedback. There was not much room for independent academic writing. As a result, when I started my PhD journey, my writing skills were out of shape. The Shut Up & Write! (SUAW) style writing weekend for higher degree by research (HDR) students was my magic saviour. I wrote a complete draft of the literature review section (over 3,000 words!) in just two days.

This chapter reflects my experiences and strategies that made my SUAW practice efficient and empowering. To better understand the reasons behind writer's block, I invite you to explore the writing process and identify the hidden threats to wellbeing that arise from the pressure to write in academia. I will then discuss the benefits of the SUAW practice and introduce the Pomodoro technique as a remedy for procrastination. Additionally, I will share my story of spending a weekend writing in the SUAW style and the strategies that unleashed my 'writing superpowers'.

What Is Writing and Why Is It So Painful?

It is amusing how we can find various excuses to avoid writing when nobody is watching (Bane, 2012; Cirillo, 2018). We could reveal a sudden urge for cleaning, making ourselves endless cups of tea, and online shopping is a whole new story. Basically, anything that postpones this dreadful moment of filling this distressful 'blank page' with words. It takes a substantial amount of courage to trust ourselves and expose our ideas in writing.

We rarely find writing enjoyable due to a substantial load on our working memory. Our 'writing brain' involves both language and nonlanguage systems, as text generation and editing require a host of executive processes (Bane, 2012; Berninger & Richards, 2002). At the same time writing must address the high social expectations of the future audience without a direct social input (Drosou et al., 2020). Meaning, we do not have a conversation partner to trigger the discourse generation. High cognitive load and lack of social input feed our self-doubt and anxiety, activating the part of the brain responsible for our survival (Bane, 2012). Therefore, we often approach writing when our brain is doing its best to protect our life and blocks out its learning function (Bane, 2012; Huston, 1998).

That is why the more we push, the more harm we cause to our wellbeing. To activate our writing brain, we need to write (Bane, 2012; Chintamani, 2014; Flower & Hayes, 1981). Importantly, while writing we should not focus on the quality of the output. It is like joining a yoga class or learning a new language. It can feel uncomfortable at first. However, with practice and a willingness to engage, we eventually reach a point where we genuinely enjoy the process. Improved performance becomes a wonderful bonus rather than the main objective. Insisting on perfectionism from the onset hinders the progress (Bane, 2012; Grimmer, 2024; Huston, 1998) and the associated self-criticism undermines wellbeing (Feraco et al., 2023).

Dangerous Freedom of Academic Writing

One of the distinctive features of academic writing is a lack of guidance (Drosou et al., 2020; Mewburn et al., 2014). As we advance in our academic careers, the amount of direct instruction tends to decrease. Up until we approach the higher degree by research stage, we are given little freedom of choice of what to write and how to write (Paré, 2014). No matter how we approached the writing process, the result would be remarkably close to the expected 'ideal' paper that lived in the heads of our teachers. All the prompts, feedback, guiding questions, and suggested supporting resources clearly steered us in a certain direction of achieving the required performance standards. From early schooling through higher education, students are frequently taught to adhere to structured outlines, particular linguistic conventions, and prescribed methodologies. Hence, for many individuals, particularly those who have spent a significant portion of their formative years under the rigid tutelage of structured assignments, the transition to an open-ended writing environment can become overwhelmingly challenging, as among all other things, the blank page presents an intimidating void of infinite possibilities (Flower & Hayes, 1981; Rose, 1984).

As a rule, HDR students do have supervisors. However, there is also an expectation that HDR students are the experts in their research area, engaged in making a unique contribution to knowledge. This unique context makes it impossible for anyone to envision the final output. Additionally, this unique positioning of being the 'expert' makes it extremely challenging to approach our supervisors or other experts in our research area with questions (Drosou et al., 2020; Mewburn et al., 2014). Hence, as aspiring researchers, we have all freedom in the world, and too much ego to acknowledge that we are struggling and need help.

Publications become our main source of support and guidance. We commit to reading to confirm the title of the 'expert' awarded to us upon commencing our research journey. Eventually, we lose our pace as our brain resists supporting our exaggerated expectations. Therefore, our challenge here requires a reconciliation of the desire for structure with the necessity of autonomy in writing. Our main challenge is in embracing the ambiguity of the blank page by acknowledging that freedom can be a source of empowerment rather than paralysing uncertainty.

The Power of Habits and Information Overload

The most common suggestion for breaking through writer's block is writing your way out of it (Chintamani, 2014). The cognitive process theory of writing (Flower & Hayes, 1981) suggests that writing involves hierarchical and highly embedded thinking processes guided by the expanding network of the writer's goals. For example, we think that we need to write a certain number of words, or we need to break our text into paragraphs, or we need to write an urgent email. The complexity and the type of goals vary to reflect the context of the immediate writing process and are changing as we write. By treating our writing routines or habits as action predispositions rather than patterns we allow ourselves to learn from our experiences (Biesta, 2015; Flower & Hayes, 1981). Moreover, with regular writing practice, some of the involved skills can become automatic (Flower & Hayes, 1981). For example, when our typing skills become automatic we stop focusing on locating the letters and punctuation marks on our keyboard.

Rather than attempting to collect all the information as a prerequisite for writing, we need to focus on establishing the writing process that can 'activate' our writing brain. Commitment to writing before we have 'all the knowledge' immediately establishes the constraints and significantly reduces the ambiguity around the expected output (Flower & Hayes, 1981). This practice reduces the load on our working memory as we only require the information for completing the task at hand (Biesta, 2015; Flower & Hayes, 1981; Huston, 1998). Remember how you tried to attach multiple video files to an email (prior to when they began being automatically saved to the cloud)? From my experience, there was always a high chance that the email would not come through. It is much easier to commit to writing when we have set routines or rituals in place (Bane, 2012). Developing a habit of writing can reduce the resistance to writing on demand and under pressure (Chintamani, 2014; Huston, 1998).

Communities and Peer Pressure

Along with a passion for our research topic, successful writing requires a substantial amount of courage, permission to be curious, and a strong support network (Amitabh, 2020). Being the 'expert' in our field of research does not mean that we must navigate the research path in solitude (Mewburn et al., 2014). My experience confirms that even though we cannot share our research process, we can still travel together with our peers. For example, membership in the 'academic writing community' can keep us motivated and accountable for each other's output. We are social creatures and therefore depend on being a part of a collective even when our work requires individual input (Paré, 2014). Given that our thoughts and actions are underpinned by our social interactions (Paré, 2014), it is only natural to agree that communities amplify our values through the diverse members' shared ownership (Amitabh, 2020). Communities of practice proved themselves throughout history to promote learning and knowledge stewardship through belonging (Wenger et al., 2002). One of the key features uniting the communities of practice is the establishment of a safe learning environment achieved through voluntary engagement, trust, and mutual respect among the members (Kaethler, 2019; Pyrko et al., 2016; Wenger et al., 2002). Moreover, communities of practice reflect the common issues experienced by the community members, which results in the evolution of the practices within these communities (Kaethler, 2019; Pyrko et al., 2016; Wenger et al., 2002).

Academic Procrastination and the Pomodoro Technique

Academic procrastination is a common issue experienced by nearly every student around the world. When it comes to completing a writing task, which as we know involves a complex combination of processes (Bane, 2012; Berninger & Richards, 2002), procrastination is usually associated with students' overindulgence in resource preparation combined with overall anxiety (Fauzan &

Aniyatussaidah, 2024). Thus, the impact of academic procrastination could range from a late or incomplete task to severe damage to our wellbeing. The Pomodoro technique is a tool developed to fight procrastination (Cirillo, 2018; Fauzan & Aniyatussaidah, 2024; Amitabh, 2020).

The success of this technique is attributed to the process and the expected outcomes (Cirillo, 2018; Amitabh, 2020). The essence of the Pomodoro technique is breaking work into 25-minute intervals with five-minute breaks in between. After four 25-minute sections of focused work, we can take a longer (15–30 minute) break. Breaking the task into a smaller chunks to be completed within a timeframe brings a sense of control and zones us out of all the unrelated thoughts and activities.

Pomodoro Technique Writing Weekend

Approximately a month before my candidature proposal was due, Edith Cowan University Support, Opportunities, Advice, Resources (SOAR) Peer Advisers together with Graduate Research Services (GRS) organised a writing weekend for HDR students featuring the Pomodoro technique (Booth, 2015). The event summary had a very loud promise. By the end of the writing weekend, we would produce an unbelievable amount of text (10,000 words). Quite skeptical about the outcome, but curious about the Pomodoro technique, I signed up for this workshop.

Surprisingly, on the day, the room was packed with my peers. The attendance was higher than at any other HDR workshop I had attended before then. On average we had six people per table. Despite the big crowd of people, the room was quiet. All of us had our laptops turned on. Everybody was typing. It did not take me long to start typing myself. I started with my writing routine, which is typing my name. Then I started retyping the first highlighted excerpt of the article I brought along. What happened next was a miracle. It felt like somebody had just switched on the light in a dark room. I automatically started paraphrasing the text. The next excerpt I was adopting instantly formed the logical connections to the first one. The writing was flowing for the entire 25 minutes.

An unusually loud sigh of relief concluded the first writing session. All of us were leaving the room for our first five-minute break with a face that represented satisfaction and anticipation. I approached the second writing session with a growing confidence. This time the air was filled with excitement. I was fully engaged in typing and did not even notice how the time of the next break approached. The same happened again and again up until we had our larger lunch break.

At lunch, we cheerfully talked about our research projects and our excitement with how much we were able to write in such a short time. Some of the workshop participants, including myself, were sincerely amused with how productive we could be. We also shared how hard it was to stay focused when we were at home alone, or at home with the family around.

To be honest, the writing session after the lunch was not as productive as the sessions before the lunch. At this point, I have already relaxed, feeling that I had some work done. My thoughts started wandering away, but everybody else was typing. Everybody else looked focused, so I felt the urge to play along and stay focused on the task at hand. I resorted to retyping the paragraph and then spending some time and effort paraphrasing it. The time was dragging, and I was waiting for the alarm to ring. Finally, we reached the short break time. This time the atmosphere in the room was not that cheerful. I was not the only one who needed a break. For the remaining sessions we were still doing the work, but the speed of execution gradually faded. The last bell has gone. The workday was over. I could not believe how much writing I had done. That evening, I came home, ate dinner, and went straight to bed. First time in a while I went to bed early as I was too exhausted for reading and did not have to worry about writing. Importantly, I did not have to worry about not writing.

The next morning, I was in anticipation of the magic of writing. I had clearer goals and expectations of the workshop and of myself. Those two days of sharing the writing space with my colleagues enabled me to complete the entire literature review for my research proposal. Those two days set me up for success as a PhD candidate. In those two days, I learned a lot about myself. I learned to trust myself.

Writing Weekend Preparation

Of course, I must acknowledge that the readings I have done were not in vain. I had physical copies of most of the articles. While reading, I highlighted the sections that appeared important, surprising, or contradictory. I was putting question marks next to the passages that made me think. When I found some passages that seemed to be good examples of presenting information, I marked them with a star. Additionally, I used margins to summarise key points and write my reflections. I also started sorting out my texts into themed piles. Prior to the writing weekend, I bought file binders to arrange the papers according to the common themes. I had an opportunity to see the big picture and organise my ideas before committing to writing. This way, when I came to the workshop, I had the brainstorming and planning parts completed. I also had a clear goal: to write a literature review. Unintendedly, I also created a template. By organising the articles into themed groups, I created subtitles for my literature review sections. All I had to do was transfer my ideas to paper; to be more precise, to a digital document.

Reflecting on all the preparation completed before the writing weekend, the 'magic' of writing I experienced was simply a natural outcome. All the conditions to unchain my writing brain were met. The writing weekend structured around the Pomodoro technique was that crucial trigger for removing writer's block by enhancing my accountability, reducing the possibility of unnecessary interruptions, and gradually replacing self-doubt with growing confidence.

Success Strategies to Overcome Writer's Block

My writer's block experience at an early stage of the PhD journey, along with participation in the SUAW–style writing weekend featuring the Pomodoro technique, can be summarised in four strategies for productive academic writing.

Start Writing Immediately

While strategies like free writing and established writing routines can help 'trick' our brains into writing, the most important step is to commit to writing in the first place. The longer you delay writing, the more fuel you add to your self-doubt. It is beneficial to jot down your thoughts and ideas as soon as they come to you. For instance, you can use the margins, sticky notes, or the comment function in your digital documents to summarise key points from your reading. Do not wait until you finish the text; otherwise, you risk losing valuable ideas. Taking notes and making comments on your current readings will significantly reduce the ambiguity of your writing task.

Scaffold Your Writing

Set smaller writing goals. While writing 3,000 words in one day is possible, it can feel overwhelming and may cause anxiety. Consider implementing productivity strategies like the Pomodoro technique by approaching writing in focused 25-minute intervals. With this approach you can achieve your writing goals and reduce the negative impact of high expectations on your wellbeing.

Restrain Yourself from Immediate Editing

Striving for perfectionism is a proven strategy for developing writer's block. That is why embracing writing as a thinking process is an important component of successful writing. Shifting the focus from the final output to the process itself will reduce the fear of failure and rejection. This way you invite your brain to believe that you are just thinking and therefore there is nothing to criticise or to be anxious about.

Be a Part of SUAW Group

Our writing performance and productivity are influenced by our work environment. Joining a SUAW group creates a sense of peer pressure that increases our commitment to writing. The accountability we feel towards other group members encourages us to take responsibility for contributing to the group's overall productivity. Often, this peer pressure is strong enough to silence the excuses we make to avoid writing, as we do not want to lose face in front of our peers. Furthermore, we benefit from the collective productivity of our peers, which compels us to 'Shut Up & Write!'

Discussion

The pressure to publish and the high expectations associated with academic writing significantly impact our well-being (Drosou et al., 2020; Grimmer, 2024; Oluwole et al., 2018; Wentzel, 2018). One symptom of this pressure is writer's block. Self-doubt (Drosou et al., 2020; Zhao & Gong, 2019) often leads to a desire for constant editing of our work. We may also get in a trap of setting unrealistic goals, such as producing a perfect piece of writing within a short timeframe (Huston, 1998). While achieving this goal is possible, it requires a shift in focus from the final product to the writing process itself. In other words, we should switch our focus from our large, ambitious goals to smaller, more manageable objectives relevant to the immediate writing task. For instance, we can concentrate on creating a title, writing a paragraph about a specific topic, or supporting our claim with an example.

At times, the nature of academic writing can leave us feeling lost and overwhelmed. In response, our brain often creates excuses to avoid writing (Bane, 2012; Cirillo, 2018; Drosou et al., 2020; Mewburn et al., 2014). This uncertainty and misinterpretation of the writing process can diminish the joy of writing (Berninger & Richards, 2002). Paradoxically, research indicates that to engage our writing brain, we actually need to be actively involved in writing (Bane, 2012; Chintamani, 2014; Flower & Hayes, 1981).

The 'magic' power of the SUAW workshops (Mewburn et al., 2014) largely stems from their ability to create an environment where we cannot distract ourselves with other tasks, such as cleaning, cooking, drinking tea, or browsing social media. The Pomodoro technique is effective because it breaks down the workload into manageable segments, helping to set realistic goals and avoid unrealistic expectations (Huston, 1998). By combining the SUAW workshop with the Pomodoro technique for productivity enhancement (Cirillo, 2018), we can divide our work time into feasible intervals. We need to focus on writing for exactly 25 minutes, followed by a break. This structure encourages us to push through any distractions, even those that might seem urgent, because we do not want to be that person who disrupted the writing flow of our peers.

Self-trust, curiosity, and peer pressure are some of the attributes of successful academic writing (Amitabh, 2020). The solitary nature of academic writing is an illusion. The sooner we recognise it, the sooner we can join a community of practice (Wenger et al., 2002) and adopt a completely new perspective on writing. Trust and mutual respect are the prerequisites for a safe and productive environment (Wenger et al., 2002) that fosters learning, self-discovery, and overall wellbeing (Grimmer, 2024; Kaethler, 2019; Pyrko et al., 2016).

Conclusion

In conclusion, the fear of a blank page, amplified by the high stakes of academic writing, creates a psychological barrier rooted in the protective mechanisms exercised by our brain. Since the phenomenon of writer's block threatens our wellbeing, the challenge extends beyond the act of writing itself; it involves reshaping our mindset. By addressing the underlying anxieties tied to exaggerated expectations and self-doubt, we can gradually transform the blank page from an intimidating void into a canvas of endless possibilities. This shift allows us to unlock our writing abilities and explore our potential for self-expression and intellectual discovery. All it takes is a commitment to set aside regular writing time and to find supportive peers who can 'Shut up & Write!' together with us.

References

Ahmed, S. J., & Güss, C. D. (2022). An analysis of writer's block: Causes and solutions. *Creativity Research Journal, 34*(3), 339–354.

Amitabh, U. (2020). *The seductive illusion of hard work*. SAGE Publications India Pvt, Ltd.

Bane, R. (2012). *Around the writer's block: Using brain science to solve writer's resistance*. Penguin Publishing Group.

Berninger, V. W., & Richards, T. L. (2002). *Brain literacy for educators and psychologists*. Academic Press.

Biesta, G. (2015). *Good education in an age of measurement: Ethics, politics, democracy*. Routledge.

Booth, S. (2015). *Writing weekend booklet*.

Chintamani, C. (2014). "Challenges in writing" – The writer's block? *Indian Journal of Surgery, 76*(1), 3–4. https://doi.org/10.1007/s12262-014-1058-x

Cirillo, F. (2018). *The Pomodoro technique: The life-changing time-management system* (Updated ed.). Virgin Books.

Drosou, N., Del Pinto, M., Al-Shuwaili, M. A., Goodall, S., & Marlow, E. (2020). Overcoming fears: A pathway to publishing for early career researchers. *Disaster Prevention and Management, 29*(3), 340–351. https://doi.org/10.1108/DPM-07-2019-0197

Fauzan, A. & Aniyatussaidah (2024). Literature review: The application of the Pomodoro technique to reduce academic procrastination levels among students in completing thesis. *International Conference of Bunga Bangsa, 2*(1), 147–157. https://journal.epublish.id/index.php/icobba/article/view/22

Feraco, T., Casali, N., Ganzit, E., & Meneghetti, C. (2023). Adaptability and emotional, behavioural and cognitive aspects of self-regulated learning: Direct and indirect relations with academic achievement and life satisfaction. *British Journal of Educational Psychology, 93*(1), 353–367. https://doi.org/10.1111/bjep.12560

Flower, L. & Hayes, J. R. (1981). A cognitive process theory of writing. *College Composition and Communication, 32*(4), 365–387.

Grimmer, L. (2024). Rethinking expectations in academia: How lowering expectations of ourselves and others improves wellbeing. In N. Lemon (Ed.), *Prioritising wellbeing and self-care in higher education: How we can do things differently to disrupt silence* (1st ed., pp. 21–31). Routledge.

Huston, P. (1998). Resolving writer's block. *Canadian Family Physician, 44*, 92–97. https://www.proquest.com/scholarly-journals/resolving-writers-block/docview/205181119/se-2

Kaethler, M. (2019). Curating creative communities of practice: The role of ambiguity. *Journal of Organization Design, 8*(1), 1–17. https://doi.org/10.1186/s41469-019-0051-z.

Mewburn, I., Osborne, L. & Caldwell, G. (2014). Writing together for many reasons: Theoretical and historical perspectives. In C. Aitchison & C. Guerin (Eds.), *Writing groups for doctoral education and beyond: Innovations in practice and theory* (1st ed., pp. 218–239). Routledge.

Oluwole, D., Achadu, O., Asfour, F., Chakona, G., Mason, P., Mataruse, P., & McKenna, S., (2018). Postgraduate writing groups as spaces of agency development. *South African Journal of Higher Education*, *32*(6), 370–381. https://doi.org/10.20853/32-6-2963

Paré, A. (2014). Writing together for many reasons: Theoretical and historical perspectives. In C. Aitchison & C. Guerin (Eds.), *Writing groups for doctoral education and beyond: Innovations in practice and theory* (1st ed., pp. 18–29). Routledge.

Pyrko, I., Dörfler, V., & Eden, C. (2016). Thinking together: What makes communities of practice work? *Human Relations*, *70*(4), 389–409. https://doi.org/10.1177/0018726716661040.

Rose, M. (1984). *Writer's block: The cognitive dimension*. Southern Illinois University Press.

Wenger, E., McDermott, R., & Snyder, W. (2002). *Cultivating communities of practice: A guide to managing knowledge*. Harvard Business School Press.

Wentzel, A. (2018). *A guide to argumentative research writing and thinking: Overcoming challenges*. Routledge. https://search.ebscohost.com/login.aspx?direct=true&scope=site&db=nlebk&db=nlabk&AN=1628952

Zhao, Q., & Gong, L. (2019). Cultural differences in attitude toward and effects of self-doubt. *International Journal of Psychology*, *54*(6), 750–758. https://doi.org/10.1002/ijop.12525

17 The HDR Writer's Wellbeing Lounge

A Community-Driven Approach to Enhancing Writing Productivity and Wellbeing for Higher Degree Research Students

Natasha Kitano, Owen Forbes, and Kirsten Baird-Bate

Introduction and Context

Wellbeing is an inherent element of Shut Up & Write! (SUAW) practices, contributing to its widespread success and universal appeal. SUAW sessions provide a space for connection and enable participants to approach writing tasks in an environment that emphasises solidarity and collective support. In higher degree research (HDR) or postgraduate research (PGR), the student experience, while often rewarding, is also marked by isolation, anxiety, and intense pressure to produce high-quality work (Jackman et al., 2022). This experience is often further complicated by students' additional work and family responsibilities. The HDR Writer's Wellbeing Lounge (the Lounge), initiated in the Graduate Research Education and Development (GRE+D) programme at Queensland University of Technology (QUT) in 2020, addresses these challenges by creating a supportive community for PGR students. The Lounge is inspired by the principles of SUAW and tailored to the unique needs of PGR students, particularly those studying remotely. This chapter explores the Lounge from the perspectives of the educator who created the concept of the Lounge and two PGR students, highlighting how this initiative fosters a sense of belonging, enhances writing productivity, and promotes overall wellbeing.

The HDR Writer's Wellbeing Lounge was established with the dual purpose of supporting PGR students' academic literacies and wellbeing. The aim was to create a community space where higher degree research students could engage in structured writing sessions while simultaneously discussing issues pertaining to wellbeing. The Lounge was initially designed to operate as a fortnightly, in-person writing session. The onset of COVID moved the sessions online and now the Lounge operates on a hybrid model to capture the differing format preferences of attendees. However, from its conception, the Lounge has followed the same format – write, reflect, relate, repeat.

DOI: 10.4324/9781003633334-21

Write, Reflect, and Relate Model

It is the rhythm of write, reflect, relate, repeat that makes the Lounge unique. In a two-hour block, attendees are guided through a series of four Pomodoro writing sprints (write). The Pomodoro technique is a time management and writing technique known to enhance productivity while reducing mental fatigue. The method features 25-minute concentrated writing "sprints" followed by short breaks and then a longer break after completing four sprints. While the students are engaging at the same time, they are working individually and are encouraged to share their individual writing goals on an online Padlet at the commencement of each session, fostering a sense of community and aligning with the concept of a community of practice (Wenger, 1999).

After each 25-minute writing sprint, students take a short break and are encouraged to reflect on their writing and prompted to consider not just writing mechanics, but also the quality of their output, what may be influencing their writing, and how they are trekking in relation to their initial set intention. Following the last writing sprint, students are given the opportunity to 'relate' and chat to their peers about a set wellbeing topic.

The Lounge is open to all enrolled PGR students at QUT, regardless of discipline, research stage, or prior participation. The program is managed by Natasha Kitano, the language and learning educator in the Graduate Research Education & Development (GRE+D) team. To ensure accessibility and maximum reach, the Lounge was promoted through multiple channels, including the university-wide PGR email list alongside other research development offerings, targeted communications through faculty-specific email channels and internal community networks (including PGR student societies), visibility on the university intranet and online student communities, institutional social media platforms, such as LinkedIn, and word-of-mouth referrals through peer networks where students were actively encouraged to invite colleagues.

The impact of the HDR Writer's Wellbeing Lounge has been widely recognised and disseminated. Articles about the Lounge have featured on the *Australian Council of Graduate Research (ACGR) Impact* blog and in academic journals, such as the *Journal of Applied Research in Higher Education*. In this research titled, 'Alone, together: how a strategy of writing, reflecting and relating helped research students deal with isolation' the aim was to evaluate two key learning preferences – social and solitary – and examine whether students' perceptions of the Lounge's success varied between these two styles. However, the present chapter focuses more on how the Lounge has enhanced both writing productivity and wellbeing for two participating PGR students. The Lounge has also been showcased at international conferences, including the International Conference on the Mental Health and Wellbeing of Postgraduate Researchers (UK) and the International Conference on Developments in Doctoral Education and Training (UK). The authors of this chapter were invited to talk about the impact of the Lounge for the award winning Podcast, *Research Culture*

Uncovered, with the University of the Leeds in the UK (Podcast link: https://research-culture.captivate.fm/episode/s9e8-navigating-postgraduate-wellbeing-the-wellbeing-lounge-at-qut).

Language and Learning Educator's Perspective

Similar to SUAW sessions, PGR students participate in focused writing sprints in the Lounge, but it is also a time where they can connect with their peers and discuss wellbeing-related topics, which promotes their wellbeing. The Lounge was launched just prior to COVID-19. Although it was unintentional, it became highly relevant at the height of the pandemic which compounded student isolation. As a synchronous online space, remote PGR students largely benefited from its creation because they had the opportunity to create or maintain relationships and alleviate their loneliness (Stuart et al., 2021). Post-pandemic, the Lounge has become a hybrid model. The motto of the Lounge is Write – Reflect – Relate – Repeat, and it is a space for PGR students to gather together to **write**, **reflect** on their writing, and **relate** to other PGR students on PGR matters. These stages of 'reflecting' and 'relating' are what set apart the Lounge format from a standard SUAW session.

One of the primary goals of the Lounge is to help students 'get some writing done'. I encourage the PGR students to start *writing* early and maintain a consistent writing routine. Many PGR students think that writing should only begin once their research is complete, rather than viewing it as an integral part of the research journey itself. I encourage the adoption of a consistent and moderate writing practice, with brief, regular sessions, which can result in more productive, less stressful, and successful writing experiences (Boice, 1990). Participating in weekly writing sessions can also help students reduce writing-related anxiety and alleviate any feelings of guilt.

Following the writing sprint, I guide students in *reflecting* on what they have written. Reflection serves as a valuable tool for consolidating knowledge and assessing writing skills to make necessary improvements (Cahusac de Caux et al., 2017).

The third stage of the Lounge process, *relate*, offers students an opportunity to build connections and forge relationships. During each Lounge session, students speak in person or join online breakout rooms where they can meet their peers and discuss PGR–related topics. The discussion topics emerged through an organic and ad-hoc process, shaped by the interests of the PGR students and recurring themes that surfaced during Lounge events. I focused on areas that consistently resonated with the PGRs, such as research skills and academic practice, personal growth, publishing throughout candidature, and building an academic identity and online profile. To support these discussions, I selected articles from a range of platforms and websites specifically tailored to the needs of PGR students. This space for interaction and mutual support contributes to students' overall wellbeing. The explicit emphasis on mental health and wellbeing taps into the existing wellbeing elements that are inherently part of peer writing groups, supporting individuals with stress and writing anxiety through collective solidarity and connection. Existing research literature has demonstrated the wellbeing benefits of peer writing groups in academic settings, and the Lounge format aims to draw out and leverage this wellbeing emphasis which is already present across SUAW communities (Doody et al., 2017; Cannell et al., 2023; Proulx et al., 2023).

The popularity of the Lounge reflects PGR students' strong desire for connection. Additionally, the Lounge addresses the increasing need for universities to prioritise student health and wellbeing, which are critical for fostering learning, productivity, and engagement (Van Kessel et al., 2021).

The Lounge has significantly influenced its participants, showcasing the effectiveness of student-centred programmes in addressing the distinct challenges faced by PGR students. Regular attendees report decreased anxiety about writing and an enhanced sense of belonging within the academic community. Additionally, the programme has fostered connections among PGR students across Australia, building a supportive network that bridges geographical divides.

As wellbeing is a topic that can potentially trigger stress there were several precautionary measures put in place to ensure student safety was paramount. Namely, participation in wellbeing discussions was entirely voluntary. Students were freely able to choose to opt in or out of these discussions, and to join at whatever level they felt comfortable. For example, some students chose not to join the breakout rooms, while others would choose to not turn their cameras or microphones on or would pass on sharing and be happy to listen. There was no requirement or expectation to engage if one was not comfortable to do so. The event co-ordinator was available at all times to consult one on one. As a further supportive measure, contact details of formal university student support services were provided. In the case of acute distress, a formal relationship and referral pathway was in place between the event host and the university counselling service.

The next section presents the perspectives of two regular Lounge attendees, providing lived experience insights into the programme and its impacts on their PGR experiences.

Student A's Experience

The HDR Writer's Wellbeing Lounge (the Lounge) was an essential source of support that made a huge difference to my productivity, wellbeing and sense of community connection throughout my PhD. Over the last decade I have experienced mental health challenges including periods of depression and anxiety, and I have worked to manage my wellbeing and develop effective coping strategies. This experience has shaped my academic path – sparking my interest in studying psychology as an undergraduate and also influencing my PhD research focus on youth mental health and statistical methods for analysing brain activity data in adolescents. This experience has also made me passionate about mental health in an academic context, which became especially relevant to me during the early phases of the COVID-19 pandemic which coincided with the start of my PhD journey. Shortly after moving to Brisbane and settling in at QUT, we went into lockdown three weeks later. I quickly packed up my life and returned to Canberra, where my PhD workspace became a corner of the kitchen table in our small townhouse, shared with three housemates who were also adapting to remote work. This sudden shift made me acutely aware of the importance of mental health support in academic settings, particularly for PGR students already facing the inherent pressures of research work.

The pandemic amplified existing mental health challenges in ways I hadn't anticipated. My usual coping strategies needed adjustment for the isolation of remote PhD work. The boundaries between work and home life blurred – my kitchen became an office, social space, and living area all at once. My housemates and I tried to maintain focus while navigating shared spaces and overlapping video calls. Starting a PhD usually means joining a research community – instead, I found myself physically isolated from other students and researchers. Without impromptu discussions about methods over coffee, or casual conversations about shared challenges, I felt quite disconnected from my peers. I wasn't alone in feeling this sense of heightened isolation and distress as a research student in the early days of the pandemic. It is well documented that PGR students broadly face higher rates of mental health challenges compared to the general population, and the pandemic added new layers of complexity to these existing pressures (Brownlow et al., 2022). Alongside the unique stresses of the pandemic, I was also trying to manage the regular garden-variety wellbeing challenges of a PhD, including writing anxiety and feeling under pressure to produce high quality outputs.

When I first learned about the Lounge, it felt like exactly what I had been missing. The Lounge offered this space that managed to tackle both the practical challenges of getting words on the page and the broader needs for connection and wellbeing support that so many PGR students need. The structure really clicked with me, with focused writing sprints combined with dedicated time for connecting and sharing around how we were doing as humans, not just as researchers. I loved how Tasha would send out articles before each session about things like supervisor relationships, perfectionism, or burnout prevention. It gave us a casual, approachable framework to start those conversations that can be tricky to initiate. The format of the Lounge was awesome – structured enough to be productive, but flexible enough to feel natural and supportive. We could concentrate on our work and then talk openly about the realities of doing a PhD, alongside managing isolation and worry during the early phases of the pandemic. The combination of practical writing time and peer support gave us a sense of solidarity and focused space to progress our work, and it was a huge help for the challenges of maintaining wellbeing in isolation. From my psychology background, I appreciated how the Lounge's design integrated evidence-based approaches to both productivity and mental health support. The Pomodoro technique provided structure, while the peer support model created opportunities for authentic connection and shared learning.

The two-hour Lounge sessions became my most productive writing time each week. But the shared presence of peers made the real difference. Seeing others working alongside me, even virtually, helped overcome the perfectionism that often stalled my progress. I consistently wrote more words during one Lounge session than in the rest of my week combined. The structured time and peer accountability created an environment where writing felt more manageable. We shared similar challenges with performance anxiety and getting words on the page, making it easier to push through difficult writing tasks together. We could focus entirely on writing during sprints, then engage fully in discussion during breaks.

The breakout room discussions really helped normalise mental health conversations among the participants in our PGR student cohort. When Tasha would step out and leave just the students to 'Relate', it created this safe space where we could feel at ease and speak freely about our struggles and victories. Topics ranged from supervisor stress to imposter syndrome, to finding work-life balance while juggling research demands. We shared practical strategies for managing supervisor meetings, workload, and maintaining boundaries. The Lounge offered a space for us to develop a shared vocabulary for discussing wellbeing that made it feel like a natural part of academic life, not something we had to hide or push aside. This helped mental health become part of our regular academic discussions, not a separate issue to handle alone. Implementing this programme at scale could help PGR students to recognise early signs of stress in themselves and others, building proactive support networks rather than waiting for crisis points.

The relationships formed in the Lounge extended beyond our writing sessions – though we have since graduated, we still check in on each other's progress and wellbeing. Particularly for me as a remote student, even after the Lounge events resumed with an in-person component, the hybrid online format provided me with a regular space to maintain a sense of connection and community belonging throughout my PhD. There's something special about connecting with people who understand what you are dealing with, who can relate to both the academic pressures and the personal challenges of maintaining wellbeing throughout a PhD journey.

This experience showed me how universities can actively support student wellbeing through structured but flexible programmes that combine practical academic support with space for genuine connection. The Lounge demonstrated that effective mental health support in academia needs to be proactive and community-driven, integrated into regular academic practices rather than treated as a separate service to be accessed only in crisis. The impact extends beyond individual wellbeing to broader academic culture – by normalising conversations about mental health and creating supportive peer networks, we can build more resilient communities and better look out for each other.

Student B's Experience

Wellbeing, reflective practice, and how women locate a sense of balance and focus while in the throes of life has always been an area of interest to me. Both personally, as well as professionally through my master's and PhD research projects, I have traced this field. It is through this lens that I recount my experience with QUT's HDR Writer's Wellbeing Lounge.

Wellbeing is a multifaceted construct that is both subjective and objective in nature (WHO, 2012, 2021). As such, this part of the chapter will begin by sharing a little more about my sociocultural context as a way of fully illustrating how the Lounge supported different aspects of my wellbeing and helped me establish a more effective writing practice.

The impetus for my master's and PhD research projects, both of which employed visual narrative methods, was my own parenting experience. As mother to three children, two with complex needs, life has always held both the joys and challenges of parenting, plus an additional layer of caregiving. Life was – is – well, full.

When my children were younger, I began to wonder how other mothers navigated this caregiving/parenting terrain and juggle what seemed to be multiplying balls in the air and compounding layers of challenge. I looked to the extant autism wellbeing literature and found that it was dominated by stories of parental stress and burden, which seemed to perpetuate negative stereotypes around autistic children and those who cared for them. While such stories were valuable, they also did not represent the full picture. Nor did they seem to offer a way forward. Missing, and needed, were positive accounts of parenting and stories that ultimately may contribute to the development of strength-based supports and services for families caring for children with disabilities.

My master's by research used visual narrative methods to explore the lived experiences of mothers of autistic children and my PhD then sharpened focus to more specifically examine how primary carers of autistic children conceptualised wellbeing. Building off the success of my master's degree, which engaged participants in a photographic journaling process, my PhD also wove visual narrative methods into the mixed-methods research design. In both projects, I found that inviting participants to reflect and make visible their wellbeing experiences centralised their voices within the research and in doing so contributed to more effective policy and practice discussions. This focus on wellbeing and reflective practice in my research made those elements of the Wellbeing Lounge resonate with me.

My PhD was undertaken as a remote student after moving from Brisbane to regional coastal NSW. While the beach was beautiful, the lack of access to campus and an academic community was noticeable. The COVID migration of university services, supports, and workshops onto online platforms was, in my experience, a blessing. For me COVID dismantled geographical barriers and opened up new opportunities for connection and learning. One of those offerings was QUT's HDR Writer's Wellbeing Lounge.

My Experience with the Lounge

Loneliness and its associated impact on mental health is often connected to the experience of undertaking a PhD with some research to suggest that this may particularly be the case for remote students (e.g., Brownlow et al., 2022; Mills et al., 2024). As a remote student, I did not experience social loneliness as such, but I more missed the synergy of campus. I missed the discussions with academics and colleagues, the option to engage in ongoing learning opportunities, the sense of community that is built with others trekking a similar path. I missed the library, the quiet reprieve from the busyness of home life where I could focus uninterruptedly on writing.

When the Lounge was established, it became my lifeline. It became my weekly connection point into something bigger than the words on my computer screen. It was my chance to refine my academic writing practice, meet other PGR candidates, and to feel a sense of resonance through a shared experience.

First and foremost, the Lounge supported my wellbeing by helping me establish an effective writing practice. It offered a dedicated writing time within my busy week – it was a few hours where I would switch off my phone, inbox, and re-arrange any caregiving needs and just write! The quiet, focused space became an invaluable part of my week and an unmovable appointment in the family calendar.

Through regular attendance at the Lounge, I then started to carve out other windows of focused writing time. As a busy mum, and sessional academic, I found that I did not always have the luxury of full days of writing. Sometimes it was just short, sharp windows where I needed to reign in my split focus and maximise the time I had.

The Lounge helped equip me with the skills and confidence I needed to engage independently. I would switch off, then switch on the Pomodoro timer and just write. Sometimes one round would lead to five rounds; I just needed to get started.

Through the Relate session of the Lounge our weekly wellbeing discussions started to cue into what qualities I needed to write effectively. For example, these discussions encouraged me to consider my circadian rhythm and how I could structure my weekly calendar in a way that was most conducive to our natural productivity. For me, this meant setting up early morning writing sessions, when my brain was fresh, and the household was still and quiet. I would then aim to arrange meetings in the afternoons or use the time when I was shuffling kids between after-school activities to engage in work that did not demand long attention spans, such as editing.

I also noticed that walking and moving helped my capacity to think more clearly. If I hit writers block, or needed to think about how ideas could fit together, then going for a walk helped ideas formulate/reformulate and connect in new ways. In particular, I found going for a walk on the beach, in nature, to be supportive of my wellbeing and writing practice.

The HDR Writer's Wellbeing Lounge 217

Image 17.1 Taking breaks by walking on the beach helped me become more conscious of how I maintained productivity and focus and supported my wellbeing.

The Relate session of the Lounge opened a space to connect to other PGR students around topics of wellbeing. The opportunity to hear from other students' stories provided a "normative framework" (Kuhn and Carter, 2006, p. 571) around the more pressured aspects of candidature. It may sound simple and obvious, yet I did find it validating to hear others too experienced the ebbs and flows of the writing process, the tussle over word length, the stress of looming milestones.

As the Lounge drew together students from across faculties it provided an opportunity to build interdisciplinary connections and hear different theoretical approaches and interesting projects beyond my faculty. In this way, the Lounge helped fill the synergistic and social connections that were initially missing at the beginning of candidature.

I began to form friendships with some of the other regular Lounge attendees and our bond became forged through the shared experiences of candidature. Our weekly writing sessions also became an opportunity to encourage one another to "keep going" when things got tough, share our variant research skills and insights, and celebrate milestone achievements. Such connections are invaluable to successful academic outcomes and wellbeing.

Collectively, the Lounge supported my capacity to focus and produce work more effectively and did so in a way that was supportive to my wellbeing. The Lounge helped me to achieve academically and honor the elements I needed to put in place to achieve in a way that was more balanced and sustainable. Valuably, the Lounge opened a space for connection and bloomed friendships that have lasted well beyond final submission.

Learnings and Recommendations

The Lounge, through its structured yet flexible approach, supports PGR students in multiple ways. We think the model of the Lounge could easily be implemented in other higher education institutions by:

- *Fostering Community and Belonging*: By creating a space for PGR students to connect, share experiences, and support each other, the Lounge helps mitigate the isolation often felt in academic pursuits. The elements of connection and community have been particularly valuable and impactful for students conducting their research remotely. The Lounge has shown that peer support can significantly enhance the PGR journey.
- *Enhancing Writing Productivity*: Regular, focused writing sessions using the Pomodoro technique help students develop productive writing habits and reduce procrastination. A dedicated writing practice also supports those who are juggling multiple demands of family and work alongside PGR completion.
- *Promoting Wellbeing*: Tapping into the inherent focus on wellbeing support that is present across SUAW communities, the 'reflect and connection components or 'relate' of the Lounge format emphasise the importance of wellbeing in the academic journey. Through reflective practices and peer support, students are encouraged to adopt a balanced approach to their research and writing tasks. Connecting and sharing openly about mental health challenges enables students to build stronger mental health literacy, model help-seeking behaviours, and share coping and self-care strategies. By introducing this subtle yet meaningful addition to the traditional SUAW format, we can tap into the existing undercurrent of wellbeing benefits that are present in peer writing groups and help cultivate a more open and supportive space to enhance students' mental health resilience and academic experience.
- *Adapting to Remote Needs*: The online format of the Lounge ensures that remote PGR students can participate fully, breaking down geographical barriers and providing equal support to all students.
- *Aligning with best practices and strategic goals*: By facilitating connections, the Lounge contributes to a more rewarding and enriching academic experience which aligns with QUT's aspirations to build supportive research environments expressed in QUT's Connections Strategy 2023–2027 (Queensland University of Technology, 2023). It is also a response to the Australian Council of Graduate Research (ACGR's) good practice guidelines

for mental health and wellbeing (ACGR, 2021) which recognise the significance of mental health and wellbeing in graduate research education and the importance of actively supporting wellbeing.

The HDR Writer's Wellbeing Lounge, we believe, has a unique approach and supports PGR students as a structured, student-centred, and community-driven initiative which can enhance writing productivity and wellbeing in higher education. We hope that this chapter contributes to the broader discussion on the impacts and experiences of SUAW programmes, demonstrating the value of fostering supportive academic environments that prioritise both academic excellence and personal wellbeing.

References

Australian Council of Graduate Research (2021, July). *ACGR Good Practice Guidelines for Mental Health and Wellbeing in Graduate Research Education* [Guidelines]. Australian Council of Graduate Research.

Boice, R. (1990). *Professors as writers: A self-help guide to productive writing.* New Forums Press.

Brownlow, C., Eacersall, D., Nelson, C. W., Parsons-Smith, R. L., Terry, P. C. (2022) Risks to mental health of higher degree by research (HDR) students during a global pandemic. *PLoS ONE* 17(12): e0279698. https://doi.org/10.1371/journal.pone.0279698

Cahusac de Caux, B. K. C. D., Lam, C. K. C., Lau, R., Hoang, C. H., & Pretorius, L. (2017). Reflection for learning in doctoral training: writing groups, academic writing proficiency and reflective practice. *Reflective Practice*, 18(4), 463–473. https://doi.org/10.1080/14623943.2017.1307725

Cannell, C., Silvia, A., McLachlan, K., Othman, S., Morphett, A., Maheepala, V., ... & Behrend, M. B. (2023). Developing research-writer identity and wellbeing in a doctoral writing group. *Journal of Further and Higher Education*, 47(8), 1106–1123.

Doody, S., McDonnell, M., Reid, E., & Marshall, S. C. (2017). Doctoral peer writing groups as a means of promoting well-being. *LEARNing Landscapes*, 10(2), 145–157.

Jackman, P. C., Jacobs, L., Hawkins, R. M., & Sisson, K. (2022). Mental health and psychological wellbeing in the early stages of doctoral study: A systematic review. *European Journal of Higher Education*, 12(3), 293–313. https://doi.org/10.1080/21568235.2021.1939752

Kuhn, J. C., & Carter, A. S. (2006). Maternal self-efficacy and associated parenting cognitions among mothers of children with autism. *American Journal of Orthopsychiatry*, 76(4), 564–575. https://doi.org/10.1037/0002-9432.76.4.564

Mills, L., Read, G. J., Bragg, J. E., Hutchinson, B. T., & Cox, J. A. (2024). A study into the mental health of PhD students in Australia: Investigating the determinants of depression, anxiety, and suicidality. *Scientific Reports*, 14(1), 22636.

Proulx, C. N., Rubio, D. M., Norman, M. K., & Mayowski, C. A. (2023). Shut Up & Write!® builds writing self-efficacy and self-regulation in early-career researchers. *Journal of Clinical and Translational Science*, 7(1), e141.

Queensland University of Technology. (2023). *Connections: QUT strategy 2023–2027.* QUT. https://www.qut.edu.au/connections

Stuart, J., O'Donnell, K., O'Donnell, A., Scott, R., & Barber, B. (2021). Online Social Connection as a Buffer of Health Anxiety and Isolation during COVID-19. *Cyberpsychology, Behavior and Social Networking*, 24(8), 521–525. https://doi.org/10.1089/cyber.2020.0645

Van Kessel, G., Brewer, M., Lane, M., Cooper, B., & Naumann, F. (2021). A principle-based approach to the design of a graduate resilience curriculum framework. *Higher Education Research & Development*, 41, 1–15.

Wenger, E. (1999). *Communities of practice: Learning, meaning, and identity.* Cambridge University Press.

World Health Organisation (WHO) (2012). *Measurement of and target-setting for wellbeing: an initiative by the WHO Regional Office for Europe / second meeting of the expert group.* https://www.euro.who.int/data/assets/pdf_file/0009/181449/e96732.pdf

World Health Organisation (WHO) (2021). *Health promotion glossary of terms 2021.* Geneva: World Health Organization. https://www.who.int/publications/i/item/9789240038349

18 Connection, Momentum, and Growth

Exploring the Benefits and Challenges of 'Shut Up & Research' for Researcher Wellbeing

Annalise Roache, Jane George, and Lisa M. Baker

Introduction

In the fast-paced world of academic research, balancing productivity with personal wellbeing is a significant challenge. This chapter explores the transformative potential of "Shut Up and Research" (SU&R) sessions, an evolution of the "Shut Up & Write!" (SUAW) model (Proulx et al., 2023), in promoting both productivity and wellbeing. We aim to provide a nuanced understanding of how SU&R sessions impact researcher wellbeing, drawing on the perspectives of various career-stage researchers who are members of the Research Accelerator group. Research Accelerator's online, structured co-working SU&R sessions combine focused work periods with social interaction, addressing the isolation and burnout that often affect researchers (Mewburn et al., 2014).

Drawing on qualitative data from the Research Accelerator community and our experiences, this chapter examines the impact of SU&R sessions on researchers' wellbeing and productivity and offers practical implementation insights. This chapter begins with a theoretical foundation linking to academic productivity and then discusses Research Accelerator's adaptation of SU&W, its structure, community dynamics, and participant-driven evolution (Mewburn et al., 2014). Data analysis highlights the benefits of these sessions—building *connection*, *momentum*, and *growth* while tackling challenges such as imposter phenomenon and boundary management.

Finally, this chapter provides actionable recommendations for academic institutions and research communities, advocating for the intentional integration of wellbeing into productivity frameworks. This work will resonate with researchers, educators, and practitioners seeking to support personal and professional needs, demonstrating SU&R sessions' potential to transform academic practice at the intersection of wellbeing, productivity, and connection.

Shut Up & Research: A Framework for Academic Community and Productivity

Research Accelerator (RA) (Academic Consulting, 2025) is an online community of practice established in New Zealand in 2020, initially in response to the isolation caused by the COVID-19 pandemic. Inspired by the Shut Up & Write! (SUAW) model (Mewburn et al., 2014), RA adapted the approach to create Shut Up & Research (SU&R) sessions—recognising that researchers engage in a range of tasks beyond writing. RA now supports a global community of postgraduate students, early-career researchers, and experienced academics across disciplines (www.researchaccelerator.nz).

The SU&R sessions are central to RA's offering. These Zoom-based sessions are designed to foster both research productivity and researcher wellbeing. Each month, they provide over 120 hours of structured, collaborative work time, combining focused work intervals with informal discussions. Members select which sessions to attend based on personal goals and availability, allowing flexible integration into individual timetables.

Key features of RA and SU&R sessions include:

- **Structured Productivity**: Sessions follow a 50-minute work block model, promoting sustained focus and momentum. Hosts guide sessions but personalise facilitation styles to meet group needs.
- **Community Support**: Informal discussions before and between work blocks enable members to share insights, address challenges, exchange resources, and celebrate research milestones, building a strong sense of belonging.
- **Flexibility and Responsiveness**: The structure of sessions and the broader RA offering continually evolve based on member feedback, ensuring relevance to diverse research activities and stages.
- **Wellbeing Integration**: Quarterly virtual retreats and everyday session practices encourage holistic wellbeing, incorporating activities such as chair yoga, meditation, and self-care prompts.

Beyond the live sessions, RA offers members access to an extensive library of self-paced courses, webinars, expert presentations, and personalised one-on-one support focused on academic writing, data analysis, and research communication. Ongoing connection between sessions is maintained through a 24/7 virtual co-working space (Welo), a WhatsApp group, and an asynchronous discussion forum hosted on the RA website. RA's strength lies in its balance between structure and flexibility, combining a focus on academic productivity with intentional support for connection, collaboration, and researcher wellbeing.

For a fuller exploration of the RA community's philosophy, structure, and broader offerings, please refer to Chapter 6.

Data Collection and Analysis Process

This chapter draws on data from Research Accelerator group members and the authors' experiences. As doctoral and post-doctoral researchers, the authors of this chapter are active participants in the RA community, regularly attending and hosting SU&R sessions. Our expertise in wellbeing and health sciences and our positionality inform our understanding of SU&R participants' perspectives. We gathered data about participants SU&R experiences via an anonymous online survey with open-ended questions, and this chapter is informed by two specific wellbeing related questions, namely *"What have been the most significant benefits and challenges you've encountered while participating in SU&R sessions? How have these impacted your mental health, wellbeing and productivity?"* and '*How has participating in SU&R sessions impacted your overall wellbeing (for better or worse)? Please share specific examples to illustrate your experience.*"

The survey and an information letter outlining the study's purpose, ethics, and publication details were distributed to approximately 110 Research Accelerator members through their weekly email. Participation was voluntary, and anonymity was ensured to encourage honest responses. Ethical guidelines, including informed consent and confidentiality, were strictly followed. A short data collection period of 10 days saw 15 responses received. The qualitative data offered valuable insights into the SU&R experience from the broad perspectives of researchers from various career stages—such as master's and doctoral students, early-career academics, and experienced scholars.

We employed three complementary but separate thematic analysis methods for data analysis, based on author preference and to allow for different perspectives and results to be raised and considered. Thematic analysis is a qualitative research method used to identify, analyse, and report patterned meaning (themes) within data, providing a flexible and accessible approach to organising and describing datasets (Braun & Clarke, 2006). Each author conducted the analysis independently before coming together to discuss and compare results. While the tools for analysis varied—one author used AI ChatGPT, one used manual analysis (via Excel), and the third used a hybrid approach using NVivo (Lumivero, 2022)—consistent findings resulted. The final analysis presented here integrates these methods, emphasising survey respondents' perspectives and language.

Real-World Insights from Participants Relating to Wellbeing and Productivity

Analysis of the perspectives provided, drawn from participants' responses and the authors' thematic analysis, illustrates the benefits and challenges of SU&R participation. Three main themes (*connection*, *momentum*, and *growth*) and six sub-themes were identified. These themes are now discussed, and their intersection with SU&R practices and participant's self-reported wellbeing is illustrated in Image 18.1.

Theme 1: Connection

SU&R sessions create a sense of **connection**, **belonging**, and mutual **support**, reducing feelings of isolation and loneliness. Participants report significant improvements in their mental health and emotional resilience, often

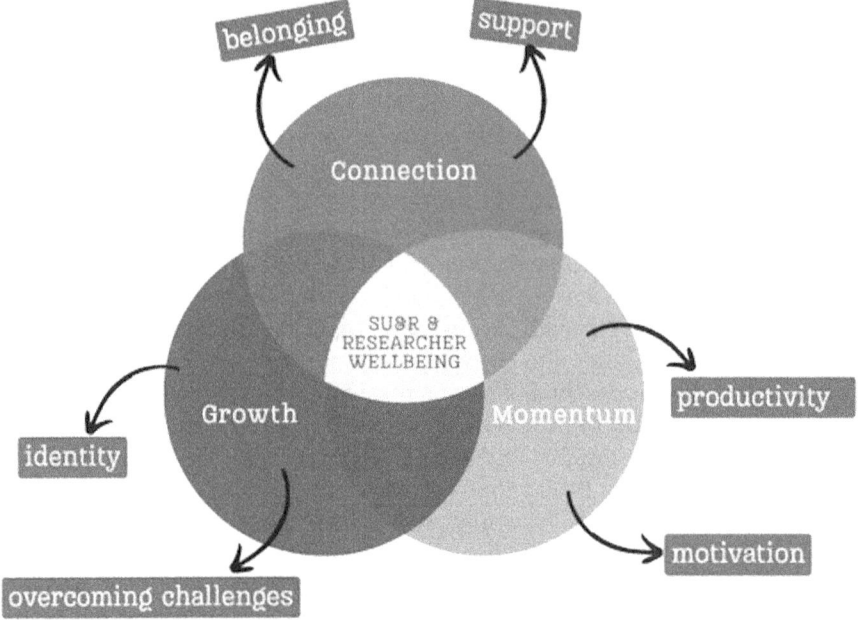

Image 18.1 Venn diagram of intersecting themes that connect SU&R practice with participants' wellbeing.

describing the sessions as transformative for their overall wellbeing. Many note that the supportive environment alleviates the emotional toll of graduate work, tempering loneliness with encouragement and camaraderie.

Participants speak of **connection** as a sense of **belonging** to the SU&R research community and a crucial element in their writing and research journey. Despite the virtual nature of interactions, members develop authentic and meaningful **connections**. As one participant reflected, "*these relationships, although 100% online, are real and integral to my progress and therefore wellbeing*". The sessions create a shared space where participants can witness and celebrate each other's milestones. Another participant notes this aspect was particularly valued,

> as taking part in SU&R makes me feel connected to others. I feel inspired when I see researchers ahead of me reaching goals and milestones. Demystifying the process of completing a PhD makes me feel less anxious about my own trajectory.

This peer-to-peer visibility and **connection** help normalise doctoral and other research challenges while creating an inclusive community where participants can see themselves represented in others' successes.

The SU&R sessions are particularly valuable in combating the inherent isolation of research. Participants consistently highlighted how the sessions transform their solitary work environments into spaces of shared experience and mutual understanding. As one participant emphasised, "*the greatest benefit has been reduced isolation. As a mainly off-campus PhD candidate, I have spent most of my time alone in the home office*". The virtual sessions create a bridge between each researcher's workspace, fostering a sense of collective presence despite physical separation. As another participant noted, these shared experiences resonate deeply with participants, "*knowing that there were others going through what I was going through. So, decreasing the loneliness of the postgrad solitary journey*". The formation of these **connections** was potent as participants found genuine commonality in their experiences, reflected in one observation, because "*in the SU&R community, I have found people like me, and the isolation is removed*". This transformation from solitary to communal work demonstrates how SU&R sessions can effectively address one of the most challenging aspects of graduate study and research projects more widely.

The supportive environment cultivated within SU&R sessions extends beyond academic collaboration into a genuine care and emotional **connection** network. As one participant described, "*we have developed supportive relationships. It's not just a quiet space to get your work done in silence and then go*". These virtual spaces become safe places where participants can share their professional challenges and personal struggles. One participant's experience powerfully illustrates the depth of this **support**,

> one morning, just before going online for SU&R, I received news that a friend had only days to live. I was upset by this but decided to go online anyway. The group was so incredibly compassionate. This made a huge difference to my grieving.

Such moments of vulnerability and compassionate response help forge lasting bonds among participants. The cumulative effect of this sustained **support** is transformative, as another participant reflects: "*I have established genuine lifetime friendships, and I completed my PhD by simply turning up for one SU&R session after another and seeing/hearing from others that they had my back*". This testimony underscores how the consistent presence and encouragement of the SU&R community facilitates progress and also creates relationships that go beyond the immediate context of academic research.

The SU&R sessions examined here purposefully create a uniquely balanced environment where serious academic work is complemented by intentional moments of fun, joy, and **connection**. The social breaks prove instrumental in transforming isolated work periods into energising and communal experiences. Participants particularly valued the playful elements, with one noting, "*I like the fun and humour – the coding song, the Zoom effects… and energising spurts of Zumba to get me out of the chair, moving and taking a mental and screen break*". This integration of movement and levity provides more than just physical breaks—it fosters genuine emotional **connections** among participants. As another participant shared, these playful moments were "*really* *energising and connecting*", creating an *"uplift of positive emotion that then translates to getting more work done"*, reflecting the connections between play and wellbeing (Farley et al., 2021).

The SU&R structure thoughtfully incorporates opportunities for both celebration and **support**, with *"talking/encouraging/commiserating spots"* always available, allowing participants to share wins and challenges. This responsive approach to emotional **support** creates a robust sense of **belonging**, as one participant noted that *"sharing wins, resources and stories with and from others helps me connect and feel a sense of belonging which is great for my wellbeing and productivity"*. Combining structured work time, playful breaks, and emotional support creates an environment where researchers can find academic progress and enhance their wellbeing (Mewburn et al., 2014).

Theme 2: Momentum

Virtual SU&R sessions emerge as powerful environments for researchers, offering structured frameworks that transform solitary research into collective **productivity** rituals. Sessions provide participants with consistent routines, accountability, and a sense of achievement, contributing to their **motivation** and **productivity**. The resulting progress helps participants feel more in control of their workloads, reducing stress and fostering a sense of increased accomplishment and satisfaction. A structured approach allows participants to balance their work-life schedules more effectively, enhancing their overall wellbeing.

The silent writing periods during SU&R sessions create optimal conditions for sustained cognitive focus and deep work. Research indicates that writers with strong self-regulation skills, including the ability to plan, set goals, organise, and self-monitor, exhibit higher **productivity**, regardless of their initial writing ability (Proulx et al., 2023). The structured environment and shared accountability of SU&R sessions foster these self-regulatory behaviours by creating clear boundaries around writing time and reducing external distractions. One participant noted that *"the effect is my productivity increases, giving a sense of accomplishment"*. The sessions' communal yet quiet nature strikes an effective balance, providing enough structure to support sustained attention while avoiding the cognitive load of constant interaction. This protected space for deep focus supports participants to potentially enter flow states (Csikszentmihalyi, 1997), where they become fully immersed in the research task aided by clear goals and time constraints, which afford regular feedback points by which participants can measure progress.

Beyond the cognitive benefits, SU&R sessions provided a valuable structure that helps participants establish sustainable writing routines. The scheduled nature of these sessions creates accountability and allows participants to protect dedicated research time within their busy schedules. As participants reported, these sessions can provide a welcome structure to their work periods, with one noting that they *"can enjoy my afternoon off when I have spent the morning 'in session'."* This approach appears to support consistent **productivity** balanced with self-care, with participants reporting more consistent output, particularly during intensive periods such as the RA quarterly retreats. Combining regularly scheduled sessions and occasional intensive writing periods helps participants maintain **momentum** in their research work while creating clear boundaries between work and rest periods—essential to sustainable academic **productivity** and overall wellbeing maintenance.

The consistent rhythm of virtual co-working sessions is instrumental in helping participants maintain **momentum** in their research journeys. Rather than experiencing their work as isolated bursts of **productivity**, participants find that regular attendance at SU&R sessions creates sustained positive progress in their research. One participant emphasised that *"every session adds to my forward movement on research in some manner – ideas, words down, resources, support"*. This incremental progress contributes to a compelling sense of advancement that encourages participants to persist in their scholarly endeavours. The commitment to regular sessions on days and times in the week that suit individual needs proves especially powerful for maintaining this **momentum**. Another participant reflected that *"being part of a regular, committed 7-day-a-week schedule has been great for my wellbeing as it has helped me to keep going with my research and feel a sense of accomplishment"*. This steady cadence of research activity, supported by the virtual co-working structure, helps participants avoid the common pitfalls of procrastination and work avoidance that often plague graduate studies and research projects more widely. Instead a sustainable pattern of consistent progress that enhances both **productivity** and wellbeing is fostered.

Theme 3: Growth

The formation of researcher **identity** emerged as a crucial outcome of the SU&R sessions, transcending their primary function as productivity spaces to become environments where researchers and graduate students can develop and strengthen their academic identities. As researchers, participants feel more grounded and self-assured, developing healthier academic identities, self-belief, and resilience to challenge. This **growth** in confidence and clarity helps participants manage academic pressures, reducing anxiety and fostering a more positive outlook on their abilities and futures. Participants often credit these SU&R sessions with reshaping how they approach their research and personal wellbeing. The collaborative nature of these virtual spaces fosters an environment where researchers can learn from peers at various stages of their research journey, creating informal mentoring relationships that contribute to their development. Through regular interaction with fellow researchers, participants gain access to diverse perspectives, shared resources and emotional support, both personal and professional, all contributing to a stronger sense of belonging within the broader academic community and a more robust researcher **identity**.

The development of researcher **identity** within SU&R sessions is intrinsically linked to forming supportive community relationships, which foster personal **growth** and professional resilience. One participant reflected that the sessions facilitated *"creating a healthy identity with support networks, breaks, and generally being much kinder to myself than I ever would've been doing the mahi* [work] *in isolation"*. This interconnection between community support, **identity** formation, self-care and compassion proves transformative, leading to what another participant described as *"a de-cloaking of mysteries, acceptance of challenges, and rock-solid belief in self: I am, I do, I write"*. The collective nature of these sessions creates a space where participants can witness others' journeys, normalising research challenges while building confidence through shared experiences. This is evident in participants' testimonies, with one noting that *"SU&R has definitely grounded me and supported me to be a better researcher"*, while another emphasised how they *"gained confidence from collaborating with people … to believe I actually could complete"*. Setting and sharing research intentions within the group adds another dimension to **identity** formation, as one participant observed that *"setting intentions and sharing these reminds me that I want to achieve as much as I can to disseminate my research"*. Community support, shared aspirations, and collective accountability create an environment where participants can develop more potent, resilient researcher identities while maintaining a clear vision of their academic goals.

Challenges and Potential Drawbacks Impacting Researcher Wellbeing

While SU&R sessions significantly benefit researchers' productivity and wellbeing, participants also reported encountering specific challenges. These challenges often emerge from the inherent tensions between individual research needs and the communal nature of virtual co-working, requiring participants to develop strategies for managing both the practical and emotional aspects of their participation.

Challenge 1: Balancing Boundaries and Managing Focus

While the community aspect of SU&R sessions was highly valued, it can sometimes create competing demands on participants' attention and time management. As one participant noted, the desire to *"catch up with people in the session on a personal level"* could lead to distraction from research tasks. While necessary for the session format, the structured timing of breaks occasionally disrupted participants' deep work periods, potentially fragmenting their concentration at critical moments. Beyond the sessions, some participants struggled with broader boundary management, particularly around weekend sessions, where they faced difficult choices between maintaining their research momentum and participating in social activities with friends and family. These challenges highlight how the very elements that make SU&R sessions effective—their regular schedule, social connectivity, and structured breaks—can sometimes create tensions that participants must actively navigate.

Challenge 2: Comparison and Imposter Phenomenon

SU&R sessions create a supportive research community; however, the visibility of peers' progress and achievements sometimes intensifies participants' experiences of comparison. As one participant reflected, "*I have to be careful not to compare myself all the time with others as I get imposter syndrome. It's easy to think I'm not doing anything well or right as others in the group seem so amazing*". This heightened awareness of others' work could trigger feelings of inadequacy, particularly when participants perceived their peers as more productive or accomplished. The regular sharing of progress and goals, while intended to foster accountability and celebration, occasionally leads participants to question their own pace and achievements, with some noting that they "*struggle with comparing my progress to others*". Paradoxically, the same community connections that could spark these comparisons also provided the supportive environment needed to process and overcome such feelings as participants gradually learned to appreciate the unique nature of each researcher's journey.

Discussion and Practical Implications

Wellbeing benefits shared by participants were self-reported; however, parallels with wellbeing science frameworks are evident. Participants report that SU&R sessions foster a sense of belonging, mutual support, and camaraderie, transforming solitary research into a shared journey. Research on the foundational and critical benefits of belonging and relatedness for wellbeing is significant, underscoring the crucial role social connectedness plays in positive mental health and wellbeing (Baumeister & Leary, 1995; Ryan & Deci, 2000). The structured and deep work facilitated by an SU&R framework supports participants' self-regulation and sense of accomplishment, both evidenced pathways to psychological wellbeing through supporting a cycle of growth and positive affect (Baumeister & Vohs, 2007; Ryff & Keyes, 1995). Researcher identity and confidence are also linked to wellbeing as participants reported they gained insights into the research process, built resilience, and developed healthier academic identities. Professional identity can buffer against burnout, and confidence in one's professional abilities supports positive emotions, engagement, and a sense of control (Ibarra, 1999).

Various studies have highlighted the need to attend to the wellbeing and self-care needs of those in higher education, including graduates, post-doctoral researchers, and academics (Evans et al., 2018; Lemon, 2021; Satinsky et al., 2021). Demands related to academic work and realities of career advancement, overworking, rankings, comparisons and scholarly production create pressure for those in academia and research, impacting wellbeing (Bergen et al., 2020; Fang, 2021). As highlighted in the participants' comments, some of the effects of these pressures can be shared and ameliorated through the *connection*, *growth*, and *momentum* benefits of SU&R sessions. Research institutions and education settings (including but not limited to universities) may consider both the structure and intentionality of SUAW or peer support writing groups for both productivity and wellbeing outcomes.

Structural Implications and Insights

Structural implications exist from the sense of belonging and identity, support, motivation, productivity, and overcoming challenges resulting from SU&R membership. One of the implicit threads from the perspectives shared in this chapter is the *ongoing* involvement and membership of those in the SU&R sessions. The sense of community, collaboration, and support experienced came from the sessions' scheduled and reliable nature. Some institutions and community writing circles offer ad-hoc or drop-in style SUAW times for researchers and students. However, the sense of belonging, community, and connection from consistent and frequent availability of online sessions (across all days of the week and hours of the day) is impactful. Participants being able to regularly and reliably connect and share research goals and personal tribulations in a supportive and stable community is key to the productivity and wellbeing of its members. Structural consistency and collegiality are vital.

The need for fluidity within the structure exists, balancing individual and collective needs. While the benefits from the consistent and reliable nature of SU&R sessions are evident, rigid expectations of fixed 'working' and 'break' times may not suit all participants. The architecture of focus intervals versus social interaction levels is essential to support participants' momentum and wellbeing. Silent work opportunities for those who enjoy deep concentration and creative flow without interruption should be balanced with the availability of social and fun opportunities.

The choice of platforms to deliver sessions is also worth consideration, noting that this chapter has focused on a virtual SU&R community. Platforms such as Zoom, Webex, or Google Meet can be used for scheduled and regular days, sessions and intervals, allowing for formality and predictability, whereas virtual 'offices' or collaboration spaces such as Kumospace or Topia support more spontaneous or autonomous research sessions, and small or large group working. We hope the insights offered in this chapter provide practical suggestions for institutions or research communities interested in implementing SU&R-style sessions. For example, this could include considerations on session facilitation, platform choices, session scheduling, and balancing work and breaks.

Wellbeing Intentionality Insight

Tangible and visible benefits of SUAW sessions for researchers and writers of self-efficacy, self-regulation, productivity, structure, skill creation, and connection are well documented and promoted (Bergen et al., 2020; Micsinszki & Yeung, 2021; Proulx et al., 2023). By sharing active SU&R community members' voices, we wanted to highlight the less noticeable or measurable outcomes. Wellbeing benefits of *connection*, *momentum*, and *growth* were clearly articulated by the SU&R community surveyed, yet this is not an explicitly stated overall intention of the community. The Research Accelerator structure includes wellbeing content and focuses during quarterly virtual retreats; however, it is apparent that participants' indirect wellbeing outcomes occur across other offerings within the community. While an intention to build the wellbeing literacy of participants (the ability to communicate intentionally about and for wellbeing; Oades et al., 2021) is not stated, the perspectives and language use of participants would suggest the SU&R structure do indeed support their use and development of wellbeing communication. Through this chapter, we hope that current and future SUAW/SU&R communities may see the psychological benefits and wellbeing literacy possibilities within their structures. Articulating to participants the intention for wellbeing in addition to productivity may highlight these probable benefits, encouraging greater engagement and improved wellbeing outcomes. Given the pressures of scholarly life, a greater focus on the intersection of *connection*, *momentum*, *growth*, and wellbeing can only be a strength of such communities.

Conclusion

This chapter has demonstrated the profound impact of SU&R sessions on the wellbeing and productivity of researchers, offering a model that blends intentionality with flexibility to meet diverse needs. Three core themes emerged: *connection*, *momentum*, and *growth*.

First, *connection* underscores the significance of community in alleviating academic isolation. SU&R sessions foster a sense of belonging, mutual support, and camaraderie, transforming solitary research into a shared journey. Participants consistently reported enhanced emotional resilience and mental health, attributing these gains to the supportive and compassionate environment of the sessions.

Second, *momentum* highlights the productivity benefits derived from the structured and intentional design of SU&R sessions. The rhythm of focused work intervals and breaks creates a sustainable pattern of research activity. This structure supports deep work and fosters self-regulation, accountability, and balance habits. By integrating these elements into their routines, participants reported increased efficiency, reduced stress, and a greater sense of accomplishment.

Finally, *growth* illustrates how SU&R sessions cultivate researcher identity and confidence. Through shared experiences, participants gain insights into the research process, build resilience, and develop healthier academic identities. The sessions provide a platform for self-discovery and professional development, reinforcing participants' beliefs in their capacity to navigate the complexities of academic life.

SU&R sessions exemplify how intentional, community-driven practices can enhance productivity and wellbeing. This dual focus challenges the traditional dichotomy between work and self-care, presenting a more integrated approach to academic life. As institutions and research communities seek to support their members, the lessons from this SU&R community offer a compelling blueprint for fostering environments where researchers can thrive.

References

Academic Consulting. (2025, January 8). *Research Accelerator*. https://www.academic-consulting.co.nz/research-accelerator/

Baumeister, R. F., & Leary, M. R. (1995). The need to belong: Desire for interpersonal attachments as a fundamental human motivation. *Psychological Bulletin*, *117*(3), 497–529. https://doi.org/10.1037/0033-2909.117.3.497

Baumeister, R. F., & Vohs, K. D. (2007). Self-regulation and the executive function: The self as controlling agent. In A. W. Kruglanski & E. T. Higgins (Eds.), *Social psychology: Handbook of basic principles* (2nd ed., pp. 516–539). The Guilford Press.

Bergen, N., Hudani, A., Khan, S., Montgomery, N. D., & O'Sullivan, T. (2020). Practical considerations for establishing writing groups in interdisciplinary programs. *Palgrave Communications*, *6*, 19. https://doi.org/10.1057/s41599-020-0395-6

Braun, V., & Clarke, V. (2006). Using thematic analysis in psychology. *Qualitative Research in Psychology*, *3*(2), 77–101. https://doi.org/10.1191/1478088706qp063oa

Csikszentmihalyi, M. (1997). *Creativity: Flow and the psychology of discovery and invention*. HarperCollins Publishers.

Evans, T. M., Bira, L., Gastelum, J. B., Weiss, L. T., & Vanderford, N. L. (2018). Evidence for a mental health crisis in graduate education. *Nature Biotechnology*, *36*(3), 282–284. https://doi.org/10.1038/nbt.4089

Fang, Z. (2021). *Demystifying academic writing: Genres, moves, skills, and strategies*. Routledge. https://doi.org/10.4324/9781003131618

Farley, A., Kennedy-Behr, A., & Brown, T. (2021). An investigation into the relationship between playfulness and well-being in Australian adults: An exploratory study. *OTJR: Occupation, Participation and Health*, *41*(1), 56–64. https://doi.org/10.1177/1539449220945311

Ibarra, H. (1999). Provisional selves: Experimenting with image and identity in professional adaptation. *Administrative Science Quarterly*, *44*(4), 764–791. https://doi.org/10.2307/2667055

Lemon, N. (Ed.). (2021). *Creating a place for self-care and wellbeing in higher education: Finding meaning across academia*. Routledge. https://doi.org/10.4324/9781003144397

Lumivero. (2022). *NVivo*. In (Version 1.7.1 (1534)) QSR International Pty Ltd. https://lumivero.com/products/nvivo

Mewburn, I., Osborne, L., & Caldwell, G. (2014). Shut up & write!: Some surprising uses of cafés and crowds in doctoral writing. In C. Aitchison & C. Guerin (Eds.), *Writing groups for doctoral education and beyond* (pp. 218–232). Routledge. https://doi.org/10.4324/9780203498811

Micsinszki, S. K., & Yeung, L. (2021). Adapting "Shut Up & Write!®" to foster productive scholarly writing in graduate nursing students. *The Journal of Continuing Education in Nursing*, *52*(7), 313–318. https://doi.org/10.3928/00220124-20210611-05

Oades, L. G., Jarden, A., Hou, H., Ozturk, C., Williams, P. R., Slemp, G., & Huang, L. (2021). Wellbeing literacy: A capability model for wellbeing science and practice. *International Journal of Environmental Research and Public Health*, *18*(2), 719.

Proulx, C. N., Rubio, D. M., Norman, M. K., & Mayowski, C. A. (2023). Shut Up & Write!® builds writing self-efficacy and self-regulation in early-career researchers. *Journal of Clinical and Translational Science*, *7*(1), e141. https://doi.org/10.1017/cts.2023.568

Ryan, R. M., & Deci, E. L. (2000). Self-determination theory and the facilitation of intrinsic motivation, social development, and well-being. *American Psychologist*, *55*(1), 68–78. https://doi.org/10.1037/0003-066x.55.1.68

Ryff, C. D., & Keyes, C. L. M. (1995). The structure of psychological well-being revisited. *Journal of Personality and Social Psychology*, *69*(4), 719.
Satinsky, E. N., Kimura, T., Kiang, M. V., Abebe, R., Cunningham, S., Lee, H., Lin, X., Liu, C. H., Rudan, I., Sen, S., Tomlinson, M., Yaver, M., & Tsai, A. C. (2021). Systematic review and meta-analysis of depression, anxiety, and suicidal ideation among Ph.D. students. *Scientific Reports*, *11*, 14370. https://doi.org/10.1038/s41598-021-93687-7

For Product Safety Concerns and Information please contact our EU
representative GPSR@taylorandfrancis.com
Taylor & Francis Verlag GmbH, Kaufingerstraße 24, 80331 München, Germany

www.ingramcontent.com/pod-product-compliance
Lightning Source LLC
Chambersburg PA
CBHW071203240426
43668CB00032B/2009